DOWN IN THE RIVER TO PRAY

DOWN IN THE RIVER TO PRAY

Revisioning Baptism as God's Transforming Work

JOHN MARK HICKS
&
GREG TAYLOR

Down in the River to Pray
Revisioning Baptism as God's Transforming Work
published by Leafwood Publishers

ISBN 0-9728425-3-5
Printed in the United States of America

Cover design by Rick Gibson
Cover photo: George Washington Puckett baptizes in the Cimarron River near Stillwater, OK, circa 1890. An evangelist, Puckett established several Christian Churches in Oklahoma. Photo used by permission of the Disciples of Christ Historical Society, Nashville, TN.
Backcover photo by Amber R. Stacy

For information:
Leafwood Publishers
1409 Hunter Ridge
Siloam Springs, AR 72761
1-877-634-6004 (toll free)

Visit our website: www.leafwoodpublishers.com

04 05 06 07 08 09 7 6 5 4 3 2 1

Dedication

For Jen and Jill

Acknowledgements

We are grateful for those who have shaped our faith and led us down into the river. Our parents led us to Christ: our mothers nurtured us and our fathers immersed us.

We are grateful for our heritage that introduced us to the river and continues to stress the importance of baptism. Our heritage encourages the continual return to Scripture for faith and practice, and we appreciate the freedom to explore the depths of God's river.

We are grateful for those who have walked alongside the river with us, encouraged us, and read early drafts of various chapters. In particular, we thank John Ogren, John Barton, Rubel Shelly, Allen Black, Gary Holloway, Rees Bryant, James H. Waltner, Robert Webber, Jill Taylor and Jennifer Hicks for their patient and insightful comments.

And we are grateful to Leonard and Holly Allen at Leafwood Publishers for encouraging us to write this book and helping it take shape in the writing and editing process.

Contents

Practical Streams

Conclusion

Preface

Gathering at the River

Baptism is more important than you think, but not for the reasons you suppose.

Many believe baptism is simply the sign of salvation already received. Others believe it is an indispensable command that legally divides those heading to heaven from those going to hell. Baptism is more important than either think.

Baptism is a performative, or effectual, sign through which God works by his Holy Spirit to forgive, renew, sanctify and transform. It is a symbol by which we participate in the reality that it symbolizes. We must not reduce it to a mere symbol or sign that only looks to the past without any present power or reality. Baptism is more important than that.

Neither is baptism, however, the technical line between heaven and hell. It is not primarily a loyalty test or a command satisfied by legal performance of the rite. We must not reduce baptism to a line in the sand. Such a reading of baptism's function reduces its significance to a technical legal requirement. Baptism is more important than that.

While baptism is both a sign and a command, it is more. Baptism points beyond itself and effectually participates in God's transforming work. God is at work through baptism to transform fallen humanity into his own image, to transform the fallen human community into a people who share the life of the divine, triune community.

God's goal is to conform humanity to the image of his Son (Rom. 8:29-30). Transformation is God's fundamental aim. Everything God does, everything God commands, serves that goal. Baptism serves that end. Baptism must never trump, negate or simply point to a faint testimony of transformation, but transformation must always shape and determine baptismal theology.

Baptism is important because it serves the end of God's transforming work. It is more important than a sign or a command because its significance lies in its function as a means of transformation into the divine image and inclusion in the divine community where divine presence empowers transformation. It is not simply one among many commands, but neither is it *the* command. Baptism is God's transforming work and serves the divine goal of transformation.

Come Down in the River to Pray

We envision twenty centuries of teaching and practice on baptism as a river flowing through time. Christians through time have wrestled with what baptism was intended to be in the life of the church, for ethics, and for an understanding of what happens before, during and after the event of baptism in the life of the believer.

Picture a river's path as it meanders smoothly, bursts into a torrent, creates oxbows and accepts tributaries and even dams. Teaching and practice of baptism is like this river. At first there was One Baptism. Baptism was assumed and practiced by every Christian. Yet, further downstream Christians killed and have been killed over their beliefs and practice of baptism. Many come to these waters of baptism in great turmoil and confusion. Because of this confusion and our need to discern a baptismal theology for today, we invite you down in the river to pray with us. We invite you not only to cognitive understanding of the depths of Christian history about baptism but also to come in and experience the sometimes icy and other times fiery waters of the river.

Down in the River to Pray is our invitation to the church for a visit to these waters. By revisiting Scripture and historical theology—

the stream of thought and practice about baptism flowing since the early church (and even before)—we may benefit from the faith and practice of Christians who have gone before us. Fighting back upstream is painstaking, but disregarding the river, in our view, is unacceptable. We have much to learn about baptism from the river.

Pre-understandings from the River of Time

We each come to biblical texts on baptism with pre-understandings that distort our reading and application of the practice. To again hear and discern the biblical context for baptism, we must begin by admitting we each come to the river on tributaries of church tradition and pre-understanding about the teaching and practice of baptism.

The story of a woman named Susan illustrates the deeply confused ideas we have about baptism today.

"I was born Catholic," Susan said, "and my mother baptized me in the church so I could have a godmother and godfather...I was an infant. She didn't know what I wanted."

Susan later attended what she called "Baptist" churches because she liked the way they explained the Bible. "My dad is still Catholic and my mom is Baptist like me," she said, "but I don't see any conflict, except later when I get married."

A Baptist pastor immersed Susan when she was a teenager. Now she has a sister who wants to get baptized to take communion. Susan said that was the wrong reason to get baptized. While Susan was searching, she was also overwhelmed in the river of church doctrine about baptism.

We, like Susan, may also be drowning in the river.

In the Churches of Christ, the community in which John Mark and I fellowship, people feel anxious, angry, and confused about what is happening to our beliefs and practices of baptism. Baptism has been a cornerstone doctrine taught in Churches of Christ. We have baptized because we believe it is a saving, Spirit-giving, forgiving moment for a disciple of Christ. Many churches defend the biblical doctrine of baptism in Churches of Christ from what they perceive as attacks on the command to baptize.

Yet Churches of Christ come to the river of baptism in need of more—not less—biblical instruction on baptism, conversion, transformation, initiation into a divine community and the Holy Spirit. Even those churches that perceive themselves in a siege and believe they are correct and biblically sound on baptism should revisit their teaching and practice of baptism. Baptism is more important than you think, but not for the reasons you suppose. While we have no illusions that this book will settle the issue, we hope it contributes to clearer belief and practice and not to confused or watered down teaching and practice of baptism in churches.

You may come to the rivers of baptism from a different stream than Churches of Christ. We know of many religiously mixed marriages. Particularly when it comes time to baptize their children, these families come to the river confused and disoriented. For example, we spoke with a Greek Orthodox member whose wife was raised Baptist and joined the Greek Orthodox Church when they were married. We asked them, "What will you do for baptism?" After all, their experiences were vastly different. They planned to baptize the baby in the Greek Orthodox Church by sprinkling. Bill said baptism would "protect" their child and add her to their faith community.

If you are Southern Baptist, on the other hand, you have a different pre-understanding and identity related to baptism than a Greek Orthodox, Church of Christ member, or Catholic. You were likely taught that baptism follows your decision to ask Jesus Christ into your heart and make him your personal savior—commonly called the "sinner's prayer." Baptism, then, was the ceremony through which you made your personal decision a public statement of faith.

If you were born into a Catholic family, the church may have taught you that baptism is a sacrament that saves you from the original sin of Adam. Your family, however, may have viewed the day of your baptism as your entrance into the church or an event that gave you a godfather or godmother.

A Mennonite may baptize because she believes it to be a real discipleship act. A Methodist, on the other hand, may baptize because he or she believes that baptism is more than a symbol but a sacrament that effectively mediates the grace of God to a human being.

These are only a few examples, and there are certainly hundreds of others. You may not identify with any of these streams and feel that you come to the river either with doubts, ambivalence, or possibly anticipation of diving into the river. Whatever stream brings you to the river of baptism, we all come to the waters with pre-understandings, emotions, and beliefs about the practice of baptism. We can all learn from the waters. Shall we gather at the river to learn from each other, dialogue and grow together?

How the Book Flows

Thirteen chapters in the book are customized for quarterly study in church classes or as individual study. We believe strongly in both individual study and also discernment in local bodies of Christ. We encourage you to discuss pre-understandings, stories, biblical texts, and tradition related to baptism in the context of a community of faith in God, Christ, and the Holy Spirit.

First, we invite you in chapter one to experience the river with us.

Second, we call you and your church to study and understand the river: chapters 2-4 lead us to fresh study of biblical texts related to baptism, chapters 5-7 lay out historic Christian thought, and chapters 8-10 contribute theological reflection to the flow.

Finally, we return to experience, but this time by revisioning the waters of baptism: chapters 11-13 apply teaching to practical concerns in the church today.

Our prayer for you is that the Holy Spirit will guide your study as you seek what God has done, is continuing to do, and will do in Christ. As you study, reflect, and revision your own and your church's belief and practice of baptism, our prayer for you is like Paul's prayer in Ephesians 3:17-23:

> I pray that the God of our Lord Jesus Christ, the Father of glory, may give you a spirit of wisdom and revelation as you come to know him, so that, with the eyes of your heart enlightened, you may know what is the hope to which he has called you, what are the riches of his glorious inheritance among the saints, and what is the immeasurable greatness of his power for us who believe, according to the working of his great power. God put this power to work in Christ when he raised him from the dead and seated him at his right hand in the heavenly places, far

above all rule and authority and power and dominion, and above every name that is named, not only in this age but also in the age to come. And he has put all things under his feet and has made him the head over all things for the church, which is his body, the fullness of him who fills all in all.

John Mark Hicks
Greg Taylor
March 2003

1 / Diving into the Divine Community

> *His voice grew soft and musical: "All the rivers come from that one River and go back to it like it was the ocean sea and if you believe, you can lay your pain in that River and get rid of it because that's the River that was made to carry sin. It's a River full of pain itself, moving toward the kingdom of Christ, to be washed away, slow, you people, slow as this here old red water river round my feet."*[1]

The preacher had built up a full head of steam when Mrs. Connin and Bevel, the boy she was babysitting, arrived for a "preaching at the river." A son of indigent parents, little Bevel most days made his own peanut butter sandwiches on stale raisin bread heels. Mrs. Connin took kindly to the boy and would pick him up from his parents' home and whenever possible took him to the preaching and healing. She suspected the boy had never been baptized and wasted no time handing the boy over to the preacher.

At first the boy thought the preaching and baptizing at the river was a joke. Everything was a joke at his house. But when the preacher asked him if he wanted to be washed in the deep river of life that was made to carry sin, to lay his trouble in the "River of Pain, and watch it move away toward the Kingdom of Christ,"

Bevel said "Yes." He imagined he would find this kingdom under the water and not have to return to his parents and eat stale bread while they slept off another hangover. The preacher said the words of baptism, plunged him in the water and held him there, and he came up spitting and spewing.

"You count now! You didn't even count before!" the preacher said.

That night Bevel's mother was furious that he was baptized. The nerve of that Mrs. Connin, she said, to have her son baptized without her knowledge then have the preacher pray for the boy's parents and their drunkenness! The next morning Bevel, alone, ate more stale bread and poured the ashes from his parents' cigarettes on the carpet and played like it was a sand pile. In despair, he got an idea: he would return to the river and find the kingdom of Christ.

He tried to dunk himself again down in the river but sprung up, gasping the way he did when the preacher immersed him. Something again was pushing him back. "He began to hit and splash and kick the filthy river." He thought he'd never find the kingdom of Christ, that it was all just another joke. He plunged in frustration again, and this time the "waiting current caught him like a long gentle hand and pulled him swiftly forward and down. For an instant he was overcome with surprise: then since he was moving quickly and knew that he was getting somewhere, all his fury and fear left him."[2]

****

Flannery O'Connor's story, "The River," about young Bevel is a poignant starting place to dive into a discussion of baptism. Like Bevel, we are so in awe of the kingdom of Christ that we dive in with abandon. Then reality strikes us as a slap across the face. Perhaps in those moments we too stand in the river of pain, knee-deep, angry that this whole thing was just another cruel joke. Was Jesus in the water with us in our baptism? Where is he now? Some of us, however, keep diving, however recklessly and ignorantly and blindly and innocently, pushing forward. Yet, the church over the centuries has been going down in the river to try to find the kingdom of God there. The current lifts our feet. The river carries us along, and we are drowned. At first we are overcome with surprise and wonder and fear. That's when we meet Christ in the depths.

The river, for us, illustrates three important themes to which we now turn:

- Divine community
- God's goal of transformation
- Historical theology in the flow of time

Divine Community

Baptism is more important than you think, but not for the reasons you suppose. Yet the very questions we ask about our baptism may knock us off course from God's intention for it. For instance, we have heard members of the Churches of Christ wonder aloud whether they were baptized for the right reasons. This line of reasoning looks not to God's work in baptism but to how much we know at baptism. A question that leads us closer to God's intention for baptism is, "Did I truly have faith in Christ at baptism?" This question centers more on God's goal for baptism: transforming us for relationship with him. Baptism serves the goal of transformation.

In baptism we are plunged into the holy names and persons of God, and because of this we belong to him wholly. Baptized into the name of the Father, Son, and Holy Spirit, we are imaging the triune community. Relationship is God's nature. When we submit to baptism we are initiated into the triune community—Father, Son, and Holy Spirit. We are making God's redemptive story our own story. The story is not left to our individual interpretation or privatized belief, nor is the story just about a personal savior. What we believe we believe in concert with millions of believers before us and as a part of the believers in the local community of faith.

Particularly for those who have never connected the movement of the triune community of God with their baptism, we believe a trip down to the river to revision our understanding and practice of baptism is vital. Because of the way immersion links us with God's work in Christ and the empowering of the Holy Spirit, baptism is certainly more important than we may have previously believed and practiced in many churches. In baptism, we dive into the holy presence of the Divine Community.

No gift in the universe exceeds the offering of community with God our Father, Christ his Son, and the Spirit's presence in our lives. Yet, we tragically underestimate the power of this gift and have instead settled for anemic beliefs and practices of baptism. The triune community of God saves, empowers, renews, and mediates grace through the events that baptism symbolizes and enacts. This action is effective and normative as an essential part of the whole conversion narrative of Scripture.

By God's divine foreknowledge and wisdom, he has taken what humanity meant for evil, the attempt to destroy his Son, and raised him to life (Acts 2:23-24). The Father exalted the Son to his right hand, and from this exalted place Christ has poured out his Holy Spirit on his people.

Peter, Bevel, and Seeking the Kingdom of God

Perhaps in the story of Bevel you envisioned a river with oxbows and banks and overhanging shade trees, a crowd gathered to hear the preacher call them to bring their trouble and "lay it in that River of Blood, lay it in that River of Pain." Now come with us to another stream in the Kidron Valley, where the spring of Gihon feeds into the city of Jerusalem. In the temple courts another preacher, the Apostle Peter, is calling a new community down in the waters of forgiveness.

Too often we neglect to hear Peter's sermon before his command to be baptized. Understanding this background is crucial to a biblical view of baptism. The dramatic growth of the church, from the day of Pentecost until now, testifies that the Holy Spirit made good on Jesus' promise to give the disciples power to be his witnesses, first in Jerusalem, Judea, Samaria, and unto the ends of the earth (Acts 1:8). They were carrying out what Matthew records as Jesus' final words to his disciples—what we call the "Great Commission," the empowering and authoritative call to make disciples throughout the world: "All authority in heaven and on earth has been given to me. Go therefore and make disciples of all nations, baptizing them in the name of the Father and of the Son and of the Holy Spirit, and teaching them to obey everything that I have commanded you. And remember, I am with you always, to the end of the age" (Matt. 28:17-20).

Christ appeared to them after his resurrection and talked about the kingdom of God. Even when Jesus spoke the Great Commission, Matthew says, "some still doubted." Moreover, Luke records the disciples, just before Christ's ascension, asking, "Lord, is this the time when you will restore the kingdom to Israel?" (Acts 1:6). Jesus' response seems patient in light of the fact that he'd answered this kind of question repeatedly in the three years he'd been with his disciples. Jesus said, "It is not for you to know the times or periods that the Father has set by his own authority. But you will receive power when the Holy Spirit has come upon you; and you will be my witnesses in Jerusalem, in all Judea and Samaria, and to the ends of the earth" (Acts 2:7-8).

Jesus instructed the disciples to wait for the coming of the Holy Spirit to give them power rather than them seeking political or personal power. The ascension may have been the most startling, mind-boggling sight they'd ever seen, because Acts says they were gazing intently into the sky. His departure didn't square with their expectations of earthly restoration of Israel. He had promised to be with them till the end of the age. What would they do now? As they stared into the sky two men dressed in white stood next to them and said, "Men of Galilee, why do you stand looking up toward heaven? This Jesus, who has been taken up from you into heaven, will come in the same way as you saw him go into heaven" (Acts 1:11).

While it would seem the disciples, by sheer power of the events of the resurrection and Christ being taken up into the sky, would have been terrified, Luke only records that they were staring intently into the sky. The two men dressed in white may have also frightened them. Because of these dramatic events, the disciples would have viewed Pentecost as an event that profoundly marked the rule of God. Indeed, they had been seeking a kingdom. Not in their wildest Galilean dreams could they have imagined this kingdom would involve God's Spirit dwelling in them and empowering them to speak. People thought they were drunk but Peter set them straight. Distilled spirits are not for morning, Peter told the crowd, but who knows when the Spirit of God will come?

In his sermon, Peter gives the divine community, the Father, Son, and Spirit, their due for their work. God, by his set purpose and foreknowledge, allowed his Son to be handed over to evil men (2:23). The Father had a higher purpose in this: he raised him from the dead (2:24) and exalted him to the right hand of the Father. Exalted, Christ poured out the Spirit that the crowd saw and heard in the disciples' proclamation (2:33). God made his own Son both Lord and Christ, and even though humanity had crucified him, he would forgive them and offer the powerful person of the Spirit to dwell in those who called on his name (2:21), repented and were baptized (2:38).

Can you visualize three thousand persons baptized in one day? The first believers may have been baptized in one of the many pools that surrounded the temple courts, such as Siloam. At the order of Hezekiah in the seventh century B.C., a tunnel diverted Gihon's waters from the Kidron Valley into the city. The water collected in pools, the last of which was Siloam, near Solomon's colonnade. Pools such as these, as well as numerous *mikva'ot* (immersion cisterns) that surrounded the Temple Mount, were used for ritual washings before the Jews entered the Temple courts.

Though these pools may have been the place three thousand were baptized, Luke does not say. The people must have been charged with awe and wonder. In response to Peter's sermon, "those who welcomed his message were baptized, and that day about three thousand persons were added. They devoted themselves to the apostles' teaching and fellowship, to the breaking of bread and the prayers" (Acts 2:41-42). To this small band of one hundred twenty followers, three thousand were added. The disciples were empowered by the Spirit and proclaimed the living Christ as a part of God's redemptive work. The Father raised and exalted the Son, and Christ then poured out the person and power of the Holy Spirit on that Pentecost morning.

The disciples were diving into the divine community. The community was not simply a community of believers—that is clear from the description of their daily interaction in Acts 2:41-42; it was also a triune community of the Father, Son, and Spirit.

God's Goal of Transformation

What was God's interest in baptism? What did God intend? We believe God's primary goal is to transform us for relationship with Father, Son, and Holy Spirit.[3] God's goal is the transformation of his creation for relationship with him. God's goal is indeed redemptive—he saves us—but he also restores our relationship.[4]

We believe all Christian churches should rediscover the transforming power of teaching and practicing the whole narrative of conversion. We believe the Christian church must face its own history and the whole scriptural witness about baptism. In so doing, we may return to baptism as an event of transformation in the life of the community of faith.

God has been about the business of choosing, cutting a covenant, and restoring his people since the first fruits of his creation chose to deny his authority in the Garden of Eden. God is, and ever will be, primarily interested in a relationship that reflects the very relationship enjoyed as Father, Son, and Holy Spirit. Peter quoted David's passionate reflection on this relationship (Acts 2:25-28):

> 'I saw the Lord always before me,
> for he is at my right hand so
> that I will not be shaken;
> therefore my heart was glad, and
> my tongue rejoiced;
> moreover my flesh will live in hope.
> For you will not abandon my soul to Hades,
> or let your Holy One experience corruption.
> You have made known to me the ways of life;
> you will make me full of gladness with your presence.'

Peter preached about the sweeping changes to which Joel and King David alluded: the "last days" in which God says, "I will pour out my Spirit on my people." The Jews, the primary group Peter addressed (Acts 2:14), were not likely to be thinking only in terms of their personal salvation but also of the restoration of Israel when they asked, "What shall we do?"

In response, Peter did something that often happens to us when our ears are tuned for certain notes and a maestro plays melodies that easily pass us by. His response to their (and our) question—"What shall we do?"—answers more about this life-flipping relationship with Christ than, perhaps, the questioners mean:

> Peter said to them, "Repent, and be baptized every one of you in the name of Jesus Christ so that your sins may be forgiven; and you will receive the gift of the Holy Spirit. For the promise is for you, for your children, and for all who are far away, everyone whom the Lord our God calls to him." (Acts 2:38-39)

With many other words, Acts says, Peter warned them, "Save yourselves from this corrupt generation" (Acts 2:40). In other words, be delivered from the crookedness of this world and its powers and allow the Messianic rule of Christ in your lives; come into the community of faith that images the relationship of the trinity and is empowered by the Spirit.

The outgrowth of the 3,000 being saved was a triune community of faith that "had all things in common" and "gave to everyone as he had need" and "continued to meet together" and "broke bread together" in each other's homes "with glad and sincere hearts, praising God and enjoying the favor of all the people." And the chapter ends with a summary statement, saying, "the Lord added to their number daily those who were being delivered." The use of the English "saved" in three places in the chapter may lead readers to believe that this chapter is essentially about personal salvation, but the language is about the total deliverance and restoration of God's people to his presence as his holy people in a transformed relationship with him. The response of "what shall we do?" was not primarily focused on a personal decision. Peter preached the upheaval of the entire world because of the "last days" events of the coming Messiah, his death, resurrection, ascension, and outpouring of the Holy Spirit. The kingdom was breaking into the world with power.

By contemplating Peter's entire sermon and the context in which he preached, the river looks much more to us like a rushing Spirit-led force of the kingdom of God. Peter called those attending Pentecost to more than individual salvation; he called them to the kingdom rule of God in their lives—a transformed relationship with the Father, Son, and Holy Spirit. And about 3,000 that day took the plunge into the kingdom.

The Stone-Campbell Movement

The Stone-Campbell Movement, the historical tradition associated with Churches of Christ, generally needs a more transformative understanding of baptism. Churches of Christ in particular have focused too much on the command of Peter and too little on his preaching beforehand. We have attempted to skip to the imperatives with too little hearing of the indicatives of God's grace. We believe the transforming power must be rediscovered in all Christian churches, but our major focus is Stone-Campbell churches. Ironically, many have obsessed about baptism so much that they have turned from the essential transforming truths about baptism to questions of technicalities and polemics against those who do not baptize in the same way.

We stand firmly for believer's immersion, but we believe something has gone terribly wrong on the way down to the river. We've been led astray or distracted from the full significance and transforming power of the whole conversion narrative, which includes faith, repentance, baptism, forgiveness of sins, and renewal by the Holy Spirit.

What went wrong on the way down to the river? On the one hand, we in the Stone-Campbell Movement often use technically exact baptismal teaching and practice as the litmus test of doctrinal purity. On the other hand, some Christians de-emphasize baptism in order to promote unity among Christians. Furthermore, members of the same churches do not even agree about the role of baptism for initiation, conversion, and discipleship. The singing at the river has descanted into sour notes and the water has turned bitter. Many churches decided on the way to the river that baptism is not the work of God but a human work to be technically accomplished rather than graciously received. Texts on baptism have been divorced from their context, re-married with other texts, while other parts of the narrative are skipped over in the rush to prove a point about the mode or essentiality of baptism. The whole conversion narrative of faith, Holy Spirit renewal, repentance, and baptism has been often boiled down to primarily faith or a focus on baptism or another singular element in the biblical witness.

Stone-Campbell churches continue to value baptism, but we are calling our own fellowship to a refocusing of the very doctrine and teaching we emphasize. We believe we need more—not less—teaching on baptism. We believe Churches of Christ in particular need a more transformative understanding of baptism.

Evangelical Churches

In contrast to Stone-Campbell churches, Evangelical churches generally need a higher view of baptism. While many Stone-Campbell descendants have focused more on the technicalities of baptism to the point of diminishing the significance of the symbolism and the effectiveness of baptism to mediate God's grace, many Evangelical churches have viewed baptism only symbolically and thus also diminished its full significance. Many view baptism as less about what God does—a sacrament—and more about what humanity does—a sign—to display before witnesses what is truly happening in the heart of the believer.

As churches lead candidates for baptism to the baptismal font or baptistery, some believe the ritual of water baptism is more about what the individual is declaring than what God is doing and proclaiming through this event. On the way to the river, others decided that baptism is a private experience rather than a communal moment of initiation into a divine community. Still others believe that baptism is merely a symbolic outward action that tells the story of the gospel through the metaphor of death to self, burial in water, and raising up out of water.[5]

Down at the river, churches are renewing the conversation about baptism—even some churches that had not previously emphasized baptism. We believe we must meet at the river; there Churches of Christ can—and indeed should—contribute to the unifying and challenging discussions among Evangelicals on the role of baptism in the life of believers.

Baptismal Theology in the Flow of Time

The river illustrates the stream of teaching and practice on baptism by the community of faith in history. At the river, we see the power of Father, Son, and Holy Spirit flowing down to us, out of the very throne of God (Rev. 22:1), and we are captivated not simply by water but by the triune source of healing, power, and rule. As we come to the river, we acknowledge that God the Father, Jesus Christ, and the Holy Spirit are the intended focus of our lives and should be the basis of reflection on baptism.

Baptism has been one common denominator in almost every Christian denomination through Christian history. Baptism is one Christian teaching and practice that has brought more people together down in the river than any other. One belief common to nearly all Christian fellowships is that baptism initiates a believer into the community of faith.[6] At the river we can see that the actual practice of baptism, however, is diverse. We see some immersing, others fetching water, calling it holy and pouring on the heads of baptismal candidates. Some include children and infants, while others include only adults.[7]

Over time, Christians at the river found that this most unifying ceremony in Christian history had become one of the most fractious. They debated on the riverbank then cut off the conversation with others farther away.

We had gone down in the river to pray and ended up drawing lines in the sand.

In the twenty-first century, the river banks are populated by Catholics who sprinkle infants for remission of original sin, Nazarenes and Baptists who are saved then called to be baptized later, Evangelicals who baptize both infants and adults, and Stone-Campbell descendants in Christian Churches and Churches of Christ who baptize for more reasons than you can count on one hand: obedience, forgiveness of sins, imparting of the Holy Spirit, pledge of good conscience, re-clothing, solidarity with Christ, burial and resurrection, and salvation.

Many in Stone-Campbell churches do not see the point of going down to the river for anything but baptism. There is no history there. But have we written off history and decided to learn nothing from the river from the first century till now? The early church had gone down in the river in response to the telling of the good news about Jesus (Acts 2:41; 9:35), and our teaching and practice does certainly derive from this scriptural model; yet we must be aware of other influences on our views and practices. If we approach these texts contextually and with humility about our own prejudices toward them, rather than for extracting proof-texts to correct others, perhaps we all may benefit from such study.

This book represents, not a retreat from the importance of baptism, but a move toward an even deeper understanding of God's intention for baptism in the context of our relationship with him. Baptism is more important than you think, just not for the reasons we often suppose.

It's time, again, for going down in the river for a preaching. Perhaps the setting of Flannery O'Connor's story of Bevel was similar to the scene dramatized in the film, *O Brother, Where Art Thou?* A preacher is calling the white robed baptismal candidates to the water and they are singing, "Let's go down in the river to pray...Lord, show me the way!"

As we have seen, however, the riverbanks are not filled with unified teaching and serenity, but chaos. Nevertheless, we are calling the church down to the river to see the vast history that flows before us, to renew our understanding of baptism in Scripture, and to embrace a vision for what's downstream from us.

Conclusion

Baptism serves the purpose of transformation for relationship with the Divine Community. And the journey we embark upon is historic and powerful, much like a river with both smooth waters and rapids we could never hope to navigate without the power of God. Baptism is, in the words of Luther, "Grace clutching us by the throat."[8] In awe we dive into the mystery of the community of God the Father, Christ the Son, and the Holy Spirit.

In baptism we are radically changed, a new worldview settles upon us. Like Bevel we know this side of the river is bleak. We're playing in the ashes and making peanut butter sandwiches on stale toast. We dive in, and at first we may be elated then perhaps disoriented, but we push forward however ignorantly and recklessly toward the kingdom of God.

Bevel found something at the riverbank that we must learn: baptism is more important than we think, but not for the reasons we suppose.

****

Principle

Our experience of baptism is important. Take a few minutes and write, perhaps for the first time, the story of your baptism, the events, ceremony, and people surrounding the occasion.

Our own story is important, yet when we visit the river again, we begin to experience baptism as something more than our own experience. When we take a fresh look at God's intention for baptism as transformation, taking our pre-understandings of baptism into account and learning Christian history related to baptism, we flow further downstream toward the throne of God who longs to transform us for relationship with Father, Son, and Holy Spirit.

Prayer

Dear Lord, we can't come to a study of baptism without some pre-understandings. Whether those ideas are shallow as a summer stream or deep as the ocean, we want to lay these ideas before your throne, to open Scripture fully and seek your goals and intentions for us, your creation. Please humble us before these Bible texts and before the church's history, teaching, and practice of baptism. May you shape us in your image, and prevent us from attempting to shape you in ours. Amen.

Questions

1. How did your baptism transform you?

2. How can our churches add to the discussion about baptism in the Christian community without being sectarian or so defensive that discussion is cut off?

3. Why is it important for us to go down in the river and envision baptismal history from the first century until today?

4. What pre-understandings do you have about baptism?

5. Why were you baptized?

2 / *The Headwaters of Baptism in Israel*

In the fifth hour, the morning work session came to an end and everybody gathered for the midday meal in the community centre. First they immersed themselves in the ritual baths. These were plaster-lined cisterns into which a staircase, occupying the whole width of a cistern side, descended. The staircase was divided by a low partition wall, symbolic rather than functional–to separate those descending from those ascending. After bathing, naked except for loincloths, they changed into neat, white dress and went quietly to the assembly hall, which also served as the refectory.[1]

—Qumran Community Ritual (1st Century A.D.)

Scenes like this historical fiction were repeated countless times in first-century Judaism. Ritual immersions in pools of water were a daily facet of Jewish life. They descended impure into the water on one side and ascended pure on the other. Cleansed, they were prepared to share in holy meals and meet God in his holy sanctuary.

****

For centuries people have been going down into rivers to pray. Almost every culture has had some kind of water or cleansing ritual as part of their religious life. In this sense, baptism is not unique to Christianity.

While some have believed Christianity adopted their water ritual from Greco-Roman culture, "attempts to find the antecedents of baptism in the mystery religions have been decisively laid to rest."[2] Most now recognize that the origin and practice of Christian baptism is deeply connected to the ritual baths of the Jewish Second Temple period (ca. 200 B.C. to 70 A.D.). More fundamentally, the Christian river flows out of the history of God with his people in the Old Testament.

The Hebrew Scriptures influenced the Christian understanding of baptism in at least two ways. First, New Testament writers regarded certain events in redemptive history as types (thus, the Greek word *tupon*) of Christian baptism. Peter calls baptism the antitype (*antitupon*) of the Noahic flood in 1 Peter 3:21. Paul uses baptismal language to describe the crossing of the Red Sea and says what happened to Israel was an example (*tupon*) for Christians (1 Cor. 10:1, 6). The significance of Christian baptism is illuminated typologically by the events of redemptive history. These redemptive events embody theological principles that are also expressed in Christian baptism.

Second, the practice of water immersion in Israelite religion foreshadowed baptism in the Christian faith. The ritual baths of Levitical priests and the mandated ceremonial washings for ritual cleansing in Leviticus lead to Christian baptism through the ritual baths of Second Temple Judaism. When Peter invited believers in Jesus at Pentecost to be baptized in the name of Jesus (Acts 2:38), baptism was not foreign to the culture and religious life of his hearers. On the contrary, the only thing new was the referent—this ritual immersion was in the name of Jesus for the remission of sins and participants received the gift of the Holy Spirit.

Redemptive-Historical Typology

Typology is a hermeneutical device by which authors see in the past meanings that are associated with present realities. For example, the Passover was a type of the Lord's Supper. The meaning of the former was ultimately fulfilled in the latter. Typology is a difficult topic and should be approached with caution. Consequently, while there may be other instances of baptismal typology in the Old Testament (e.g., Naaman in 2 Kings 5), we have restricted ourselves to two. The Flood and the Exodus are directly linked to a Christian theology of baptism in the New Testament.

The Noahic Flood and Baptism (1 Peter 3:18-21)

> For Christ also suffered for sins once for all, the righteous for the unrighteous, in order to bring you to God. He was put to death in the flesh, but made alive in the spirit, in which also he went and made a proclamation to the spirits in prison, who in former times did not obey, when God waited patiently in the days of Noah, during the building of the ark, in which a few, that is, eight persons, were saved through water. And baptism, which this prefigured, now saves you—not as a removal of dirt from the body, but as an appeal to God for a good conscience, through the resurrection of Jesus Christ.

The succinct statement that "baptism…now saves you" is astounding. Indeed, it is scandalous for some. Peter attributes to baptism some kind of soteriological function and his exact meaning has been the subject of considerable debate.

The Noahic Flood is typological of the saving function of baptism. The eight persons who found refuge in the ark from the destructive floodwaters were, in fact, "saved through water" (*dieswthesan di' hudatos*), and this prefigured how Christians are also saved through water (that is, water baptism saves us). Baptism, just like the Flood, is a saving event. Just as God saved Noah through cleansing the old world with water, so God saves his people from their old life through baptism. In the Noahic Flood, water judged the old world and cleansed it, and baptism judges the old life and cleanses it. To use a Pauline metaphor, baptismal water kills the old person, buries it and then renews it. Noah passed through the waters into a new world, just as Christians pass through baptism into a new life.

Peter, however, quickly qualifies his meaning. He does not want to foster a misunderstanding or misapplication of his point. The power of this salvation is not inherent in the water. The water does not literally save, but God saves through the water by the power of Christ's work. The death of Christ, where the righteous died for the unrighteous, is the power of salvation. The resurrection of Christ, where life overcomes death, is the power of salvation. Baptism saves us, not by the power of the water, but "through the resurrection of Jesus," just as—as Peter wrote earlier—God gave us a "new birth into a living hope through the resurrection of Jesus" (1 Pet. 1:3).

Peter's qualification points us to the significance of baptism. It is no mere cleansing of the outer person. It is not like a Jewish ritual bath that only cleansed the outer person from ceremonial impurities or like an ordinary bath that only removes the dirt from the body. On the contrary, it addresses the inner person. It is the "appeal to God for a good conscience." Baptism has an inner dimension—it is a function of conscience.

The exact nature of this function, however, is debated. The Greek term behind the word "appeal" (*eperotema*) is ambiguous. While the NRSV translates Peter's phrase as an "appeal to God for a good conscience," the NIV translates it "the pledge of a good conscience toward God." In other words, is baptism the appeal for a good conscience (thus, a cleansing of the inner person) or is it the pledge of a good conscience (thus, a commitment of loyalty to God). Is baptism a "prayer" (Moffatt's translation) for a clean conscience or a pledge of allegiance? Both fit the inner/outer contrast in the text—baptism is not simply an outer act like removing dirt from the body, but it is an inner appeal or pledge of the soul. Both suppose that baptismal candidates actively appeal or commit themselves to God through baptism. This would seem to exclude those who cannot make such an appeal or commitment.

The term itself is problematic. It only appears here in the New Testament. In the second century the word commonly appeared in legal documents. It referred to the practice of "answering" the question of whether one would keep the contract. Viewed in this way, baptism is the "answer of a good conscience" which pledges to keep the baptismal covenant. If, however, the noun is viewed through the lens of its verbal form (*eperotao*), which means "request," then the word refers to the believers' request through baptism for a good conscience. This is a better fit with Peter's contrast. Baptism is not the cleansing of the outer body, but rather it saves through the cleansing of the inner person as believers address God in that moment. Baptism is the sinner's prayer for a good conscience; a prayer for the application of God's saving act to cleanse the conscience.[3] As Colwell writes, "what is a sacrament if it is not a human prayer and promise in response to a promise of God and in anticipation of its fulfillment?"[4] We go down in the river to pray for a good conscience. We go down in the river seeking transformation.

What is the meaning of "now" in Peter's statement? Some have thought that perhaps this was part of a baptismal liturgy so that at the moment of baptism this was the pronouncement over the candidate, that is, "baptism now saves you" as you are immersed. But it is better to see this "now" as a redemptive-historical term. It is an "eschatological" (or apocalyptic) now where we experience the end-time salvation in the present. Just as the Flood was a cataclysmic event that destroyed the old world through cleansing, so the baptismal experience is a destruction of the old person through cleansing. Just as Noah and his family were "saved through water," so we are saved through water. Just as Noah and his family transitioned from an old to a new world, so through baptism we move from an old world under judgment to a new beginning in a renewed life. The old passed away and everything became new—for Noah, and for us! Baptism is an apocalyptic, or eschatological, moment. We have been born anew (1 Pet. 1:23).

The Identity of Israel and Baptism (1 Cor. 10:1-5)

> I do not want you to be unaware, brothers and sisters, that our ancestors were all under the cloud, and all passed through the sea, and all were baptized into Moses in the cloud and in the sea, and all ate the same spiritual food, and all drank the same spiritual drink. For they drank from the spiritual rock that followed them, and the rock was Christ. Nevertheless, God was not pleased with most of them, and they were struck down in the wilderness.

The most momentous redemptive event in the history of Israel was the Exodus when Israel crossed the Red Sea. They escaped Egyptian bondage and were led to a new relationship with God at

Mt. Sinai. At the Red Sea Israel saw the salvation of God (Ex. 14:26-15:18). No other event in the history of Israel evoked more profound images of redemption and salvation than this one. There were, of course, other events, even related to water, that were redemptive in character. For example, Israel experienced God's salvation at the river Jordan when they crossed over into the land—God brought them from Shittim (the east bank of the Jordan) to Gilgal (the west bank of the Jordan; cf. Micah 6:5). But the Exodus is the paradigmatic redemptive event in Israel's history.

Paul characterizes this redemption as a baptism "into Moses," which is Paul's baptismal language when he describes Christian baptism as "into Christ" (Rom. 6:3; Gal. 3:27). Indeed, earlier in 1 Corinthians Paul noted that Christians find their identity and unity in the fact that Christ died for us and that we were baptized into the name of Christ rather than "into the name of Paul" (1 Cor. 1:13, NIV). Paul wants us to understand our baptism as a comparable moment of deliverance and redemption. Just as they were baptized into Moses, so we are baptized into Christ.

The point of "into Moses" is identity. Israel gained a new identity at the Exodus. There God declared to the nations that Israel belonged to him and Israel entered into a relationship with God through Moses. Likewise, those who are baptized into Christ also are given a new identity as part of the people of God.

This identity means that there is a new relationship of loyalty. God is jealous for his people (1 Cor. 10:22). The identity is a privilege and a gift, but it is no guarantee. Just because God redeemed Israel at the Red Sea did not mean that God would excuse behavior inconsistent with that identity. Indeed, many died in the wilderness because of their sin. The privilege of redemption carries with it grave responsibilities, just as the new life of a Christian emerges out of a grave. We are redeemed in order that we might be conformed to the image of Christ. We must not rest in our redemption while neglecting God's transforming work.

Baptism is an experience of redemption. We are baptized into Christ, freed from sin and bound to God in a new relationship. But this gift is no guarantee. Rather, it is a call to responsibility. Christians, just like the Israelites, easily fall prey to the sin of presumptuousness. We abuse our privileges and expect God's grace.

We presume our status, and Paul warns that "if you think you are standing, watch out that you do not fall" (1 Cor. 10:12). But God calls us to ethical responsibility and discipleship. He is jealous for the relationship and calls us to reflect his own values in our lives. We must not presume upon the gift and turn the grace of God into a license for sin.

Baptism is a wonderful divine gift. God redeems us, gives us a new identity and frees us from bondage through his mighty work. Baptism, however, is no substitute for transformation. Baptism serves the goal of transformation as God works through baptism to transform a people for himself, but without transformation baptism is meaningless.

Ritual Baths in the History of Israel

One of the foundational principles of Christianity, according to the preacher in Hebrews, is the "instruction about baptisms" (6:2; *baptismon didaches*). The plural may seem rather curious to contemporary Christians. But first-century readers were well aware of the pervasive character of bath rituals in first-century Judaism. They also knew the baptismal regulations in Leviticus, which the preacher also mentioned in Hebrews 9:9 as "various baptisms" (*baptismois*). It was imperative for the preacher that his readers discern the difference between Christian baptism, which lies at the foundation of Christian faith and repentance (Heb. 6:1-2), and the ceremonial baptisms of the Levitical order which could "not perfect the conscience of the worshiper" (Heb. 9:8-9). Their Christian baptism ushered them into a new reality of which Levitical baptisms were only shadows.

Levitical Immersions

There were many ritual washings in Torah regulations (Lev. 8:6; 11:32; 14:8, 9; 15:5, 6, 7, 8, 10, 11, 13, 16, 18, 21, 22, 27; 16:4, 24, 26, 28; 17:15; 22:6; Num. 19:7, 8, 19; and Deut. 23:12). These washings were immersions or baths in water. For example, Leviticus 15:16 prescribes the washing of the "whole body." If first-century Jews were united on anything, they agreed immersion was the biblical mode of ritual purity. In view of this diversity on practically every other religious concern, Sanders asks, "What, then, are we to make of the happy harmony on immersion and pools?" Their agreement was "exegetical" as they read the regulations concerning Levitical washings as immersions.[5]

In fact, according to Webb, water sprinklings or affusions were unknown in Israel except in two cases. "Sprinkling persons with water," he writes, "is used only in two contexts: cleansing the Levites prior to service (Num. 8.7) and cleansing corpse impurity in the red heifer rite (Num. 19.1). In both cases additional cleansing procedures were involved (8:7-8; 19:12, 19)."[6] These sprinklings were water mixed with blood or other sacrificial elements. In all other cases in the Levitical prescriptions, water rituals were "washings" or "baths" (immersions)—terms that identify the rituals as immersions. Naaman, for example, was told to "wash" (*louo*) in the river Jordan (2 Kings 5:10, 12, 13), and he dipped (*ebaptisato*), that is, baptized or immersed himself in it (2 Kings 5:14). "Washing" and "dipping" were equivalents—they were ritual baths. Normally, sprinkling in the Israelite rituals is a sprinkling of blood, or sometimes a sprinkling of ashes (Ex. 9:8-10). Only a single text outside of Numbers in the Old Testament refers to the sprinkling of water—Ezekiel 36:25. Even here, however, the water is characterized as "clean," which means that it is mixed with sacrificial elements such as blood or ashes. It is not "clean" water in the sense that it is only water, but it is a mixed water of purification as in Numbers 19.

Levitical baptisms served a significant function in the life of Israel. Two functions are especially significant for understanding Christian baptism. First, ritual immersions were part of priestly life. Second, they were important for ritual purity in cases of physical defilement.

Before the consecration of the priests, Aaron and his sons were bathed (Ex. 29:4), and before the tabernacle was put into service they were bathed (Ex. 40:12). On the Day of Atonement, the high priest bathed before putting on sacred garments (Lev. 16:4). He also bathed after taking off the sacred garments (Lev. 16:24). The one who led the scapegoat outside of the assembly bathed before he returned to the camp (Lev. 16:26), and the one who burned the bull and goat outside the camp bathed before he returned to the camp (Lev. 16:28). These immersions separated the individuals from the impurities of life and they separated them from the agents of sin bearing. It was not so much a moral purification as it was a setting apart—the high priest is set apart for his holy task on the day of atonement and the priests were set apart for their ritual tasks. They were "cleansed" before they entered the presence of God or stood in God's presence on behalf of the people. They were "sanctified" or "consecrated" before they entered the holy presence. They were washed or cleansed in order to enter God's presence.

Hebrews 10:22 applies this typology to the Christian experience. The leading verb of Hebrews 10:22 is "draw near" (used elsewhere in Hebrews 4:16; 7:25; 10:1; 11:6; 12:18, 22). It describes the worshiper's access to God (cf. Lev. 9:5, 7, 8; 10:4, 5; 21:17, 18, 21, 23). The high priest approached God by entering the Holy of Holies and Christians approach God through Christ (Heb 7:25). Because Jesus is our high priest, we draw near to God in full assurance with sincere hearts.

The preacher draws the parallel further. Just as the high priest immersed himself before entering the Holy of Holies, so Christians are washed before they draw near to God. The preacher in Hebrews uses the identical language of Leviticus: wash, body and water (cf. Lev. 16:4, 23, 26, 28). Given the preacher's interest in baptisms in Hebrews 6:2 and 9:9, he clearly parallels the ritual immersion of the High Priest on the Day of Atonement before he approaches God with the immersion of believers who have been washed before they approach God. Of course, this is no mere external cleansing. Rather, the heart is also sprinkled with blood just as the body is washed with water. Blood, not water, is always the object of "sprinkling" in Hebrews (cf. 9:13, 19-22; 12:24). Water refers to an immersion ritual in line with the Levitical baptisms and the bath of the High Priest on the Day of Atonement. Though some understand "water" as a metaphor for "Spirit," this fits neither the immediate (high priest on the Day of Atonement typology) nor the remote (baptisms in Hebrews) context, and it does not fit the language of washed "bodies" (physical) in the inner (hearts sprinkled) and outer (bodies washed) combination. But this immersion, in contrast to the Levitical immersions (Heb. 9:8-9), is an outer/inner cleansing moment—by the sprinkling of the blood of Jesus our baptism prepares us for entrance into the presence of God with a cleansed conscience. Those who approach God to enter the Holy of Holies are sprinkled with the blood of Jesus and washed with pure water.

In addition to priestly functions, water immersions were also important for ritual purity. After exposure to diseases, everyone bathed for ceremonial purity (Lev. 14:8-9). After bodily discharges, everyone bathed for ceremonial purity (Lev. 15:5-11, 13, 16, 18, 21-22, 27). After eating something killed by wild animals, everyone bathed for ceremonial purity (Lev. 17:15). After touching anything unclean, everyone bathed for ceremonial purity (Lev. 22:6).

Old Testament washings were external regulations that could not cleanse the conscience (Heb. 9:9) and were intended only for physical contagion and communicable impurities. "In contrast," Webb writes, "when the state of uncleanness was caused by moral contagion...the responses varied, but actual ablutions were not prescribed in such cases...Dealing with sin itself usually required a sacrifice to provide atonement."[7] The Levitical washings were concerned with ritual purity and physical defilement, not with moral purification.

This is the point of the preacher in Hebrews. The Levitical baptisms could not perfect the conscience (Heb. 9:9). There is a difference between Levitical baptisms and Christian baptism. New Testament washings are external regulations that involve the cleansing of the conscience (Heb. 10:22; cf. 1 Pet. 3:20-21). The difference between the two is not the baptism itself, but the sacrifice that grounds the different baptisms (Heb. 9:13-14; 10:2-4, 11-12, 19-22). The blood sprinkled upon the heart in the context of Christian washing or baptism is the blood of Jesus that is able to cleanse the conscience whereas the blood of animals was not able to do so.

Ultimately, both forms of ritual washing, whether priestly or in relation to physical contagion, served a more fundamental purpose. They both represented some kind of cleansing which enabled the worshipper to draw near to God. The outer contamination or ritual impurity hindered their approach to God. The water rituals were outward cleansings whereupon worshippers were admitted into the presence of God.

Second Temple Immersions

The immediate backdrop for Christian baptism, other than the theological typology upon which the preacher in Hebrews draws, is the Jewish baths or immersion rituals of the Second Temple period (200 B.C.-70 A.D.).[8] Immersions in water were common in Palestinian Judaism. Our window into these immersions is primarily through three identifiable practices: (1) Jewish purification baptisms; (2) Jewish proselyte baptisms; and (3) Qumran baptisms.

The significance of Jewish purification immersions in the first century has only recently come into prominent discussion.[9] There was a time, for example, when some argued that there was not sufficient water in Jerusalem to immerse three thousand people on Pentecost. However, the existence of numerous immersion pools (*mikva'ot* [pl]; *mikveh* [sg]) has rendered this point mute, though some continue to repeat the argument.[10] Within the environs of the Temple, there were sufficient "baptistries" for the immersion of many more than three thousand people.

The first ancient *mikva'ot* identified as such were discovered at Masada in the early 1960s. *Mikva'ot* were generally dug out of the bedrock—much like a cistern—and were filled with rainwater. Usually, there were two sets of stairs—one for descending into the water for self-immersion and then one ascending out of the water. Others have since been discovered at the Herodium, Herod's winter palace in Jericho, private homes in Jerusalem (almost every private residence in the Upper City had its own), but especially around the Temple Mount in Jerusalem (at least 48).[11] A total of 150 had been found in Jerusalem as of 1993.[12] Indeed, several have been discovered outside the Jerusalem wall where many devout Jews immersed themselves before entering the holy city.[13] Others immersed themselves in the evening when they arrived home. Some, according to the Babylonian Talmud (*Tosaphoth Jadaim*, 2:20), immersed themselves every morning and were called "baptists of the morning."

Complete immersion was required for ritual purity. The Mishnah tractate *Mikvaot* (9.1) requires that "for immersion to be valid, no part of the body's surface may be untouched by the water."[14] Purity was necessary for entering the Temple Mount, before making a sacrifice, and as a result of contact with unclean elements or after engaging in unclean activities. The Mishnah tractate *Yoma* (3:3) states that no one could enter the Temple without ritual purity through immersion. This is confirmed by the numerous *mikva'ot* surrounding the Temple Mount. Most, if not all, immersed themselves before entering the Temple or before eating holy meals.[15] Josephus (*Antiquities*, 12.3.4) confirms this by reference to a second-century B.C. decree that only those who had purified themselves could enter the Temple. Thus, daily immersion was not uncommon in Palestinian Judaism. The practice is reflected in the New Testament as devout Jews would not only immerse themselves daily but also their utensils, beds and other items (Mark 7:4 ["wash" is "immerse," *baptisontai* and "washing" is "immersing," *baptismous*]; Luke 11:38 ["wash" is "immerse," *ebaptisthe*]). While some have questioned the immersion of such items as a bed, the Mishnah prescribes the immersion of furniture and beds that had become unclean (*Mikva'ot* 7.7). And while some read Luke 11:38 as if it is about the washing of hands, the text is more probably about daily immersions, which was apparently the practice of priestly families as well as some Pharisees.[16] Some Jewish-Christian sects apparently continued this practice. The fourth-century Christian writer Ephipanius (*Panarion*, 17) identified a first-century group whom he called the "Hermerobaptists" (daily baptizers) who believed that daily baptisms were required for moral purity.

The need for purification is one of the reasons synagogues were built near water (lakes, rivers) or with their own *mikva'ot*. The oldest excavated synagogue in Palestine is near Jericho. It was in use for about one hundred years between 130-30 B.C. The synagogue building contained two *mikva'ot*.[17] Purification rituals continued in the Post-Temple era. *Mikva'ot* have been found in numerous synagogues throughout the East and even in Western Europe (a medieval *mikveh* is visible in Cologne, Germany). Apparently, some believed that a ritual immersion was necessary before entrance into the synagogue. "Confirmation of this practice comes from Ben Zoma," writes Grasham, "who, when questioned about the need for purificatory baths before attending worship, said that all who cross over to the sacred area of life need an immersion."[18]

Another backdrop to Christian baptism may be Jewish proselyte immersions. While impossible to be certain, there is a growing consensus that proselyte immersions predated Christian baptism, although some believe that it did not become an initiatory rite until after the destruction of Jerusalem when it replaced the sacrificial offering. Indeed, the oldest explicit record of proselyte baptism as part of a conversion ritual for Gentiles is found in the Mishnah (*Yebamoth*, 47a, which may reflect a first-century practice, but it is uncertain).[19] Nevertheless it is difficult to believe that ethnic Gentiles were not asked to undergo some kind of ablutions before they offered a sacrifice in the temple when even devout Jews were asked to do so.

If the Jewish faithful were expected to cleanse themselves from ritual impurities through frequent immersions in water, it would follow that pagan converts would also undergo some kind of immersion ritual or at least participate in the immersion rituals which were expected of devout Jews. While improbable that there was a proselyte immersion that served as an initiation or conversion rite in the early first century, it is probable that they were immersed after their circumcision for ritual purity.[20] Baptism as an initiatory rite was probably introduced after the destruction of the temple and became common in the second and third centuries. Some have argued that the immersion mystically connected the convert with the experience of Israel at the Red Sea. In either event, it appears that Christian baptism owes its heritage more to Old Testament and Second Temple immersions than to anything specifically linked to proselyte immersions. Nevertheless, the existence of proselyte baptism is part of the cultural fabric in which Christianity developed and grew.

A third backdrop to Christian baptism during the Second Temple period is the Qumran (the Dead Sea Scrolls community) practice of immersion. Some think this is the primary context for the baptism of John the Baptist.[21] *Mikva'ot* were identified at Qumran in 1973.[22]

The Temple Scroll identifies several reasons for ritual immersions. They are connected with ritual impurity, cleansing of moral failure, and initiation into true/pure Israel. The initiatory immersion was purificatory which involved a change of status. There were also daily immersion rituals in Qumran, which were connected with repentance and the coming of God's future reign.

Theologically, immersions in the Qumran community were understood as prefigurements of the eschatological (end-time) washing. The *Manual of Discipline* describes the coming kingdom with the metaphor of a bath (1QS 4:18-22).[23] When Qumran members immersed themselves, they anticipated that eschatological moment.

While all three practices (ritual immersions, proselyte immersions and Qumran immersions) formed part of the cultural context in which Christianity flowered, none are exactly equivalent to Christian baptism with its emphasis on moral purification, transformative living, forgiveness of sins and the gift of the Holy Spirit. Nevertheless, no first-century Jew would have been surprised by Peter's call for an immersion in water. Such immersions were common. The surprise would have been the "high" theology associated with that immersion as it effectively symbolized and signified the work of God in Christ. The surprise was the Messianic character of this baptism, which we will address in the next chapter.

Conclusion

Christian baptism did not arise out of nothing. Rather, it is part of the redemptive-historical work of God among his people through Israel. God used water to judge and cleanse a world, and now he uses water to judge the old and cleanse a new people for himself through Christian baptism. God used water as a boundary marker for redemption in the Exodus, and now he uses it as a marker of redemption through Christ. God used water as a cleansing ritual among his people in order to prepare them for entrance into his presence, and now our bodies are washed as he sprinkles us with the blood of his Son so that we might enter the holiest place.

When we go down in the river to pray, we join the whole history of God's people there. We experience the destruction and renewal of the Noahic Flood and are united with Israel as they crossed the Red Sea. Dirty we go down in the river and clean we come out because God hears our appeal for a good conscience and cleanses us by the blood of his Son. The river is significant, not because it is water, but because it is connected with God's work through Israel. It is one of the threads that connects the history of redemption from beginning to end. It is a river that flows from the past through the present into the future. It begins and ends at the throne of God, but it flows through human history as a point that connects us with God and the past as well as the future people of God.

Principle

Water rituals represent a transition—from the old world to the new world (Noah), from bondage to freedom (Israel) and from impurity to purity (Levitical rituals). Water rituals cleanse the participants and prepare them for entrance into something new, free and pure. They sanctify a people for God's holy presence.

Prayer

Father, we thank you for the way you have prepared your people throughout history. We thank you for the history of your redemption by which you gathered a people for yourself. May we remember that history and embody its values in our communities of faith today. Never let us forget that you have prepared us for yourself through your people Israel. We thank you for your covenant of love with Israel and the renewal of that covenant in Jesus, your Son, by your Spirit. Amen.

Questions

1. What is the typological significance for baptism of the Noahic flood? How are the destructive waters purifying?

2. What is the typological significance for baptism of the Exodus? How do we experience that Exodus in our own baptism?

3. What is the typological significance for baptism of Levitical washings? Why is washing important in relation to divine presence?

4. Why is "water" such a vivid image in biblical and Jewish history? Have contemporary Christians lost the dynamic character of that image?

5. How does "water" connect the present with both the past and the future? Why is it important to situate Christian baptism in the context of God's redemptive history? How does this give more significance to the water of Christian baptism?

3 / The Restoration of Israel: Spirit and Baptism in Luke-Acts

In the last days it will be, God declares, that I will pour out my Spirit upon all flesh, and your sons and your daughters will prophesy, and your young men shall see visions and your old men shall dream dreams. Even upon my slaves, both men and women, in those days I will pour out my Spirit; and they shall prophesy... Then everyone who calls on the name of the Lord will be saved.

—Peter, quoting the prophet Joel (Acts 2:17-18, 21)

The pilgrims could not believe their ears. They had come from countries throughout the whole Roman Empire, each with their own language and dialect. Yet, they heard Galileans speaking in their native tongues! Some sneered and said they were just drunk. Others wondered about the significance of this remarkable event.

But they were not drunk, and something phenomenal was happening. God had poured out his Spirit. God had begun the restoration of Israel. Peter quoted the prophet Joel with his promise of the Spirit, restoration and salvation for those who call upon the name of the Lord. He told the story of Jesus' ministry and death. He announced the resurrection of Jesus and his exaltation as Lord and Messiah.

The pilgrims were astonished. "What should we do?" they asked. "Repent, and be baptized every one of you in the name of Jesus Christ so that your sins may be forgiven," Peter responded, "and you will receive the gift of the Holy Spirit."

Three thousand people welcomed the message. Though most, if not all, had already immersed themselves as they entered the temple that day in one of the *mikva'ot* that surrounded the Temple Mount, they were immersed again. But this time they were immersed upon (*epi*) the name of Jesus, calling upon (*epi*) the name of the Messiah.

A new community was formed. They were now a Messianic community. Israel began anew that day. They gathered at the temple daily to pray and hear the teaching of the twelve. They broke bread together in their homes as they praised the God of their salvation. They shared their food, their possessions and their lives with each other.

The pilgrims came to Jerusalem to seek Yahweh at his Temple, and the God of Abraham, Isaac and Jacob poured out his Spirit upon them through the exaltation of Jesus of Nazareth as the Christ.[1]

****

Baptism figures more prominently in Luke-Acts than in any other text of the New Testament. Luke gives more attention to the baptism of John the Baptist than the other Gospel writers and the conversion narratives of Acts consistently emphasize baptism as the faith response of those who heard the gospel proclaimed. The Greek terms for baptism appear more in Luke-Acts than in the rest of the New Testament.

However, Luke's two accounts are narratives, not church manuals or directories, and certainly not "systematic theologies" of baptism. Luke narrates the story of John, Jesus and the early church, and while baptism is a prominent element in the narrative, it is not its centerpiece. Baptism does not function independently in the narrative, but serves the larger concern that drives Luke's gospel story.

New Testament scholars have increasingly recognized, even to the point of general consensus, that Luke's dominant motif is the expectation of the "restoration of Israel." Luke narrates that restoration. N. T. Wright has demonstrated that this was the ardent expectation of Israel in the first century and that Israel still viewed itself under the curse of the exile but living with the hope of restoration.[2] The disciples expected this throughout Jesus' ministry, and after his resurrection they asked him (Acts 1:6): "Lord, is this the time when you will restore the kingdom to Israel?"

Therefore, the purpose of Luke-Acts is to narrate the restoration of Israel—first in the person and ministry of Jesus, and then in the pouring out of the Spirit upon the church. Jesus is the presence of the kingdom in a fallen world and when he ascended to the right hand of the Father, he sent the Holy Spirit as a continued divine presence among his people. He reconstituted the people of God and restored Israel by pouring out his Spirit.

Baptism, as Jon Weatherly points out, functions "less as the church's sacrament and more as an action that evokes the fulfillment of Israel's hopes."[3] Baptism is a prophetic act—it performatively and effectively signifies God's salvation of Israel. It embodies the hope of Israel and declares God's saving action for Israel in Jesus Christ. The conversion narratives in Acts—which include faith, repentance, baptism, forgiveness of sins, and the Holy Spirit—testify to the coming of the kingdom. God restored the kingdom to Israel through pouring out his Spirit and calling his people to faith, repentance and baptism. This is the context of Luke's baptismal theology.[4]

The Baptism of John

John comes to Israel as the prophet of the coming restoration. In typical prophetic fashion, "the word of God came to John" (Luke 3:2). His mission is defined by Isaiah 40:3. Matthew, Mark and Luke all quote Isaiah's fundamental mission of the voice "crying out in the wilderness"—he prepares the way for the Lord. But only Luke extends the quotation to Isaiah 40:5. The final line in Luke's quotation is, "and all flesh (*pasa sarx*) shall see the salvation of God." This anticipates the language Luke quotes from the restoration text of Joel 2 in Acts 2:17-21. According to Luke's quotation of Joel, God pours out his Spirit on "all flesh" (*pasan sarka*) and "everyone who calls on the name of the Lord shall be saved." And the events on that Pentecost day were "what was spoken through the prophet Joel" (Acts 2:16).

John's mission is to announce the coming of the kingdom of God as the fulfillment of God's promise to restore Israel. His mission and message are filled with language and motifs of Jewish expectation. It anticipated the "last days" when God would judge the world and restore his people, when God would both curse and bless. It is the language of "eschatological" (last things) anticipation. Something is about to change; God is doing a new work—a work of judgment and a work of blessing. Consequently, John asked the "vipers" that had come to him about who had warned them "to flee from the wrath to come." God is about to come and "cut down" every tree that does not bear "good fruit" and throw it "into the fire" (Luke 3:7-9). Judgment is coming.

In the light of this coming judgment, John calls for repentance and transformed living. Those who come to him for baptism should share their possessions (Luke 3:11), pursue economic justice (Luke 3:12), and treat people fairly (Luke 3:13). John rebuked sinners and called them to repentance in light of the coming judgment, even rebuking Herod the Tetrarch for his evil (Luke 3:19). Those who come to him for baptism must exhibit "fruits worthy of repentance" (Luke 3:8). This resonates with the Old Testament expectation of the "last days" and the coming of God to judge and save his people. Joel 1:13-20 has a similar call to repentance. Even there "fire" devours Israel (Joel 1:19). John is the prophet who has appeared at the end of days, the last of a long line of prophets, to proclaim divine judgment and call Israel to repentance.

Despite the bad news, John also has "good news" for Israel (Luke 3:18). His message of judgment and prophetic baptismal call created an "expectation" within Israel (Luke 3:15). They expected the coming of the Messiah and wondered whether John himself was that Messiah. In response, John offers hope. He is not the Messiah, but the Messiah is coming, and "he will baptize you with the Holy Spirit and fire." He will gather his people as he gathers wheat into a barn, but he will also winnow out the chaff and "burn it with unquenchable fire." The Messiah will execute judgment through a baptism in fire, but he will also bless his people through a baptism in the Holy Spirit. John prepares a people for the coming of the Messiah by announcing both judgment and blessing—judgment for those who refuse to hear his message of repentance and blessing for those who respond to it.

Herein lies the significance of baptism for John. John proclaimed a "baptism of repentance for the forgiveness of sins." He invited his hearers to respond to the announcement of judgment and blessing by submitting to an immersion water ritual. As we saw in the previous chapter, such rituals were pervasive in Jewish culture. However, John's baptism is noticeably different from the normal Jewish water rituals with which Palestinians would have been familiar.

While their water rituals were self-administered, John is "the Baptizer." He does the baptizing. The only parallel to this in known Jewish literature is the ordination of the Aaronic priesthood when Moses immersed Aaron and his sons (Ex. 40:12-15; Lev. 8:6-13). John, as the Baptizer, functions as a prophet who initiates Israel into a new era, the "last days." His baptism is a prophetic act—an act that both anticipates the coming Messianic age and effects the forgiveness of sins through faith-repentance.[5] It is a repentance-baptism that cleanses the whole person as preparation for participation in restored Israel under the leadership of the Messiah. John administers this grace as God's prophet to proclaim God's saving work for Israel. He announces—just as he announces the coming kingdom—a "baptism of repentance for the forgiveness of sins" (Luke 3:3). Submission to John's baptism evidenced repentance and involved a cleansing from sin.

There is another difference between John and the ritual washings of first-century Judaism. John is concerned about moral purification rather than ritual purity. His washing is for the forgiveness of sin. His call for moral reformation means his baptism is no mere removal of ritual impurities, but it is also an absolution from sin.[6] God cleanses his people through John's baptism.

As Acts 19:4 points out, John's baptism looked forward to the coming of Jesus, but it was effective for repentance and forgiveness. Since it was effective, those who were baptized by John apparently did not need rebaptism when the Spirit was poured out in Acts 2.

Elements	*Levitical Washings*	*John's Baptism*	*Christian Baptism*
Water Immersion	Yes	Yes	Yes
Remission of Sins	No– Outward Only	Yes (Luke 3:3)	Yes (Acts 2:38)
Holy Spirit	No– Not Yet Given	No– Not Yet Given	Yes (Acts 2:38)

Figure 1

There is no indication, for example, that the apostles were rebaptized or that Apollos was rebaptized (Acts 18:24-28). John's baptism was a genuine moment of redemption, but it was incomplete. It was incomplete not only because it pointed to the future coming of the Messiah, but also because it did not involve the presence of the Holy Spirit. The similarities and differences between Old Testament washings, John's baptism and Christian baptism are identified in figure one.

Though most Jews underwent some kind of water immersion for ritual purity, John called them to a baptism for the remission of sins—for moral purification. But John recognized that his baptism was incomplete and that the one coming would baptize in the Spirit. The pouring out of the Spirit was yet in the future (cf. John 7:39), but the remission of sins was a present promise for those who underwent repentance-baptism by the hands of John. Peter, however, announced a fuller experience when he promised that both the remission of sins and the gift of the Holy Spirit followed repentance and baptism (Acts 2:38). Christian baptism is the fulfillment of the anticipations not only of Levitical washings but more explicitly John's baptism.

John's message and mission prepared the way for the Lord. John prepared Israel through moral reformation and purification (cf. Zech. 1:17). Israel repented and was cleansed. A people were prepared to receive the coming Messiah. They were prepared for the coming of the Spirit who would indwell this reformed and purified people so as to identify them as restored Israel and empower them for service to the nations. Through John God prepared a people upon whom he would pour out his Spirit and send to the "ends of the earth" (Acts 1:8).

The Baptism of Jesus

Luke's description of Jesus' baptism is succinct but filled with significant language that is played out in his narrative.

> Now when all the people were baptized, and when Jesus also had been baptized and was praying, the heaven was opened, and the Holy Spirit descended upon him in bodily form like a dove. And a voice came from heaven, "You are my Son, the Beloved; with you I am well pleased." (Luke 3:21-22).

Given the theology of John's baptism in Luke, it is quite surprising to read that Jesus was baptized along with "all the people." The people and Jesus shared the same baptism—a baptism of repentance for the forgiveness of sins. Jesus underwent the cleansing ritual that announced the coming of restored Israel. But why does Jesus need cleansing?

The baptism of Jesus has been a central aspect of Christian imagination, piety, and art from the beginning. The earliest piece of Christian art, and the most frequent scene depicted in the earliest centuries, is the baptism of Jesus. The Christian festival of Epiphany, celebrating the baptism of Jesus, was practiced in the East as early as the late second century, which is well before Christmas was ever instituted. By the late fourth century, Epiphany was the most significant feast in Syria. This emphasis was rooted in the belief that the baptism of Jesus was the "dominant model for Christian baptism."[7] The baptism of Jesus is a pattern for Christian baptism; it is the first Christian baptism. It participates in the reality of John's baptism as a cleansing ritual but it also participates in the "last days" of Christian baptism as the context for the reception of the Holy Spirit.

On the one hand, Jesus identifies with sinners through the waters of John's baptism. He undergoes a ritual designed for penitent sinners. He goes down in the river with "all the people" and identifies himself with a people who need cleansing. Jesus dives in with his people who are looking for the kingdom of God. Through baptism Jesus joins himself to his people and experiences solidarity with them. This is, of course, exactly what Jesus did in his own death. Quoting Isaiah 53:12, Jesus characterizes his own death as one that was "counted among the lawless" (Luke 22:37). When Jesus went down in the river, he counted himself among the lawless—not because he was himself a sinner, but because he identified with his people. He shared their corporate identity and underwent a cleansing ritual designed for sinners.

On the other hand, Jesus experienced something that his people had not yet experienced, and would not experience in Luke's narrative till the day of Pentecost in Acts 2. When Jesus was baptized, "the Holy Spirit descended upon him" (Luke 3:22). In this moment, as Peter later recalled in Acts, Jesus was "anointed…with the Holy Spirit and with power" (Acts 10:38). This anointing involves several ideas. First, it is the promise of divine presence. The Holy Spirit now abides with Jesus and leads him (cf. Luke 4:1). God is present with his Son. Second, God anoints his Son with his Spirit. It is a divine commission. The Son is given the Messianic task—it is the Spirit-anointed task of the Messiah to "preach good news to the poor" (Luke 4:18). This anointing involves the power to carry out that task so that the Messiah demonstrates the presence of God's kingdom by casting out demons by the Spirit of God (Luke 11:20; cf. Matt. 12:28). Third, this anointing is a public divine declaration of God's relationship to his Son (Luke 3:22). God owns his Son in this moment.

Jesus' baptism is a model or paradigm for Christian baptism. We undergo the same repentance-baptism as John proclaimed, but we also experience the divine blessing of the Holy Spirit. God gives his Spirit to us, anoints us with his Spirit as we are empowered for ministry, and publicly declares our relationship to him as his own children (cf. Gal. 3:26-4:7).

Further, in this baptism Jesus commits himself to the way of the cross. Immediately after his baptism, the Spirit of God leads Jesus into the wilderness where he is tempted by Satan to turn from the way of the cross. But Jesus' water baptism is his commitment to experience the baptism of suffering (Luke 12:50). Jesus' own baptism in water anticipated this baptism into death, just as our baptism in water is both a participation in the death of Christ and an act of discipleship that commits us to the way of the cross as well. If we follow Jesus into the water, then we must also follow him to the cross (cf. Luke 9:23-26).

Baptism is about what God does. Through John God announces the coming restoration of Israel and prepares a penitent and cleansed people. The anointing of Jesus with the Spirit testifies to the reality of the "new age." The baptism of Jesus is the beginning of the "new age." From the baptism of Jesus on, we live in the "last days" when God pours out his Spirit and restores Israel. God has acted to save his people and the waters of Jesus' own baptism churn with eschatological fervor. God's saving act enlivens the mundane waters of the Jordan by the power of the Spirit; the river is now living water that flows down to us, but that living water is only meaningful because the Messiah was willing to suffer for us by undergoing his own baptism of fire.

Conversion Narratives in Acts

Since the work of G. R. Beasley-Murray and R. E. O. White,[8] New Testament scholars in the late twentieth century increasingly recognized that baptism is part of the New Testament conversion narrative.[9] Luke's second volume, Acts, most clearly demonstrates this. Conversion narratives in Acts are replete with baptismal language. Men and women, Jews and Gentiles, hear the gospel, believe it and are baptized. Here are a few examples:

> Acts 2:37, 41 — "when they heard this…those who welcomed his message were baptized."
> Acts 8:11-12 — "they listened eagerly to him…but when they believed…they were baptized, both men and women."
> Acts 8:13 — "Simon himself believed. After being baptized, he stayed constantly with Philip."
> Acts 8:35-36 — "Philip…told him the good news about Jesus…they came to some water and the eunuch said, 'Look here is water. Why shouldn't I be baptized?'"
> Acts 16:14-15 — "Lydia, a worshiper of God, was listening to us…The Lord opened her heart to listen eagerly…When she and her household were baptized…"
> Acts 16:32-33 — "They spoke the word of the Lord to him and to all who were in his house…then he and his entire family were baptized without delay."

TEXT	HEARD	BELIEVED	REPENTED	IMMERSED	HOLY SPIRIT	SAVED
Pentecost Acts 2:14-41	Heard 2:37	Believed 2:37	Repented 2:38	Immersed 2:41	At Immersion 2:38	Remission of Sins 2:38
Samaria Acts 8:5-13	Heard 8:12	Believed 8:13		Immersed 8:12-13	After Immersion 8:15-17	
Eunuch Acts 8:35-39	Heard 8:35	Believed 8:36		Immersed 8:38-39		Rejoicing 8:39
Saul Acts 9:1-18; 22:1-16; 26:9-18	Heard 9:4-6	Believed 22:10	Repented 9:9	Immersed 9:18	At Immersion 9:17-18	Washed Away Sins 22:16
Cornelius Acts 10:34-48 11:4-18; 15:7-11	Heard 10:44; 11:14	Believed 10:43	Repented 11:18	Immersed 10:48	Before Immersion 10:46-47	Purified Hearts 15:9
Lydia Acts 16:13-15	Heard 16:14	Believed 16:14		Immersed 16:15		
Jailor Acts 16:30-34	Heard 16:32	Believed 16:31	Repented 16:33	Immersed 16:33		Rejoiced 16:34
Corinthians Acts 18:8	Heard 18:8	Believed 18:8		Immersed 18:8		
Ephesian Disciples Acts 19:1-7	Heard 19:2	Believed 19:2		Immersed 19:5	After Immersion 19:6	

Figure 2

Acts 18:8 — "many of the Corinthians who heard him believed and were baptized."
Acts 19:5 — "On hearing this, they were baptized in the name of the Lord Jesus."

These texts call attention to the frequency with which baptism immediately follows receiving the word or believing the gospel. Baptism was the concrete way in which the gospel was received. Luke tells his story in such a way that the conversion narrative has constitutive elements. Even when these are not explicitly mentioned in every case, the narrative assumes them. But what is explicit is extremely important in Luke's storytelling. Figure 2 summarizes Luke's conversion stories in Acts.[10]

This chart may impact people differently, but it seems clear that Luke, as a narrator, intends to provide a holistic picture—conversion is the total experience of salvation, which includes immersion. The conundrum in the picture is the role of the Holy Spirit, which we will defer to the final section of this chapter. The "conversion narrative" in Luke involves faith, repentance and baptism in response to the gracious message of God's saving work in Christ.

Conversion narratives in Acts read rather differently than the more popular conversion narratives in the Evangelical world. Nowhere does one read that conversion is asking Jesus into one's heart through offering the "sinner's prayer." Rather, the one who would call upon the name of Lord is baptized upon the name of Jesus. When Ananias in Damascus finds Paul, he is told to "arise and be baptized…calling upon the name of the Lord" (Acts 22:16). Baptism is the "sinner's prayer" in Acts.

What Shall We Do?

As the narrative shifts to the beginning and growth of the Christian community after the Jesus' death and resurrection, we find a community that follows Jesus into the water and experiences the presence of the Holy Spirit just as Jesus did. Acts 2 recounts the beginning of this baptized, Spirit-anointed community.

Acts 2 is easily skewed. On the one hand, some readers focus on the chapter's baptismal language and leave the impression that the main point of Acts 2 is baptism. On the other hand, some fail to see how significant Acts 2:38-39 is for the announcement of the restoration of Israel. The former tend to lift Acts 2:38 out of its context so that it has a quasi-independent and autonomous function while the latter do not connect it with the language of restoration/redemption in the chapter.

Peter's sermon announced the beginning of the "last days." What the prophet Joel foretold and what John the Baptist anticipated, Peter declared a reality. God has poured out his Spirit upon his people and the restoration of Israel has become a reality. Salvation has come to Israel, to "everyone who calls on the name of the Lord," and this salvation is evidenced by the presence of the Spirit. Luke anticipated this constellation of events and ideas in Luke 24:46-49: repentance, forgiveness, name of the Lord, for all nations, witnesses to the whole earth, and the power of the Spirit.

Acts 2:38, as Peter's response to the pressing question, "what shall we do?" functions as a summary of the human response to the gospel in Luke's narrative. Green counsels us to take "with the greatest seriousness the pattern-setting words of Peter in Acts 2:38."[11] Just as the baptism of Jesus functions paradigmatically in Luke's narrative, these words function normatively in Acts. Peter's call for repentance and baptism is analogous to John's call for repentance and baptism. Both seek to prepare a people for God's presence and the coming kingdom of God. But it is different for Peter. He proclaims a reality and promises not merely the forgiveness of sins, but the presence of the Holy Spirit. Whereas John's baptism was a baptism of repentance for the forgiveness of sins, Peter announces a baptism of repentance for the forgiveness of sins and the consequent reception of the Holy Spirit.

The normative human response to the announcement that the kingdom has come and that God invites us into his community is faith, repentance and baptism. God has restored Israel and poured out his Spirit upon it. If we take this "normative" perspective seriously as a narrative indicator, then "even when Luke does not enumerate each item of human response and salvific promise comprised in Peter's pronouncement (and he rarely does), those responses and salvific gifts are to be presumed present unless we are given explicit reason to think otherwise."[12]

Because Acts 2:38 has been the focus of so much polemical discussion, its grammar and meaning have been hotly contested. For example, does "for" (*eis*) in the phrase "for the remission of sins" mean "because of "or "in order to" the remission of sins? In other words, are we baptized in order to receive the remission of sins or because our sins have already been remitted? The consensus, except in some Baptist circles, is that *eis* has a forward reference, just as it does in Matthew 26:28.[13] Acts 2:38 is the promise of forgiveness for those who respond to the gospel message. Another example is that some believe that "for the remission of sins" only modifies "repent" and does not modify "baptism." Consequently, they read the text in this way: "Repent (plural) for the remission of your sins and let each one of you be baptized." But the plural "repent" is simply distributed with "let each of you." The referent remains the same—everyone addressed is commanded to repent and be baptized.[14]

But the most significant function of Acts 2:38-39 within its narrative context is often overlooked. Joel prophesied that God would pour out his Spirit on "all flesh" (Acts 2:17) and John's work prepared the way for "all flesh" to see the salvation of God (Luke 3:6). Peter announces that salvation comes to those who repent and are baptized in the "name" of Jesus. To be baptized "in (*epi*) the name" of Jesus is to participate in restored Israel as people who "call on (*epikalesetai*) the name of the Lord" (Acts 2:21, 38). They are baptized "upon the name of Jesus" just as they "call upon" the name of Jesus for salvation (cf. Acts 22:16). These baptized believers from all over the world constitute a new community as the restored Israel. As others are baptized in the "name of Jesus," the Samaritans in Acts 8:16 or Gentiles in Acts 10:48, they too join that same community. The restored people of God transcend ethnic and social boundaries; it includes "all flesh."

"What shall we do?" Peter's answer is to receive what God has done for you through repentance and baptism.

The Conversion of Saul

Besides Cornelius (Acts 10, 11, 15), no other conversion narrative receives as much attention as the conversion of Saul (Acts 9, 22, 26). Cornelius represents the redemptive historical shift whereby uncircumcised Gentiles are invited to share fellowship with restored Israel. The conversion of Saul legitimates Paul's standing as the apostle to the Gentiles whom God has united with restored Israel (cf. Acts 9:15-16; 22:21; 26:17-18). Consequently, the primary focus is not to provide a "pattern" for the sequence of conversion events, but to bear witness to God's intent that his people would include "all flesh" (Acts 2:17) and his witness should go to the "ends of the earth" (Acts 1:8).

Nevertheless, Saul's conversion story illustrates the connected nature of faith, repentance, baptism, forgiveness of sins and the Holy Spirit that is characteristic of conversion narratives in Acts. As an enemy of the Christian faith, Saul intended to persecute Christians in Damascus, but as he journeyed there he encountered the risen Christ. He was struck blind and led into Damascus by his companions. For three days he fasted as he devoted himself to penitent prayer (Acts 9:9, 11). Saul sought the Lord and was heard. After three days, the Lord sent Ananias.

Ananias explained to Saul that he had come that "you may regain your sight and be filled with the Holy Spirit" (Acts 9:17). And when Ananias laid his hands on him, he received his sight. Then Ananias announced that Saul was God's chosen witness to "all the world" and asked him, "And now why do you delay? Get up, be baptized, and have your sins washed away, calling on his name" (Acts 22:15-16). Paul got up and was baptized (Acts 9:18).

When was Paul converted? That is a loaded question. Does "converted" mean when his sins were washed away or when he became a believer? The narrative must be read as a whole rather than piecemeal. It relates the story of an unbeliever who becomes a believer who seeks the Lord through prayer intensely for three days and a preacher who heals and baptizes the penitent believer. If "conversion" means the whole process of becoming a Christian, Saul was converted in the context of his baptism after three days of prayer and fasting. If, however, we are asking when he became a believer in the risen Christ, then it was on the road to Damascus. The narrative is about the transformation of an enemy of the cross into God's witness to the Gentile world. The process is significant, but it is a process filled with events—Saul "sees" Jesus on the road to Damascus, he fasts and prays for three days, he is healed through the hands of Ananias and is baptized by Ananias.

We should not devalue any of these "events." On the one hand, some who would emphasize that baptism was the point at which Saul's sins were washed away miss the transformative nature of his experience with the risen Christ. Saul was a changed man before his baptism. He had come to faith in Jesus. On the other hand, some who would emphasize his experience on the Damascus road as the "converting moment" miss the significance of his healing and baptism as the conclusion of the conversion narrative where Paul is assured of his relationship with Jesus and is received as a member of the Christian community. His baptism was a washing away of his sins as he called upon (*epikalesamenos*) the name of Jesus (Acts 22:16; cf. Acts 2:21).

Further, when did Paul receive the Holy Spirit? He did not receive that divine presence on the Damascus road because Ananias came that Paul might receive the Holy Spirit. But did Paul receive the Holy Spirit when he was healed as Ananias laid his hands on him? Or did he receive the Holy Spirit when he was baptized? From the perspective of Acts 2:38, we might argue the latter, but the narrative offers no decisive answer to those questions. The narrative assumes that faith, repentance, baptism, forgiveness and the reception of the Spirit are part of the whole experience. Whatever the sequence, the conversion narrative involved all of the above and was not complete without them.

What about our Children?

Since Acts describes the missionary push of the church towards the "ends of the earth," the conversion narratives are first generation in character. There are no "second generation" conversions in Acts. There are no descriptions of children who "grow up in the church" and seek confirmation of their faith in Jesus. Indeed, there are no explicit references to children in Acts at all.

There are references, however, to "household" baptisms. Lydia and "her household *(oikos)* were baptized" (Acts 16:15). The jailer "and his entire family (*hoi autou pantes*, literally, all the ones belonging to him, which is synonymous with "household") were baptized" (Acts 16:33; Acts 16:34 refers to his "household" [*oikon*]). "Crispus, the synagogue ruler, and his entire household (*oiko*) believed in the Lord" just as many Corinthians "believed and were baptized" (Acts 18:8; cf. 1 Cor. 1:16 where Paul writes that he had baptized the "household [*oikon*] of Stephanus"). "Households," of course, could have included children, but the Greco-Roman "household" also included slaves, extended family and even employees. The term is inclusive and it is impossible to determine who actually constituted these households and whether infants or children were present.

We acknowledge the *prime facie* force of this language. It lends itself to the inclusion of infants or small children. But there are several considerations that discourage that reading. First, several of the texts characterize the household as not only undergoing baptism, but also that the household heard, believed or rejoiced. Second, we would not presume to think that an unbelieving slave would have been baptized in one of these households. The prior question is whether faith is necessary for baptism before we assume who was baptized or who was not baptized as part of a household. Third, the semantic range for "household" is comparable to language used in baptistic communities today. For example, a Baptist might rejoice that a "whole family" was converted but only mean that those who were old enough to believe did believe even though there may have been an infant in the family.

Ultimately, the question of infant baptism cannot hang on these ambiguous texts in Acts. They neither include nor exclude infants from baptism. Rather, the discussion rests upon whether personal faith is necessary for baptism or whether one (such as an infant) may be baptized on the faith of another (such as the faith of the parents or the faith of the church as a whole). Yet, in Lukan theology, baptism is not simply about faith, but also repentance. It is, as Timothy George has described it, "repenter's baptism as well as believer's baptism."[15] Would we accept vicarious repentance? May one repent for another? The theology of "baptism of repentance," which is rooted in Luke's baptismal theology, excludes the participation of those who are unable to commit to following Jesus as a matter of personal faith. Luke's baptismal theology, then, prevents us from reading his descriptions of "household" baptisms as inclusive of infants or small children. It would read more into the language than Luke intended.

The Ephesian Disciples

As we saw at the beginning of this chapter, the baptism of John was significant for the beginnings of Christian baptism. Jesus himself received the baptism of John, but transformed it by his own coming and the gift of the Spirit. With the inauguration of the Messianic kingdom and the pouring out of the Spirit, the intent and purpose of the baptism of John was fulfilled. Christian baptism replaced John's baptism.

Apparently, however, some continued to practice John's baptism almost twenty years after his death. In Ephesus, Priscilla and Aquila encountered an eloquent and learned preacher by the name of Apollos who "taught accurately the things concerning Jesus, though he knew only the baptism of John" (Acts 18:25). They helped Apollos gain a better understanding, but apparently—at least as far as the record is concerned—he was not baptized. We may assume that Apollos had received John's baptism before it had been fulfilled and that Apollos only needed to understand the shift that had taken place through the pouring out of the Spirit. Apollos went to Corinth and was welcomed by the believers there.

Paul, however, arrived in Ephesus and encountered some of the fruits of Apollos' ministry before Priscilla and Aquila had gently corrected him. Paul found twelve "disciples" in Ephesus who had "not even heard that there is a Holy Spirit" (Acts 19:2). They had been baptized "into John's baptism" (Acts 19:3). Given the proximity of the Apollos story with this one, we may assume that John himself had baptized Apollos while Apollos had baptized these "disciples." Paul judged their baptism deficient because they had received the mere promissory baptism when the fuller one had already arrived. John's baptism was about the "one who was to come," but that one had already come and poured out his Spirit. Given their baptismal deficiency, Paul rebaptized them, though actually they were, for the first time, "baptized in the name of the Lord Jesus" (Acts 19:5). Then, through the laying on of Paul's hands, "the Holy Spirit came upon them."

Despite their deficient baptism, Luke describes the twelve as "disciples." What does Luke mean by "disciples"? Some maintain that Luke is calling them Christians since "disciple" is his primary term for describing Christians in Acts and it always refers to tians in Acts, unless this is the one exception.[16] Thus, Luke nizes some believers as disciples (Christians) who had not experienced a proper baptism. But this would also mean that he recognizes some believers as disciples (Christians) who had not yet received the Holy Spirit. Others, however, argue that Luke "uses the term early in the episode from the limited perspective of Paul rather than the omniscient perspective of the narrator."[17] Luke did use the term "disciple" for John's followers in Luke 5:33 and 7:18. Thus, they are disciples of John rather than Jesus. But Luke is the narrator and he describes the twelve from his perspective rather than Paul's. Further, they are not disciples of John. If Apollos, who taught Jesus right though he baptized wrong, had baptized the twelve, then these Ephesians were disciples of Jesus who had received the defunct baptism of John. When Luke means "disciples of John" he says so (as in Luke 5:33; 7:18), but when he simply denominates them "disciples" he means "disciples of Jesus."

Consequently, these twelve Ephesian disciples were followers of Jesus who had received neither Christian baptism nor the Holy Spirit. Their conversion was incomplete, though their allegiance was to Jesus. If they had been in the situation of the Samaritans who had received Christian baptism, Paul would have simply laid his hands on them in order that they might receive the Spirit. If they had been in the situation of Cornelius, Paul would have simply baptized them in the name of Jesus. But their situation was unique. They had neither been baptized in the name of Jesus nor received the Holy Spirit, though they were disciples of Jesus. Paul did not berate them or dismiss their allegiance to Jesus, but upon their faith in Jesus, he baptized them in the name of Jesus and laid his hands upon them. Now their conversion was complete.

Priscilla, Aquila, and Paul model how we should approach disciples of Jesus whose conversion is incomplete though their allegiance to Jesus is genuine.[18]

Conversion Narratives and the Holy Spirit

In the conversion narratives of Acts people hear the message of the gospel, believe it, are immersed in response to it and enjoy its benefits. Some of these elements are present in some stories, but not in others (e.g., explicit references to repentance). While

Luke's purpose does not demand a consistent, repetitive retelling of conversion stories in some kind of standardized language, his consistency is fairly telling. The conversion stories involve hearing the gospel, believing it, repentance, baptism, and entrance into the community of faith.

However, there is one element that is clearly problematic: there is an inconsistent "pattern" in the book of Acts regarding the reception of the Spirit. Those baptized on Pentecost received the Holy Spirit as a promise connected with baptism or at baptism (Acts 2:38). Those baptized in Samaria received the Holy Spirit a significant time after baptism (Acts 8:15-17). Those baptized at Cornelius' house received the Holy Spirit before baptism (Acts 10:47).

Which of these accounts is the ordinary pattern of God's work, if there is one? Perhaps it is inappropriate to find an "ordinary" pattern. After all, God is free to distribute his Spirit as he desires. Nothing constrains God's gift except his own decision. Furthermore, it is inappropriate to impose on Luke's stories a grid that determines the "ordinary" order when he is unconcerned about that point. Thus, whether there is an "ordinary" pattern or order depends upon Luke's own narrative.

Though his narrative contains an inordinate pattern regarding baptism and the Holy Spirit, Luke recognizes that two of his stories are extraordinary because he explains them. His editorial comment in Acts 8:16 concerning the Samaritans indicates that Luke is aware that this is an anomalous situation. That the Samaritans did not receive the Spirit when they were baptized, but only when Peter and John laid their hands on them (Acts 8:15) needed explanation. Luke explained why Peter and John were present because the reader, based on Acts 2:38, would have expected that they would have received the Spirit in connection with their baptism. Luke, thus, recognizes the exceptional nature of the situation. He does not explain the difference in terms of a supposed distinction between the "miraculous" and "ordinary" gift of the Spirit. Rather, he emphatically says that they did not receive the Holy Spirit. The exceptional circumstance is directly related to their ethnic and social standing as Samaritans. God, through Peter and John, bore witness to the inclusion of the Samaritans within restored Israel (cf. Acts 1:8).

Luke also indicates that Cornelius' circumstance is extraordinary. Cornelius was an uncircumcised Gentile and no uncircumcised person had ever been included within Israel. God poured out the Spirit upon the house of Cornelius before he was either baptized or circumcised. As a result Peter asked, "Can anyone withhold the water for baptizing these people who have received the Holy Spirit just as we have?" (Acts 10:47). God's action bore witness to the fact that he accepted the inclusion of the Gentiles within restored Israel. When his Jerusalem brothers objected to the baptism and hospitality of an uncircumcised Gentile, Peter asked, "If then God gave them the same gift that he gave us when we believed in the Lord Jesus Christ, who was I that I could hinder God?" (Acts 11:17). The significance of this extraordinary situation is highlighted by the fact that Luke tells the story of Cornelius' conversion three times (Acts 10, 11 and 15) and each time his entrance into the Christian community is defended. The fundamental defense is that God poured out his Spirit on Cornelius and thus he could not be denied baptism.

Despite the fact that these situations are extraordinary and that Acts 2:38 functions as the ordinary means, we should not underestimate the significance of God's use of extraordinary situations. God is sovereign. He gives the Spirit when and where and to whomever he desires. God is not bound to the ordinary means. We rest upon God's promises in Acts 2:38, but God is not limited by Acts 2:38 in the distribution of his Spirit.

Further, recognizing this diversity in Luke's narrative alerts us to something exceedingly more important. While our book is focused on baptism and its theological themes, Luke's main concern was not baptism. Rather, Luke is much more concerned with the presence, work and power of the Spirit. Baptism serves the larger theme of a restored community indwelt and empowered by the Spirit. Too often, based on Acts 2:38 and the search for the assurance of our forgiveness, we orient Luke's narrative to baptism as if this is his primary point. But if we recognize that the "pouring out of the Spirit" upon restored Israel is Luke's primary point, then baptism, while important, will assume a secondary role.

When we think of the gift of the Spirit and baptism, we must recognize that the presence of the Spirit is more important than baptism. Luke gives more emphasis to the Spirit than to baptism by a three to one margin if one only counts the number of times the words are used in his narrative. But a word count is not the main indicator. Rather, it is the link between the pouring out of the Spirit and the restoration of Israel. The salvation of Israel is the presence of God's cleansing and empowering Spirit.

Yet, despite this caveat, Luke's theology expects that baptism and the giving of the Spirit are always in close proximity. When the baptized Samaritans do not have the Spirit, Luke explains the anomaly. When an unbaptized Cornelius receives the Spirit, Luke explains the circumstance. In both episodes, baptism and the Spirit were expected correlates, and though they were separated the narrative ultimately united them—everyone who received the Spirit was baptized and everyone who was baptized received the Spirit. Indeed, when Paul encountered some disciples in Ephesus he asked them, "Did you receive the Holy Spirit when you became believers?" Paul expected that they had, and when he discovered that their baptism was deficient, he baptized them and the "Holy Spirit came upon them" (Acts 19:2, 6). Conversion, baptism and the Holy Spirit are interwoven. Luke's narrative connects them and no conversion narrative leaves the impression that there might be a Christian who has the Spirit but is unbaptized or that there is one who is baptized but has not received the Spirit. When either is the case, the other follows in order to complete the conversion narrative.

Conclusion

John the Baptist announced the coming of a new age. Jesus went down into the river. The new age began as he came up out of the water and was anointed by the Holy Spirit. The Father was present with his Son, acknowledged him as his Son, and empowered his Son for the mission he had given him. The Son of Man had come to redeem Israel and to be a light to the nations. Through him "all flesh" would see the salvation of God.

We follow Jesus into the water. We go down in the river to pray—to offer the sinner's prayer in repentance and baptism. We go down in the river to receive what God has done for us—the remission of sins—and to receive God's gift, the Holy Spirit. We come out of the river cleansed and gifted. We are cleansed from our sin and gifted for transformation and ministry. We become part of a new community, the restored Israel. With this new identity and the presence of God's Holy Spirit we bear witness to the world that the triune God has inaugurated a new age of communion with humanity.

****

Principle

The new age was announced by John's baptism, broke into the fallen world through the baptism of Jesus, and was given to the world in the presence of the Holy Spirit through faith, repentance and baptism.

Prayer

Father, we thank you that in your grace you have restored Israel and that you have poured out your Spirit on all flesh. We acknowledge that only by the power of your Spirit may we become like you, and we give thanks for the presence of your Spirit among us. We rest in the promise of your Son and the word of your apostles that through baptism we receive both the forgiveness of sins and the gift of the Spirit. Just as we have followed Jesus into the water, we vow that we will follow him to the cross. Amen.

Questions

1. Would those baptized by John need rebaptism after the pouring out of the Spirit in Acts 2? Why, or why not? What does this say about the significance of John's baptism?

2. How much teaching have you heard about the baptism of Jesus? What has been the major focus of that teaching? How does this relate to what you have read in this chapter?

3. Is it fair to speak of an "ordinary" means of conversion in the book of Acts?

4. What do you think is the significance of the irregular pattern of baptism's relationship to the giving of the Holy Spirit in Acts?

4 / United with Christ: Baptism in Paul's Letters

Your baptism is nothing less than grace clutching you by the throat: a grace-full throttling, by which your sin is submerged in order that ye may remain under grace. Come thus to thy baptism. Give thyself up to be drowned in baptism and killed by the mercy of thy dear God, saying: "Drown me and throttle me, dear Lord, for henceforth I will gladly die to sin with thy Son." [1]

—Martin Luther

Karl Barth, who quotes Martin Luther, adds, "This death is grace." About grace, the Apostle Paul would say nothing less. In this chapter we look at baptism through the eyes of Paul.

****

Baptism followed and represented a seismic shift in Paul's life when the Lord appeared to him on the road to Damascus. "Saul was still breathing murderous threats" (Acts 9:1, TNIV) against disciples of Christ when light flashed all around him. He fell to the ground. The words, "I am Jesus of Nazareth, whom you are persecuting" must have echoed in his mind in Damascus as he fasted three days in blindness. A devout and respected Jew named Ananias laid hands on Saul and his sight returned, he received the Holy Spirit and was baptized. Luke narrates Paul's conversion (Acts 9) and later shows Paul in Jerusalem recounting the story (Acts 22). Paul's own story of baptism figures into both accounts and is significant as we move toward his teaching on baptism. He did not originate the practice of baptism in the church. On the contrary, Paul was found by baptism.

God revealed an entirely new world view to Paul (Gal. 1:11-17). Just as Paul reflects on his own baptism as an event of apocalyptic importance—revealing a new age breaking into this world—so he also wants disciples of Christ to view their baptism in this frame. Therefore, Paul develops the significance of baptism in the first-century church as an apocalyptic moment in which they unite with Christ in the new age.

Just as Paul described baptism as an essential part of his calling, so Paul assumes baptism is a normative and natural part of the life of a believer. With this assumption, he lays out the implications of this event. Our sinful past was who we were. Now our identity is in Christ and made so through union with him in his death and resurrection, which is shown through the objective sign of water baptism and the reception of the Holy Spirit. It is not baptism itself that saves but the Christ-event that is proclaimed through the act of baptism: Christ's death, burial, and resurrection, ascension, enthronement, intercession, and second coming. Paul's language describes baptism as a God-revealing, Christ-uniting, and Spirit-empowering occasion of transformation. Baptism for Paul is an apocalyptic sign of a seismic shift from an old identity, ethic, and world view to a radically new identity in Christ, an ethic of life in the Spirit, and a restored and hope-filled world view. Baptism is the objective sign that the old world has passed away and everything has become new in the life of the believer.

Paul's Redemptive-Historical Framework

We examine here primarily the strongest passages on baptism in Paul's letters: Romans 6:1-7; Galatians 3:26-29; Colossians 2:9-12; 1 Corinthians 1:11-17, 6:11, 12:13; and Ephesians 4:5. The best way to understand baptism in Paul is to look at the strongest references to baptism within the context of his argument, then move toward understanding passages that allude to baptism.

One of the problems we face on the way down to the river is that we often isolate Pauline texts on baptism and attempt to extract meaning from them, but in the process we lop off the theological trunk and are left with disconnected branches. Some read Romans 6, for example, searching to prove that baptism is by immersion or that baptism is essential for salvation. This attempt doubly deprives us: not only are we unlikely to get final answers to those questions from this text since Paul does not specifically address those questions, but we also miss its incredible theological implications.

In order to understand Paul's view of baptism, we must see baptism in its apocalyptic framework so that we do not divorce it from its theological, sociological, ethical, or eschatological bases. Paul never lays out for his churches or for us, "Paul's 13-Week Study on Baptism." Paul does not preach specific sermons on baptism but instead comes to baptism in the context of larger discussions about church divisions, human sin and ethics, the grace of God, faith in Christ, the movement of the Holy Spirit, and future hope. We will, therefore, approach Paul's baptismal texts through understanding his apocalyptic or redemptive-historical framework.

Paul mentions some form of baptism or washing at least sixteen times in his letters.[2] He does not speak of baptism randomly but within a redemptive-historical framework that includes at least three categories. A key question that shapes these categories is, "What has God done?"

New Identity. First, Paul speaks of a new identity that is rooted in what God has done for us. It is an identity that breaks down all the barriers of the old world. The operative question is, "Who are we?"

New Ethic. Second, based on this identity and God's redemption, we live a new kingdom ethic. Our ethic is now other-worldly and is not conformed to the ethics of the old world. The operative question is, "How shall we then live?"

New Worldview. Third, anticipating the completion of God's work gives us a new hope. The future is now a present reality through the presence of the Spirit who engenders hope and sanctifies a people for God. This category might better be explained with an exclamation, "Look with new eyes at what God is doing!"

One indicator of this focus on what God has done is Paul's consistent reference to baptism in the past (aorist) and indicative tense. Paul assumes his readers and hearers have already been baptized, and he builds a theological and ethical understanding on the reality of their participation with Christ through baptism. Baptism connects us with the Christ-event, the central shaping event of our new identity, new lifestyle, and new world view.

With Romans 6:22 as the theme text, figure 1 illustrates this framework. God's work of salvation is past, present and future, which may be depicted as justification (righteousness), sanctification (the work of the Spirit), and glorification (eternal life). For example, God has declared us righteous, is making us righteous, and in the future will fully conform us to his righteousness. Romans 6:22 is perhaps the most compact description we could use to explain Paul's redemptive-historical framework: "But now that you have been freed from sin and enslaved to God, the advantage you get is sanctification. The end is eternal life." Paul points to a past reality of sin. He reminds disciples that they have been set free from the past, yet this new freedom is not meant for a lawless life. Paul responds to such faulty thinking, exclaiming, "May it never be!" (Rom. 6:1). Since they have new ownership—the ones in whose name they are baptized, Father, Son, and Holy Spirit—they are identified with their owner. They are slaves to God and their new identity is grounded in God's redemptive work in Christ by the power of the Spirit.

Furthermore, the owner has a new set of house rules, a new ethic. The new ethic, however, is not the basis of salvation but is the result of being justified in Christ. The new ethic is not fueled by willpower to keep the law but empowered by the Holy Spirit. So, the advantage or fruit of this righteousness through faith in Christ is holiness (sanctification) that results in eternal life. Lest we believe the holiness comes from ourselves, Paul reminds disciples that the wages of sin is death but the gift of God is eternal life in Christ Jesus our Lord (Rom. 6:23).

Paul calls disciples of Christ to live in an apocalyptic tension between their past and their future. This is their new world view. We are united with Christ in baptism and the event of Christ's death, burial and resurrection has life-changing implications for the present and future. This apocalyptic understanding of baptism means that the sign points to a reality behind and beyond what we can see. It is the present experience of that future reality. The future has broken into the present in order to reshape the old world into the new world, the old person into a new person. Baptism, for Paul, is an apocalyptic sign of this new identity, new ethic, and new world view.

Figure 1 places some of Paul's theological words into the three categories of new identity (past), new ethic (present), and new world view (future). At one end is baptism that unites disciples with Christ's death. This union with the Christ-event is the identity marker that frames one side of Paul's thought world. On the other side is the return of Christ. Baptism unites us with the resurrection of Jesus. Our lives not only take place between these two events but our entire existence is grounded in them. Baptism symbolizes, embodies, clothes us in, and unites us with these two realities—it illustrates God's apocalyptic work of breaking into the past and present with future realities that matter now. The future—not only the past—is breaking into the old world that is falling apart around us. We have hope. We live in these in-between times as if the new world has already arrived. Christians are a new creation in an old world. Baptism proclaims a reality beyond this world. Paul's call to the river is to receive a radically new identity, ethic, and world view. But what does this new identity mean and what does it look like through Paul's eyes? That is the focus of the next three sections.

Word Group	*Past*	*Present*	*Future*
Theological Meaning	**New identity rooted in a redemptive past**	**New kingdom ethic between times**	**New expectant worldview**
"Righteousness"	Romans 3:24; 5:1	Romans 6:13,16,18,19	Galatians 5:5
"Sanctification"	1 Corinthians 6:11	2 Corinthians 7:1; 1 Thessalonians 4:3-8	1 Thessalonians 5:23
"Salvation"	Ephesians 2:5,8	2 Corinthians 2:15	Romans 5:9,10; 13:11
"Glory"		2 Corinthians 3:18	Romans 8:30
"Redemption"	Colossians 1:14; Ephesians 1:7		Romans 8:23: Ephesians 1:14
"Set Free"	Romans 6:18,20; 8:2	Galatians 5:13	Romans 8:21
"Received-Having the Spirit"	Galatians 3:2-5	Galatians 5:22-25	1 Corinthians 15 "Spiritual"

Figure 1: Pauline Redemptive-Historical Theology

A New Identity Rooted in God's Redemptive Timeline

Baptism connects believers with a new identity rooted in God's redemptive timeline. The word "timeline" is used here because God's redemptive work is continuous, not only in the past, which may be implied in "history." Paul's strongest declaration about baptism, in Romans 6, comes as he discusses identity: how Jews and Gentiles enter and thrive in the kingdom of God.[3] One of Paul's primary concerns is to develop a unified identity in Christ. While Jews and Gentiles view their identities in social categories, Paul takes pains to view them through union with Adam and Christ. He explains that all have sinned, Jews and Gentiles, and no one has an excuse for disobedience (Rom. 3:23). We are, therefore, united in sin with Adam and all humanity (Rom. 5:12-19). Further, while the Jews may look down upon the unbelieving Gentiles, the Jews have no right to claim the covenant based on acts of righteousness. Abraham, after all, was not considered righteous on the basis of his law-keeping or circumcision but through faith (Rom. 4:4). Paul says the law came in to show sin for what it is—utterly sinful—so that humans of all races would have no excuse (Rom. 1:20; 5:20).

In chapters 5-8, Paul then flips the categories. Paul does not mention Jews and Gentiles in these chapters but sets up new categories: Adam and Christ. Just as Paul begins chipping away at the old identity markers of Jews and Gentiles by showing all are united in sin (Rom. 5), so he also plants new identity markers through union with Christ (Rom. 6). This is the social, ethical, and apocalyptic context in which baptism is mentioned: through union with Christ we put on a new communal identity. This new identity is illustrated in at least three major realities: we are united with Christ, buried and resurrected with Christ and clothed with Christ.

Planted in Union with Christ

The new identity in Christ means that we are united with Christ in baptism. We are planted in union (*synetaphemen*) with Christ in the likeness of his death. In baptism we participate in Christ's death, not our own. The tomb is not ours but Christ's. Just as we do not go down into our tomb but Christ's, so also our resurrection is not by our own power or something we can claim as our own. Paul first compares Christ's resurrection to our living a new life (Rom. 6:4).

The power of baptismal renewal is not our action but the life of the resurrected Christ. Our life is Christ's life. His exaltation is our exaltation. Paul says that if we are united in death with Christ, certainly we will (future) be united with him (6:5) in his resurrection. We are identified with Christ, and this constitutes our new identity—we are one with Christ and are no longer identified with Adam.

It is important, therefore, to distinguish between Christ's resurrection and ours. He does not say "our resurrection" but in a parallel way says that if we have been planted in union together with Christ, so we will also be in that same likeness with his resurrection. He uses a different word and tense for Christ's resurrection from the word and tense for our resurrection. Christ was raised (*egeiro*). We, on the other hand, will stand up (*anastasis*) with him. The difference in the words and in the tenses points to two dimensions in Paul's argument: first, we have hope because God's kingdom has broken in, and second, we have an ethical basis upon which to act now.[4]

With Paul's typology of Adam and Christ, his redemptive-historical world view, and the language of being planted in union with Christ in mind, consider again the impact of Romans 6:1-6:

> What then are we to say? Should we continue in sin in order that grace may abound? By no means! How can we who died to sin go on living in it? Do you not know that all of us who have been baptized into Christ Jesus were baptized into his death? Therefore we have been buried with him by baptism into death, so that, just as Christ was raised from the dead by the glory of the Father, so we too might walk in newness of life. For if we have been united with him in a death like his, we will certainly be united with him in a resurrection like his. We know that our old self was crucified with him so that the body of sin might be destroyed, and we might no longer be enslaved to sin.

Paul begins Romans 6 as if taking a deep breath and responding to those who are not only unconcerned with Adam's disease but are rolling in more and more toxic sewage as if to say, "Let's pile on sin so God's grace will pile on the greater." You can almost hear Paul's teeth grind as he exclaims, "Are you out of your minds?

No! The day you were joined to Christ, do you ask how much you can cheat on him?[5] No way! You were baptized. Don't you know what baptism proclaims? You were planted in union with Christ in the likeness of his death. You were planted in this way to grow up together" (Rom. 6:1-4, paraphrase).

For Paul the initiating rite of baptism is always bound up with, in, and through the redemptive story—the Christ-event. Therefore, our new identity in Christ expressed through baptism is indeed a decisive moment of union with Christ in his death, a divorce from sin, and a re-orientation to a new ethic of the kingdom that means dying daily to sin. The new identity means that through faith in Christ and the power of the Spirit we are made new in the attitude of our minds, and the Spirit leads us to put off falsehood, to not let anger rule us, to resist the devil, to stop stealing, to build others up, to get rid of bitterness, slander, and malice, to be kind, compassionate and forgiving, to submit to one another out of reverence for Christ (Eph. 4-5). If we are united with Christ in baptism, we take on his identity and the Spirit helps us in our weakness.

Buried and Raised with Christ

Baptism also connects our identity directly to the work of God in Christ. We cannot overstate the importance of this connection. Without this connection to Christ, we are dead (Eph. 2:1-5). Paul's language of being buried with Christ in baptism in Colossians 2:12 is similar to Romans 6:4. In both passages the sense is that the grave we are buried in is not our grave but Christ's. We are planted in union with Christ in his tomb (Rom. 6:5). Paul's language describes our relational connection "with" (*syn*) Christ. Not only are we buried with Christ in baptism but also in the same sentence Paul says we are raised with him through faith in the power of God, who raised Christ from the dead.

In Colossians Paul, after the prayer and thanksgiving section, first declares that Christ's identity is foundational for ours: "He is the image of the invisible God, the firstborn of all creation" (1:15). "He is the head of the body, the church; he is the beginning, the firstborn from the dead, so that he might come to have first place in everything" (1:18). God is pleased to dwell in Christ and through him to reconcile all things to himself.

The larger context surrounding the reference to baptism in Colossians 2:12 is Paul's concern that the Colossians are depending on "human tradition and the elemental spiritual forces of this world rather than on Christ" (Col. 2:8, TNIV). Perhaps a group within the church or an external group had been insisting that, in order to stay on God's good side, the church needs mystical, ascetic or legal rituals. To address this situation Paul contrasts the fullness of Christ with the emptiness of these elemental spiritual forces. Spiritual fullness is not found in ascetic rituals but in Christ. The fullness of God is in Christ, in bodily form (Col. 2:9). Paul connects disciples to this identity in Christ. We have been reconciled by Christ's physical death in order to be presented as holy (1:22; 2:13, 20). Our identity is bound up in the fullness of God in Christ. Discerning Christ's identity leads to understanding our identity in Christ. Conversely, when we fail to discern Christ's identity, we fail to discern our own.

Paul illustrates further how we identify with Christ in his death and resurrection. He describes how sin is stripped from us, not like traditional circumcision, but by the death of Christ on the cross. The phrase, "circumcision of Christ," might be confused as a synonym for baptism, but it makes more sense as a graphic figure of Christ's own flesh being stripped off in crucifixion. Our connection to Christ is through this cruel death he suffered for us. Paul says, "when you were buried with him in baptism, you were also raised with him through faith in the power of God, who raised him from the dead" (Col. 2:12). Paul's images are potent. Our sin is cut away as Christ's flesh was shredded on the cross. We die to sin only in connection with Christ's own death. The death is not ours but his. Here is where Paul connects baptism, not with circumcision as if the replacement for it, but with a burial. We are buried with Christ in his death. As surely as Christ took away sins at the cross, we died to sin in baptism which represents and proclaims the whole Christ-event.

Not in our own death but in Christ's death, we die. Not in our own resurrection but in Christ's resurrection, we are raised with Christ. There is, however, an important phrase that we often miss: "through faith in the power of God." The power of God raised Christ from the dead, and it is by God's power that we are identified with Christ's fullness, his death and resurrection. The same power of God that raised Christ from the dead is at work in us (Eph. 1:19-20). We identify with God's power exerted in Christ's death and resurrection through our faith. This does not mean that our faith effects its own resurrection.[6] The resurrection is not ours any more than the death is ours. Both are God's work in Christ. God blesses us through faith and baptism with a profound connection to his work in Christ's death and resurrection.

Clothed with Christ

A third lens through which Paul views our baptismal identity is being clothed with Christ. Identity is a major concern for Paul in Galatians. Galatians 3:26-29 is a key to Paul's concern that the Galatians return to their identity that had been shaped by the gospel (1:6-9). He contrasts their new identity with their formerly divided identities of man and woman, slave and free, Jew and Gentile. In Christ these distinctions were obliterated. Paul says that all who were baptized "put on" (*enedysasthe*) Christ like a new set of clothes.[7] The Galatians had worn garments of various identities, but now were putting on Christ (Gal. 3:27), putting on a new identity.

In Galatians baptism is mentioned within a swirl of controversy over those who had changed Paul's gospel and were misleading the church to believe that God's promises depended on law-keeping (circumcision). Paul's omission of comparing baptism with circumcision, as he did in Colossians, is perhaps intentional, because he did not want baptism to be misused as circumcision was. Paul declares that the new basis for claiming the promise is to find one's origin in Christ (3:29) rather than in law-keeping.

In the case of the Galatians, for instance, when they put on Christ in baptism, they put on a whole new social identity as children of God rather than Jews and Gentiles, male and female, slave and free. This new identity swept into their lives like a tornado ripping a house off its foundations. A person is a person, and no longer were they to believe that God somehow favored Jews over Gentiles. Grace was freely offered no less to women than to men. Slaves and women were on equal footing with freedmen and men because of the new clothes they wore in Christ. They had entered into a new humanity, and the old walls of identity had been broken down.

Paul's use of "in" (*en*) illustrates how he understands identity in this new community. Including "in Christ," "in the Lord," and "in him," he uses the preposition 165 times in his letters. Paul's most common expression of "in Christ" (*en Christos*) describes a new creation (2 Cor. 5:17), a relationship, a transformed union (Rom. 8:10).

When Paul speaks of the new communal identity in Christ in 1 Corinthians, two questions arise: "Who died for you?" and "Into whose name were you baptized?" Paul uses the preposition, "in" or "into" when sorting out the divisions in Corinth in 1 Corinthians 1:13-17. He asks rhetorically, "Were you baptized into (*eis*) the name of Paul?" He says he's thankful no one can say they were baptized into his name. The preposition "into" (*eis*) ties together the two concepts of being baptized into the name of Christ and the experience of being united with Christ in death and the new world view that comes along with this union.

Paul uses these prepositions to help frame the language of what God is doing specifically to connect us with Christ in baptism. God poured out his mercy to us through Christ (Rom. 1:5; cf. 1 Thes. 5:9). Christ died for us. We are united and buried "with Christ" to be "in Christ" (2 Cor. 5:17). The significance of the prepositions is that they describe the work of God in us. They are small words but holy connectors, linking us to God's work in Christ. If, therefore, we are "in Christ," we have a radical new identity. Becoming children in Christ happens through faith and is mediated through the objective sign of baptism (Rom. 6:3-4; Gal. 3:26-29).

For Paul, baptism embodies these realities of identity: we are united with Christ, have been buried and raised with Christ, and are clothed with Christ. We are in Christ. Through Paul's eyes, going down in the river to pray means we exit a destructive community and enter an entirely new community of those who have united with Christ in death and resurrection. We come up from the river with a new kingdom ethic. In the next section, we look at how this new ethic flows out of the river of God's grace.

A New Kingdom Ethic for Between Times

Through Paul's eyes, baptism leads to a new ethical life. Here we consider Ephesians in order to see the basis for new ethic: the identity-shaping grace of God that made us alive when we were dead in the water. Paul in Ephesians grounds this new ethic and world view in God's grace.

Ephesians includes one specific mention of "one baptism" (4:5), one direct figurative reference to baptism, which is a reference to Christ "washing (the church) with water through the word" (5:25-26), and possible allusions to baptism (1:13; 4:30; 5:14). Since baptism is alluded to, specifically mentioned, and spoken of in the same terms of being "in Christ" (2:13; 3:12, 17, 21), the whole letter helps us understand the meaning of living between death to transgressions (Eph. 2:1; cf. Rom. 6:2-3) and our life "in Christ." James D. G. Dunn calls baptism a "concertina word"—a single word that includes a variety of concepts. Inversely, a variety of concepts can allude or specifically refer to baptism. So baptism not only refers to concepts such as washing, being in Christ, and being clothed with Christ, but Paul may also be thinking of baptism at times when he says we are "in Christ," "buried with him," or "clothed with Christ."

Pauline ethics are formed on the basis of God's grace. Language runs throughout Ephesians that orients recipients to grace and the ethical outgrowth of this new identity (Eph. 2:8-10). On the firm ground of God's grace, therefore, Paul calls the Ephesians to live a life worthy of their calling (4:1). The imperatives flow out of the indicative foundations of God's grace (2:8-10; 3:7, 14-21). The whole of chapters 4-6 are grounded in God's work for us through Christ and the Spirit. Exhorting the Ephesians, Paul reminds them that they were taught to put off the old self, to be made new in the attitude of their minds and to put on a new self, created to be like God in true righteousness and holiness (4:22-23). In their new life orientation they have been sealed by the Holy Spirit for the day of redemption (4:30).

As Paul defines for the Ephesians what the new life looks like in terms of relationships to husband and wife, slave to master, children to parents, Jew to Gentile, he points again to baptism. In this section filled with imperatives for the ethical life, Paul lists baptism in his seven "ones": "There is one body and one Spirit, just as you were called to the one hope of your calling, one Lord, one faith, one baptism, one God and Father of all, who is above all and through all and in all" (4:4-6).

Baptism is in honored company in Ephesians 4, but this does not tempt us to elevate baptism to the status reserved for the Father, Son, and Spirit. It does, however, strongly suggest an important place in the theology of Paul for the relationship between the experience of baptism and our relationship with Father, Son and Holy Spirit. Mentioning baptism is Paul's way of addressing the redemptive dimension of unity. God the Father has by the Spirit and in Christ created one body for one hope through one faith experienced in one baptism. We are not certain whether this was a familiar hymn, but we are certain that it is a powerful expression of the foundational oneness of God's people. This means that when we talk about unity, we must speak of baptism; when we talk about redemption (soteriology), we must also talk about baptism. When we talk of baptism, we must talk about one faith, one body, one Spirit, one hope of our calling, one Lord and Father of all. Baptism is a vital part of the fabric that unifies us. To speak only of faith and to ignore baptism is to undermine this fabric.

Live on the Basis of Grace

Ephesians is one of the best examples in Paul's letters of the distinction between the indicatives of grace (Eph. 1-3) and the ethical imperatives built on the basis of this grace (Eph. 4-6).[8] To illustrate, Watchman Nee offered one of the most compelling if not simple outlines of Ephesians: sit, walk, stand.[9] Nee says the grace of God calls us to sit until we understand the ocean of God's grace (Eph. 3:16-21)—the indicative language of grace. Only out of grasping this grace (Eph. 1:8) ought we to get up and attempt to walk a life worthy of this grace and calling (Eph. 4:1f.)—the imperative language of ethics. Finally, in walking the life of discipleship and sanctification we are empowered to stand against Satan and his minions in the spiritual battle (Eph. 6:10-18).

The new life "in Christ"—linguistically linked to baptism—affects ethics. Paul's ethical world view grows out of the new life "in Christ." Foundational to Pauline ethics, therefore, is a realization of our sin as well as God's grace for us in that condition. We live on the basis of *grace*. We *live* on the basis of grace.[10] Perhaps this relationship of grace and ethics may now seem natural to us, but this was not likely a popular thought in Paul's time. While

Greek and Roman religious ideas of ethics had already developed, the chief concern remained with ritual and outward acts of devotion.[11] No Greek or Roman god had done or would ever do what Jesus Christ did for Paul's audience and for us. The Christ-event primarily distinguishes our identity but also distinguishes Christian ethics from other systems. The moral impulse, therefore, says J.L. Houlden, "finds its deepest source in Christ's death, which for Paul operates at a level more profound than that of inspiration: baptism 'into Christ' brings about the destruction of the believer's orientation to sin."[12]

A fitting response to God's grace is praise and good works (Eph. 1:3-14, 15-23; 3:14-21). Life is connected to praise, and the worshiper goes on to live out what God has done first for us (cf. Mt 5:16; 7:21; 25:1-46; Heb 10:24). Christians, while enthroned with Christ, are embedded in the life of the church and community. We are connected to the divine community but also to the faith community. We forgive as God forgave us (Eph. 4:32), do all that is good and right and true (Eph. 5:9), and respect, love and honor in our relationships (Eph. 5:33; 6:1, 5). Within this context, Paul expounds on a covenant ethic of gratitude toward God, based on the work that God has done through Christ and for the purpose of honoring God, for the praise of his glory (Eph. 1:12; 3:21). In other words, Paul is telling the Ephesians that they have been saved from the former way of life in order to live a new ethical life with future expectancy of exaltation with Christ.

Paul was not simply building a foundation for Christian ethics for the Ephesians but was also addressing church conflicts with Christians living in a culture that opposed Christian ethics. Paul's ethical teaching is contextual, based on indicatives but born out of specific church problems. Paul opposes the attempt to establish the indicatives by doing the imperatives (Galatians problem with legalism), just as he opposes acceptance of grace with no discipleship (Corinthian problem—one of them—with cheap grace). In Colossians, for example, there is also a linguistic connection between the work of God in Christ on the cross and the new lifestyle that God calls us to in Christ (Col. 2:12; 3:1-4). Paul uses the same image of being raised with Christ in order to discuss holy living. He says since we have been raised, set our hearts on things above where Christ is seated (3:1). The exhortations not only follow but also blend with the divine basis for their new lifestyle in Christ: namely, we are empowered to live the holy life by union with Christ both in death and in his resurrection. This identity with Christ is the basis for our new identity.

The blessings of the indicative are not an end in themselves, but they are a means to an end of a transforming relationship and discipleship, to the praise of God's glorious grace (Eph. 1:3-14). We are saved for the purpose of glorifying God through our faith and discipleship. We are his craftsmanship, created for good works in Christ. For Paul, going down to the river to pray means uniting with Christ in his death and resurrection and rising to new ethical imperatives that are moored in God's grace.

Baptism into One Head and One Body

In addition to Paul building on grace and new life as the basis of ethics, he also points to baptism as both indicator and mediator of oneness in Christ's body. We are baptized into the head, who is Christ. The clearest example of this is in 1 Corinthians. When church unity and the gospel were at stake, Paul pointed back to the foundations of disciples' faith. Paul speaks of baptism in 1 Corinthians in the context of the implications baptism has on divisions and unity in the church (1 Cor. 1:11-17; 6:11; 12:13). When Paul called for unity in Corinth he appealed to two central "events" in the life of God's people: the death of Christ for them and their baptism into the name of Christ.

In 1 Corinthians 1:11-17, for example, Paul brings baptism into a discussion of divisions in the church in Corinth. Christians were baptized not in Paul's name or any other name but in the name of the triune God (1 Cor. 1:13-17). Misappropriation of baptism to human leaders created divisions in the Corinthian church, and Paul re-appropriates the message of their baptism to draw them back together into the head of the church, who is Christ, and the body of Christ, who are brothers and sisters in fellowship of one Spirit. Paul's principle applies not only to individuals but applies to groups and whole churches that preempt Christ as head. We are baptized into Christ and his body, the church, not into a denominational affiliation. Paul's later reference in 1

Corinthians to baptism shows the stark contrast between Paul's ethic with the Corinthians' divisions (1 Cor. 12:13): "For we were all baptized by one Spirit into one body—whether Jews or Greeks, slave or free—and we were all given the one Spirit to drink."

In addressing immorality in the Corinthian church (1 Cor. 6:12-20), Paul asks how they could think of being united in sexually sinful ways after being united with Christ. After describing a list of their past sins, such as greed and homosexuality, Paul says this is their former identity. Paul had already established that baptism is in no other name than Christ. Now he shows that this new life "in Christ" demands union with no other, because no other died for us (1 Cor. 6:11): "But you were washed, you were sanctified, you were justified in the name of the Lord Jesus Christ and in the Spirit of our God." Paul's ethics draw from the foundation of union with Christ or identity with Christ. If we were united with Christ, how could we also unite with sin? His emphasis on our identity in Christ illustrates the unique nature of Paul's ethic and of importance of baptism as a sign of the new life. In other words, it matters how we act morally and ethically in the marketplace because of who we are. Paul's language of identifying ourselves with the name of the Father and of the Son and of the Holy Spirit is similar to Christ's words in his Great Commission (Matt. 28:19). Because we are identified and named with God, so we must reflect God's image. The moment of baptism, therefore, is a transforming event that gives both a new identity and a new ethical basis on which to live (1 Cor. 6:1-20).

For Paul, baptism is a holy moment where transformation occurs in the life of the believer and leads to a transformed life. It is an event that unites us with the Christ-event. He points back to baptism in his letters when it seems his readers have forgotten their calling, have become divided, have slipped into antinomianism, or have elevated Jewish rituals over the grace of God. Baptism is a sign of a new ethical lifestyle grounded in the grace of God and lived out in the body of Christ, the community of faith.

A New Expectant World View

Our hope is a present experience of future realities. By God's grace we can view with Spiritual eyes beyond what our physical eyes can see. In Christ, we experience the power and presence of the future right now. God's Spirit in us is our seal of the promise of future glory. This reorients the way we see the world. Our hope is not simply for the future but we also live expectantly now and live in the now as if the future were already here. Future hope breaks into our world and God has the last word. This is the apocalyptic hope we have in Christ.

According to Paul, baptism has a future redemptive dimension. It is an apocalyptic sign; an in-breaking of the future into our lives in the present and the expectant hope of the fullness of the reign of God in the future. Figure 2 illustrates Paul's apocalyptic world view described in Romans, the Adam and Christ contrast of Romans 5. The old world and new world, death and life, are baptismal themes that match Paul's apocalyptic world view. Paul follows this discussion of Adam and Christ by reminding Christians that their baptism is a union with Christ that changes everything in their world. Paul connects all of Adam's descendants with one simultaneously unifying and destroying idea: we all have the same disease that killed him. Through one man sin came. In our humanity we are in solidarity with the sin of Adam. Adam represents but does not bear full responsibility for our own sin. Through the second man, however, the grace of God has come.

God's kingdom rule breaks into our Adamic world of sin. Through repentance and baptism we join in solidarity with Christ by faith through the Spirit (Rom. 6). Through union with Adam, death has become a plague in humankind. Through union with Christ, the ground of God's grace is the overflowing antidote, and it is mediated through the sign of baptism that connects us with the Christ-event. The act of disobedience of the first man brought death to all. The obedient and graceful act of the second man brought life to all humanity.

The circle of figure 2 illustrates the world of Adam, and the past and future facing arrows represent God's kingdom rule—the *eschaton* or end times—breaking into our world. The *eschaton* is breaking in from the future we already have in Christ. God's future has broken in through his past redemptive work and gives us an "already, but not yet" sense of that hope. This means that God's work in establishing his reign in this world has already begun though it is not yet complete. We live in this in-between time, after

Christ has come but before his second coming. God has decisively established the "already" reality of Christ. But God has yet to complete his work. We live in this sense of expectancy about what God has done, is doing, and will do. This in-breaking shapes Paul's understanding of what we share "in Christ": a new identity, a new ethic, and a new world view.

Paul summarizes this Adam and Christ analogy in Romans 5:21: "so that, just as sin exercised dominion in death, so grace might also exercise dominion through justification leading to eternal life through Jesus Christ our Lord." The argument flows from chapter 5 to 6 easily with no breaks, and strong connections are formed with the words sin (*hamartia*), grace (*charis*), law (*nomos*), in Christ (*en Christos*), death (*thanato*), and increase (*pleonazo*).

Paul's letter to the Corinthians is a good example of how the apostle connects identity, ethic, and world view. The Corinthians' former identity was based in pagan cults, bigotry and hate. In a compact sentence, Paul throws down the gauntlet between a heinous past and a glorious future: "And this is what some of you used to be" (1 Cor. 6:11a). He follows this declaration with a reference to the stark dividing line between their old life and the new: "But you were washed, you were sanctified, you were justified in

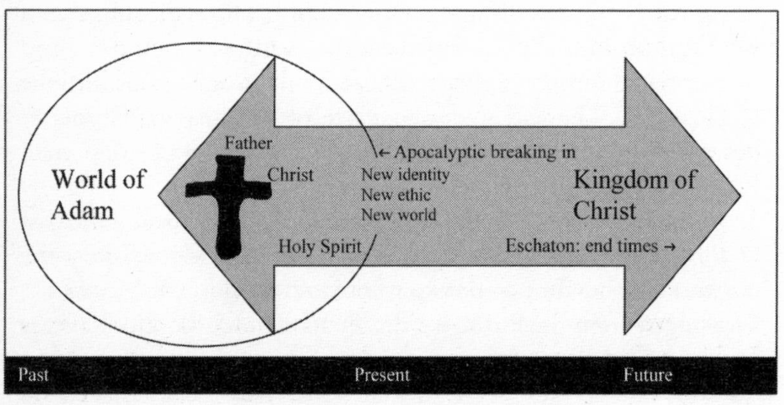

Figure 2: Paul's Apocalyptic World View

the name of the Lord Jesus Christ and in the Spirit of our God" (6:11b). Then Paul, with a sense of surprise, asks, "Do you not know that wrongdoers will not inherit the kingdom of God?" (6:9a) He continues by saying, "Do not be deceived! Fornicators, idolaters, adulterers, male prostitutes, sodomites, thieves, the greedy, drunkards, revilers, robbers—none of these will inherit the kingdom of God" (6:9b-10).

In Christ, however, we will inherit the kingdom. In Paul's view, life in Christ entails a drowning of the old orientation to sin, a transition into a new orientation, and a future expectation of exaltation with Christ in a new age. Richard P. Carlson has a helpful three-part understanding of Paul's outlook on the role of baptism as negation, inauguration, and anticipation.[13] Through baptism the old orientation to life is negated, we are inaugurated into a new orientation in Christ, and we anticipate being exalted with Christ in the final epoch. Christ has gone with us into the deep, and from the depths we may see the radiance of Christ breaking into the darkness.

Because we have seen the future breaking into our world through changed lives, we have hope for a future world. Baptism is a figure of hope. We die and rise up. Baptism may not be far from Paul's mind with this death-to-life language in Ephesians 5:15. Paul exudes resurrection language, using a metaphor of a sleeper awaking, rising from the dead, and receiving the light of Christ. Paul says with resolution, "for everything that becomes visible is light. Therefore it says, "Sleeper, awake! Rise from the dead, and Christ will shine on you" (Eph. 5:14). There is a sense in which our rising is present but also future. We rise up and walk in newness of life, but this living is filled with hope. Our identity in Adam was hope-less, but our identity in Christ is hope-filled.

We're called to arise and look to a distant shore. Our baptism is a God-given objective sign of assurance that we will someday reach that shore—yet the resurrection power and our assurance is not in the water but in the event embodied in our baptism: the Christ event (cf. 1 Pet. 3:21-22). The certainty of the future is based on Christ's resurrection. Because Christ has been raised, we also expect to be raised (Col. 2:12). The power of the resurrection is the power to destroy death and fully establish the reign of God in the end times (1 Cor.15:1-58). Our seal of assurance is God's

Spirit (Eph. 1:13-14), and by faith we receive the sign of baptism that unites us with the redemptive work of God in Christ.

Conclusion

Baptism for Paul is an apocalyptic sign of a new identity, ethic and world view. Through Paul's eyes, baptism is the "concertina" word that binds these together. In baptism, the past and future collide in a present reality: we are truly united with the earth-moving power of the Christ-event.[14] The kingdom of Christ breaks in and we dive into the divine community to seek it. In baptism, our world is upended. We are drowned to the old life. We get a view of a new life in Christ and the hope of exaltation with him in the end times.

The symbolic and theological covenant of baptism is a constant reminder of the discple's identity. Our baptism reminds us that the gospel is to be lived out in ethical connection between the event of Christ's death, burial, and resurrection and his second coming. Hence, Paul's references to baptism in the past tense were a call for Christians to remember who they were in Christ, as disciples of a higher calling than the way in which they formerly lived (Eph. 4:1; Gal. 3:27; Rom. 6:1-5).

Baptism not only symbolizes the washing of forgiveness, but we are also truly washed and forgiven (Titus 3:5-7). Baptism not only symbolizes participation or union with Christ in his death (Rom. 6:3-5), but we do truly unite with Christ through baptism into Christ's burial and resurrection (Col. 2:12). Baptism not only symbolizes a new identity, but we actually do enter a new community (Gal. 3:27), and we are genuinely, not just symbolically, initiated into the body of Christ (1 Cor. 12:13). Baptism is a normative sign through which we participate—not merely symbolically but in body and soul—in God's flood of grace.

Through the lens of the context of Paul's letters, baptism shines as a holy moment through which God mediates his grace through Jesus Christ, into whose name and death we are joined in baptism, with whom we have been raised to newness of life, and with whom we hope to be raised when he returns. With Paul we can say, "O the depths from which we have arisen in Christ!" We dove into the divine community. But in this death is grace. As Paul says in his doxology (Rom. 11:33-36):

> O the depth of the riches and wisdom and knowledge of God! How unsearchable are his judgments and how inscrutable his ways! "For who has known the mind of the Lord? Or who has been his counselor?" "Or who has given a gift to him, to receive a gift in return?" For from him and through him and to him are all things. To him be the glory forever. Amen.

****

Principle

For Paul, baptism is an apocalyptic sign that connects us to the Christ-event: his death-burial-resurrection-enthronement-intercession-second coming. Therefore, baptism does not merely symbolize new life but actually gives us a new identity. It does not merely symbolize washing but genuinely empowers a new ethic through the power of the Spirit. Baptism not only symbolizes a break with Adam's world but through faith in union with Christ gives us a whole new world view.

Prayer

Drown us, Lord. Drown us in your grace by your Spirit, through the waters of refreshing and cleansing, so that we can be in your presence. Lord, show us just a portion of all that you have done, and that will overwhelm us. Our feeble faith is like a tiny pebble in the sea. May the mustard seed of our faith be lost in the ocean of your grace. Give us hope in the present for the future and may the power of your future be present in our lives to shape us into your image. Give us the power to live our new identity through the new ethic you have given us that bears witness to our new world view. Amen.

Questions

1. Is your baptism more of a faith response or a work of God? Explain.

2. How does baptism unite us in Christ's death?

3. How does baptism unite us with Christ's resurrection?

4. In what way does baptism transform the way we view the past?

5. In what way does baptism transform our future?

6. How does baptism transform our daily lives.

5 / Quiet Water: The Early Church

Irene who lived with her parents ten months and six days received [grace] seven days before the Ides of April and gave up [her soul] on the Ides of April.

An early tomb inscription[1]

Irene was born to Christian parents, but she was not baptized at her birth. Instead, her parents expected she would grow up in the faith, undergo catechesis and be immersed when she was older. But infant mortality was high. Many died in childhood.

When Irene fell seriously ill, her parents worried that they would never see her live into adulthood. She would never confess her faith and enter the church through baptism. When death was imminent, they brought Irene to the church for baptism. It was an "emergency situation"—they did not want their child to die without baptism because they believed baptism was so important, and they believed God's grace was for their child as well as for themselves.

Consequently, seven days before her death, Irene received the grace of baptism and was reckoned among God's "believers." Her parents were comforted.

****

The river is quiet and smooth at the beginning. As far as the explicit record of second-century Christianity is concerned, the church normally immersed believers for the remission of their sins. The history of baptism in subsequent centuries is a history of exceptions to, variations from and adaptations to that tradition. The river flowed effortlessly through this early history and adapted to changing situations without churning the waters of controversy. Though the church shifted from normatively baptizing adult believers in the second century to the common practice of infant baptism in the fifth century, the waters of controversy never heated up. There was no significant opposition to this development in the first centuries of the church—the only controversy surrounding it was not "whether" they should be baptized, but "why" they should be baptized.[2] High infant mortality, a "high" view of baptismal grace and the shift from a persecuted minority to a state religion were contributing factors to acceptance.

While the second-century church reflects a remarkable consistency in the discussions of baptism, a wider diversity emerges in the third. While there is no example of infant baptism and only an incidental reference to the exceptional character of pouring (in contrast to immersion) in the second century, the third century witnesses the emergence of both. This diversity, while minor at first, grew through the fifth century and by the end of the medieval period a consensus had been established that was the opposite of the practice of the second-century church. Whereas the immersion of adult believers was the normal practice in the second century, pouring water on infants as baptism was the standard practice of continental western Europe by the fifteenth century. However, one constant was a consensus understanding that baptism was for the remission of sins and that an unbaptized saved adult was a rare exception.

Second-Century Consensus

There are few lengthy descriptions of baptismal practice from the second century.[3] Mostly we have scattered allusions. Tertullian (Carthage, North Africa; died ca. 220) provides the most extensive picture of baptism in the first book written on the subject (ca. 200). It was written against several Gnostic sects that rejected water baptism, and he used the opportunity to explain the theology and practice of the church in North Africa, which he regarded as consistent with the church throughout the Mediterranean basin.

Tertullian details the baptismal procedure with which he was acquainted (also in *On the Crown*, 3). Baptism was preceded by a period of teaching (catechesis). Though Tertullian does not specify the length of time, Hippolytus of Rome in the early third century recommends three years (*Apostolic Tradition*, 17). Most scholars believe that the first six chapters of the *Didache* (probably from Syria; ca. 100) were designed for catechesis. It lays out the path of a moral life. Candidates for baptism were expected to understand Christianity's ethical demands. Tertullian writes (*On Repentance*, 6): "We are not washed in order that we may cease sinning, but because we have ceased, since in heart we have been bathed already." Only those who "are persuaded and believe that what we teach and say is true," writes Justin Martyr in the mid-second century, "and undertake to be able to live accordingly" are baptized (*Apology*, 1.61). Only penitent believers are baptismal candidates and there is no explicit record of infant or child baptism. Tertullian is the first to explicitly mention infant baptism but he rejects it by retorting: "Why does the innocent period of life hasten to the 'remission of sins'?" (*Baptism*, 18). He opposes infant baptism and encourages people to delay their baptism till they understand the meaning of their commitment.

Candidates, according to Tertullian, spent the nights previous to their baptism in "repeated prayers, fasts, and bendings of the knee, and vigils" with an emphasis on "confessing their sins" according to the example of those who came to John's baptism (*On Baptism*, 20). Both the *Didache* (7.4) and Justin Martyr (*Apology* 1.61) also commend fasting prior to baptism, including the baptizer and the wider community. In the third century these preparations also included some bathing rituals, exorcisms and Scripture readings (*Apostolic Tradition*, 20). These practices indicate the seriousness of the baptismal moment which included repentance, confession and mourning over past sins.

As the candidates approached the water, it was blessed which seems to represent the sanctifying presence of the Spirit (*On Baptism*, 4). The believer then went down into the water naked

(*Apostolic Tradition*, 21) and was then clothed with a new white robe after baptism. The old clothes symbolized the old life, nudity symbolized full submission to God, and the new clothes symbolized new life. Though the kind of water appears to have been initially significant (*Didache*, 7, values running water), by the end of the second-century immersion in any pool of water was regarded as acceptable. Tertullian writes that it "makes no difference whether a man be washed in a sea or a pool, a stream or a fount, a lake or a trough" because the water was "sanctified by the Holy One" (*On Baptism*, 4).

Standing in the water, the candidate renounced Satan and his angels (*On the Crown*, 3). Early third-century traditions included an exorcism (*Apostolic Tradition*, 21). The believers then confessed their faith in a three-fold manner: belief in the Father, Son and Holy Spirit with a corresponding triune immersion (*On Baptism*, 6, 13 and *On the Crown*, 3). According to Hippolytus, believers are immersed after they confess the Father, and immersed again after confessing the Son, and immersed a third time after confessing the Holy Spirit (*Apostolic Tradition*, 21). Triune immersion is probably implied in the *Didache* (7), but Justin Martyr mentions only one immersion. The three-fold pattern, however, became standard.

Immersion is the consistent witness in the second century with the exception of the *Didache* (7). The manual instructs the church in this manner: "Having said all these things beforehand, baptize in the name of the Father and of the Son and of the Holy Spirit in living water. If there is no living water, baptize in other water; and, if you are not able to use cold water, use warm. If you have neither, pour water three times upon the head in the name of the Father, Son, and Holy Spirit." Clearly, the writer prefers immersion ("baptize" equals immerse) and he distinguishes between the act of baptizing (immersing) and the act of pouring. Pouring is an exceptional circumstance, though the circumstance is not identified (we may presume a lack of water or sickness).

In contrast, all other descriptions of baptism in the second century are immersions. "The act of baptism," Tertullian writes, "is carnal, in that we are plunged in water, but the effect spiritual, in that we are freed from sins" (*On Baptism*, 7). Early writers, such as Barnabas (*Epistle of Barnabas*, 11) and Shepherd of Hermas

(*Mandate*, 4.3.1) describe descending into water and ascending out of it. An early fragment of a non-canonical gospel quotes Jesus as saying his disciples "have been dipped in the waters of eternal life" (*Oxyrhynchus Papyri*, 5:840).

The theological meaning of baptism is described through various metaphors: new birth (regeneration), remission of sins, cleansing, victory over Satan, resurrection and sealing by the Spirit.[4] Tertullian reflects many of these metaphors. Through baptism we are "set free from sins," we "are set free [from sin] and admitted into eternal life," and "we, little fishes, after the example of our *icthus* [fish] Jesus Christ, are born in water" (*On Baptism*, 1, 7). The baptism of Jesus was the model for Christian baptism, and just as Jesus was declared "Son" coming out of the water, so we are declared "children of God" as we come out of the water. The fish symbol, so common today, was also prominent in the late second century. Tertullian views it through a baptismal lens.

Other Christian writers reflect these themes as well. For example, the Shepherd of Hermas (ca. 110) uses a variety of images. "Your life was saved and will be saved through water," he writes (*Vision*, 3.3.3). In baptism "we descended into the water and received the forgiveness of our former sins" (*Mandate*, 4.3.1) and those who "descend…into the water dead…ascend alive" (*Similitudes*, 9.16.3). Justin Martyr says we "obtain in the water the forgiveness of sins" and we are "regenerated" through the "washing in water," quoting John 3:5 (*Apology*, 1:61). Irenaeus, Bishop of Gaul in the late second century, encourages his readers to remember that "we have received baptism for remission of sins in the name of God the Father, and in the name of Jesus Christ, the Son of God…and in the Holy Spirit; and that this baptism is the seal of eternal life and is rebirth unto God, that we be no more children of mortal men, but of the eternal and everlasting God" (*Apostolic Preaching*, 3).

There is no thought in the second century that anyone could have been regarded as saved or a member of the Christian community without baptism. The only exceptions to this consensus were the martyrs. Because catechumens might experience martyrdom without warning, Tertullian regards their situation as exceptional. The baptism of blood "stands in lieu of the fontal bathing when that has not been received, and restores it when lost" because it identifies with the baptism of Christ's own suffering (*On Baptism*, 16). Otherwise, according to Tertullian, "bare faith" without baptism is insufficient. "The comparison with this law [John 3:5] of that definition [Matt. 28:19], 'Unless a man have been reborn of water and Spirit, he shall not enter into the kingdom of the heavens'," Tertullian writes, "has tied faith to the necessity of baptism" (*On Baptism*, 13).

According to Tertullian, after baptism believers were dressed in white robes and anointed with oil just as the Levites were anointed at their priestly ordination. The newly baptized are thus newly anointed with the Holy Spirit just as Jesus himself was after his baptism. Apparently, this anointing was also the time when they received the laying on of hands as a symbol of this blessing (the presence of the Holy Spirit), analogous to Jacob blessing his grandsons in Genesis 48 (*On Baptism*, 7-8). Afterwards the baptized are greeted with a kiss of peace and ushered into an assembly of believers where they partake of their first communion (the Lord's Supper; so also in Justin Martyr, *Apology*, 1.61 and the *Didache*, 7). Along with the bread and wine, they are also given milk and honey to symbolize their entrance into the promised land (*On the Crown*, 3).

Theologically, Tertullian's description of the initiatory ritual held three events together: immersion (cleansing) in water, anointing with oil (reception of the Spirit) and first communion (experience of community fellowship). It was an initiation into the church and into the fellowship of the divine community. It followed the model of Jesus, the "prescribed law" of the Great Commission in Matthew 28:19 and the tradition of the church. The second-century church, as far as the record goes, shared this perspective, though it had developed a more formal and extensive ritual than present in the early second-century Didache.

Third-Century Divergence

Baptismal practices diverged in the early third century. While the second-century consensus remained the normal Christian experience, varying circumstances began to shape baptismal practice. The river diverged, without great controversy or consternation, on the subject and mode of baptism.

In his *Apostolic Tradition* (ca. 215 A.D.) Hippolytus gives considerable attention to teaching catechumens. However, the document also reflects the practice of baptizing children (21.3): "First you should baptize the little ones. All who can speak for themselves should speak. But for those who cannot speak, their parents should speak or another who belongs to their family." Given that baptisms were generally held at Easter or Pentecost (cf. *On Baptism*, 19), the context may reflect some kind of "household baptism" where the whole family becomes part of the Christian community. This would account for the varying ages of the children. There is no hesitancy in Hippolytus' account, which indicates it was not unusual though it may not have been the normal custom.

Tertullian opposed infant baptism in Carthage, North Africa, which means that some were practicing it before the end of the second century. Indeed, Origen (d. 254), the renowned scholar of the Egyptian church, believed that the "church received a tradition from the apostles to give baptism to infants too" (*Commentary on Romans*, 5.9). Consequently, it appears that by the beginning of the third century infant/child baptism was practiced in some quarters of the church. Since both Origen and Hippolytus believed infant/child baptism was apostolic, this indicates that it was fairly widespread and had roots at least in the late second century.[5]

The most extensive discussion, however, of infant baptism in the third century is found in Cyprian (d. 258), Bishop of Carthage in North Africa. He and a council of sixty-six bishops judged "that the mercy and grace of God is not to be refused to any one born of man" because God's grace does not discriminate according to age (*Letters* 64.2). Cyprian offers a theological rationale for baptizing infants as soon as opportunity permits. The church should not hinder an infant because, although it has no sins of its own, it has "contracted the contagion of the ancient death at its earliest birth." Therefore, the church should offer the grace of baptism for "the reception of the forgiveness of sins—that to him are remitted, not his own sins, but the sins of another" (*Letters* 64.5). Infants need grace (baptism for the remission of sins) because they bear the guilt of Adam's sin.

Scholars have debated which came first—was Adamic sin (or some kind of contamination) the rationale for baptizing infants or was the church already baptizing infants for pragmatic reasons for which they needed a theological rationale? Ultimately, infant baptism is defended, as it is by Cyprian and later Augustine, because it is a means of grace for the forgiveness of original or Adamic sin. This became the fundamental theological rationale for infant baptism in the Western (Catholic) church. However, it was not the rationale in the Eastern (Orthodox) church, which focused on initiation into the divine communion. By the fifth century both traditions commonly baptized infants, but for different reasons. This difference is best explained if the origins of infant baptism are rooted in something other than a theological ground for infant baptism.

Ferguson has argued that infant baptism arose out of the practice of emergency baptisms.[6] Tomb inscriptions indicate that some children were not baptized in their infancy but were baptized days before their death. These inscriptions begin to appear in the third century and increase in the following centuries. Generally, the tomb inscriptions refer to baptism with the phrase that a child "became a believer" or "received grace" on a particular day before her death. These children received baptism just prior to their death at ages ranging from twelve years to eighty days. One was found in the Roman Catacomb of Priscilla (ca. third century):

> Sacred to the divine dead. Florentius made this monument for his well-deserving son Appronianus, who lived one year, nine months, and five days. Since he was dearly loved by his grandmother, and she saw that he was going to die, she asked from the church that he might depart from the world a believer.[7]

It appears that newborn infants "were not routinely baptized in the period of our early inscriptions. Baptism was administered before death, at whatever age."[8] It seems likely that infant/child baptism arose out of a sense of emergency to give these dying children "grace" prior to their death and insure their entrance into the heavenly kingdom. Since infant/child mortality was so high in the ancient world, emergency baptism ultimately became a just-in-case baptism, which church theologians and bishops began to defend with theological rationales. "Emergency procedures" became "regular practice" by the beginning of the fifth century.[9]

The third century also provides the first clear evidence (other than the Didache) of the practice of pouring for baptism. The circumstances of these cases are exceptional. They apply to those who are sick or weak. Consequently, they are called "clinical baptisms" because they are baptisms administered to people who are bed-ridden due to sickness (the Greek word for bed is *kline*, thus clinical). The first and most famous example is the case of Novatian in Rome in the early third century.[10] Because he was sick and was feared near death, he was baptized by pouring on his bed. Later, however, Novatian recovered and ran for election as Bishop of Rome. Many of the clergy opposed his nomination because "it was not lawful for someone who had received pouring in bed on account of sickness to become a member of the clergy." Apparently, while baptism by pouring was recognized in exceptional circumstances, it was not accepted as normative or sufficient for leadership in the church.

Cyprian, however, argued for the legitimacy of pouring as a form of baptism. While he would not offer pouring as a standard option for baptism, he believed that those who obtained "grace" in their "sickness and weakness" through sprinkling or pouring were legitimately baptized. When "necessity compels," those who are "sprinkled or affused" receive the whole benefit of God's mercy because even Ezekiel (36:25) and Moses (Num. 19:13) bear witness to the benefits of sprinkling. Thus, "the sprinkling also of water prevails equally with the washing [immersion] of salvation" (*Letters* 75.12). Pouring was sometimes an option in more standard baptismal rituals: "If water is scarce, whether as a constant condition or on occasion, then use whatever water is available" (Hippolytus, *Apostolic Tradition*, 21). Nevertheless, in every case in the third century, pouring or sprinkling was the exception. It was an occasional necessity rather than the normative practice of the church. However, the mid-third century *Acts of Thomas* (132), though its date is disputed and it has undergone significant redaction through transmission, reflects a seemingly normal picture of non-immersion baptism.

Despite this emerging diversity of practice, there was no divergence in the third century regarding the meaning and necessity of baptism. Indeed, Cyprian's argument for infant baptism assumes that it is necessary for the forgiveness of sins (*Letters* 72.7: "But it is manifest where and by whom remission of sins can be given; to wit, that which is given in baptism."). Origen believed infants were "baptized for the remission of sins" (*Homily on Luke* 14.5), though the sin was not Adamic but the sin of the souls in their pre-existent state. Baptism for the forgiveness of sins is the universal consensus of the third century, though the exception for unbaptized martyrs was still present (Cyprian, *Letters* 72.21). Cyprian, in an apparent expression of common agreement, offers a few other exceptions, e.g., catechumens who die before baptism and those ignorantly baptized by heretics (*Letters* 74.2).

Fourth and Fifth Century Convergence

The fourth-century church experienced major changes. It was a significant turning point in Christian history. Church leaders debated major theological topics such as Trinity and Christology. But, most significantly, Christianity became a legal religion at the beginning of the fourth century and by that century's end it was the only legal religion. The Roman Empire became Christian. When Constantine proclaimed Christianity legal in 313 A.D. and then Theodosius made it the only legal religion in 391 A.D., adult conversions became increasingly rare in Christianized sectors of the empire. Children grew up in the church. Christianity was their national religion. As a consequence, infant/child baptism became the norm. The river of baptismal history was cemented and remained constant for the next thousand years.

While infant baptism became increasingly the standard, it was neither universal nor the norm throughout the fourth century. Major Christian theologians such as Gregory Nazianzus (d. 389), Basil (d. 379), Ephraim the Syrian (d. 373), Ambrose (d. 397), Chrysostom (d. 407), and Augustine (d. 430) were baptized as adults though they were raised in Christian circumstances. Tomb inscriptions in the fourth century indicate that some children were not regularly baptized in infancy but underwent emergency baptisms at varying ages. By the end of the fourth century, however, infant baptism was widely practiced. Indeed, the Council of Carthage (419 A.D.), under the leadership of Augustine, anathematized anyone who rejected infant baptism.

Despite this growing consensus, leaders in the East and West disagreed regarding the rationale or theological significance of baptism for infants. In the West, under the predominant influence of Augustine, infants were baptized for the remission of sins—the remission of original sin or Adamic guilt. Interestingly, during the Pelagian controversy of the early fifth century, infant baptism was the presupposition and Adamic guilt was the conclusion of the argument. In other words, Augustine argued for Adamic guilt because infants were baptized rather than arguing that infants needed baptism because of Adamic guilt. While the West would root the necessity of infant baptism in the remission of Adamic guilt (original sin), this was not the original theological rationale for infant baptism.

The Eastern Church generally did not believe that infants were burdened with Adamic guilt. They baptized infants and children for much broader reasons. Baptism has many more blessings than just the remission of sins, and children were baptized to enjoy these gifts even when they did not need the remission of any sin. Chrysostom, Bishop of Constantinople, provides a representative statement in his *Baptismal Instructions* (3.6):

> You have seen how numerous are the gifts of baptism. Although many men think that the only gift it confers is the remission of sins, we have counted its honors to the number of ten. It is on this account that we baptize even infants, although they are sinless, that they may be given the further gifts of sanctification, righteousness, filial adoption, and inheritance, that they may be brothers and members of Christ, and become dwelling places for the Spirit.

Infants are baptized in order to incorporate them into the life of the church, to experience the grace of God, and to partake in the presence of the Spirit. Through baptism they become heirs of eternal life in the kingdom of God.

While the Western church tended to baptize infants for the remission of sins, the Eastern Church tended to baptize infants in order to bring them into the fuller experience of the Christian faith. Wright has argued that infant baptism may have originated in child baptism where children were treated as catechumens rather than outsiders. They were regarded as undergoing catechesis or instruction in their developing life and then at a level of maturity affirmed their faith through baptism, even at young ages.[11] For example, Gregory Nazianzus thought that unless "danger presses," children should receive baptism towards the beginning of their fourth year "when they may be able to listen and to answer something about" baptism (*Orations*, 40.28). In the East, children were regarded as catechumens but when death was imminent, they were baptized no matter what their age.

The desire to baptize children and infants in mortal danger reflects a high view of baptism's soteriological meaning. The church believed, both East and West, that no one could enter heaven without baptism. For example, Chrysostom (*Homilies on John*, 25) commented on John 3:5 that "if it should come to pass, (which God forbid!) that through the sudden arrival of death we depart hence uninitiated, though we have ten thousand virtues, our portion will be no other than hell." Unbaptized children or infants were regarded as lost (particularly in the West) or at least reserved for some kind of middle state that was neither heaven nor hell (particularly in the East). All agreed that unbaptized infants miss heaven. Consequently, every effort was made to baptize them if they were in any kind of mortal danger.

Some contemplated "unbaptized" scenarios. Ambrose dismissed them: "No one is excepted: not the infant, not the one prevented by necessity" (*Abraham*, 2). Gregory Nazianzus entertained the question of whether a person in good health could go to heaven unbaptized if that person had a firm resolution to be baptized at the next opportunity, but was prevented from doing so by sudden death. His opinion is that such a one would neither go to heaven nor hell but experience—like unbaptized infants—a "middle state" of some kind (*Oration*, 19). Augustine, on the other hand, based upon the example of the thief on the cross, believed that on occasion some might experience a conversion of the heart even when baptism has not been received because there was no opportunity for baptism (*On Baptism*, 4.31-33; cf. also 4.22). In later years, however, Augustine doubted his own argument because he was uncertain whether the thief had been baptized earlier in his life (*Retractions*,

2.18; cf. also *On the Gospel of John*, 13.7). Nevertheless, the sixteenth-century Council of Trent enshrined the "baptism of desire" or "baptism of intent" exception in their declaration of the necessity of baptism.[12]

Throughout this period, immersion or dipping was the normative mode of baptism, even if these immersions were sometimes only partial in character. While exceptions still continued, the primary documents of baptismal instruction and liturgies evidence immersion as the preferred method. For example, Cyril of Jerusalem (d. 386) in his *Catechetical Lectures* (17.14) argues that just as the one "who plunges into the waters and is baptized is encompassed on all sides by the waters," so the same one is baptized by the Spirit inwardly. Basil states that while our bodies are "buried in water," the Spirit at the same time pours life into our soul (*On the Holy Spirit*, 15.35). Chrysostom (*Homilies on the Gospel of John*, 25.2) describes it this way: "For when we immerse our heads in the water, the old man is buried as in a tomb below, and wholly sunk forever; then as we raise them again, the new man rises in its stead. As it is easy for us to dip and to lift our heads again, so it is easy for God to bury the old man, and to show forth the new." Sprinkling and pouring remain the exceptions that prove the rule.

Conclusion

The Orthodox (Eastern) churches, particularly the Greek Church, maintained the unity between immersion, confirmation (anointing) and first communion. The rite of initiation into the community involved all three, and infants born into Christian families received all three (normally, they received a sip of the wine, but not a piece of the bread). Contemporary Orthodox churches continue this three-fold initiation for both infants of Christian families and adult converts. Orthodox churches envision baptism as a mysterious entrance into the communion of God and the communion of the church. It begins the journey of transformation and is the first taste of salvation through participation in the divine life by the presence of the Holy Spirit.

The Roman Catholic Church ultimately separated immersion and confirmation. While practice varied, even into the sixteenth century when Queen Elizabeth was baptized and confirmed three days after birth, the Catechism of the Catholic Council of Trent (1566) "deemed confirmation inexpedient before the age of seven."[13] Infant communion effectively ended in the Western church in the thirteen century as the doctrine of transubstantiation began to dominate the theological landscape. Due to scruples about spilling the wine (blood of Christ), the church withdrew the cup from the laity, including infants. Immersion, though still the dominant mode in the thirteenth century according to Bonaventure and Aquinas, gradually gave way to pouring (affusion).[14] The Council of Ravenna (1311) officially sanctioned affusion. By the sixteenth century all Catholic churches poured, except the English church, which continued to immerse until the mid-seventeenth century. For Roman Catholics, baptism is where infants receive the forgiveness of Adamic sin, but confirmation at a later age is when believers receive the transformative presence of the Holy Spirit through the laying on of priestly hands.

While there is much that the Orthodox and Catholic hold in common regarding baptism,[15] the differences reflect the problems encountered when child or infant baptism became dominant. Why baptize infants or children? The Western answer was that infants and children, like adults, are sinners, but the East answered that children and infants should receive the grace of communion even though they were not sinners. This question gives rise to the next major shift in baptismal theology, detailed in the next chapter. The river no longer flowed gently but was churned by rapids as Western Reformers began to question aspects of Catholic baptismal theology in the early sixteenth century.

****

Principle

For the early church, baptism meant grace; it was a means of grace and necessary for entrance into the community of faith. The grace of baptism was a divine gift that the church judged should not be withheld from dying children, and as the Western church adopted civil religion and Adamic theology, it administered baptism to all children.

Prayer

Father, we recognize that we are not the first ones to think about or experience your gracious gift of baptism. We acknowledge our debt to those who have gone before us, and we pray for humility to understand them and ourselves better so that we might know your gift better and experience it more richly. Amen.

Questions

1. Imagine you are a third-century parent with a dying child. Do you understand why Irene's parents brought her to baptism? Why did the early church baptize infants, and why was "emergency" baptism such a formative factor in the development of infant baptism?

2. How does the move to a "national church" (state religion) institutionalize infant baptism and normalize its practice in the fifth century? What are the contributing factors to that normalization?

3. Are you "put off" by the ritual and symbolism of baptism in the early centuries, or do you think we should pay more attention to ritual and symbolism in our baptismal practice today?

4. Are you surprised by the church's insistence on the necessity of baptism? What do you think of the exceptions to the rule? Do exceptions undermine the word "necessary" for salvation?

6 / *Troubled Water: The Reformation*

It is therefore the earnest commandment, order and warning of these our Lords that no one in town, country or domain, whether man, woman or girl, shall henceforth baptize another. Whoever hereafter baptizes someone will be apprehended by our Lords and, according to this present decree, be drowned without mercy.[1]

—Zurich City Council, Switzerland, March 7, 1526

On January 17, 1525, the Zurich City Council heard the "First Disputation" on infant baptism. The council was unconvinced and so the next day it decreed the exile of those who refused to baptize their babies. On January 21, they prohibited Conrad Grebel, Felix Manz and George Blaurock from conducting home Bible study meetings. That evening, however, fifteen people met in the house of Manz's mother in Zollikon, a suburb of Zurich. Blaurock, a former priest, asked Grebel to baptize him and then Blaurock baptized the rest by pouring water on their heads. After baptism, they broke bread together as a new fellowship of believers.

On January 30, Blaurock and Manz, along with others, were imprisoned in Zurich. Fined, they were eventually released in late

February but they continued preaching. Blaurock even baptized a friend the day after his release.

The city held another "disputation" from November 6-8, 1525 that was attended by 900 people. Grebel, Blaurock and Manz advocated believer's baptism. The council decided against them, and they were imprisoned indefinitely on a diet of bread and water. They were sentenced to life imprisonment on March 6, 1526. However, on March 21 they escaped and pursued their ministries in secret.

The city council made rebaptism and even attendance at Anabaptist meetings a capital offense. Felix Manz was recaptured and was the first Anabaptist executed in Zurich. On January 5, 1527, Manz was tied down with weights and thrown into the river Limmat, drowned because of his baptismal theology. Grebel died of illness in 1526, but Blaurock, who was beaten and exiled by the Zurich authorities after Manz's drowning, ultimately suffered martyrdom in Innsbruck, Austria, in 1529.

****

The sixteenth century gave birth to the Reformation—a watershed era in Christian history. Western Europe experienced a religious revolution of mammoth proportions. Protestantism emerged as a competing Christian tradition in opposition to Roman Catholicism. More than any other theological issue, except justification and the Lord's Supper, baptism was the center of attention. It not only separated Protestantism from Catholicism, but also divided Protestantism. The gentle flowing river of baptism cascaded into three distinct Protestant streams: Lutheran, Reformed and Anabaptist. The quiet water of the early church became the troubled water of the sixteenth century.

In late medieval Catholic Europe not only did baptism mediate the forgiveness of original sin, but in baptism the infant's soul was infused with a quality of grace. This grace provided the seed of justification because righteousness is a life-long process of dying with Christ through one's life. Baptism is the infusion of a quality of grace that is the beginning of sanctification by which justification takes place. Thus, baptism is necessary for the forgiveness of

Adamic sin and for the infusion of grace by which one comes to faith (appropriated at confirmation) and through which one perseveres in faith until death. The grace of justification, then, is something that takes place within the human soul and the seed of that justification is given through baptism. When that seed is planted and grows through sanctification one is justified as a result of transformed living.

Baptism, then, has an internal efficacy. The medieval expression is *ex opera operato* ("by the working of the work," Council of Trent, session 7, canon 8). Grace truly resides in the visible sign (water) by virtue of its rightful administration. The Church, by the authority invested in it by Christ, confers grace in the baptismal act. Grace moves from the church through the baptismal act into the soul of the infant. It is a divine work accomplished in the infant's soul. The infant is forgiven of Adamic sin, receives an infusion of grace as the beginnings of a sanctified life, and becomes a member of the Catholic Church with access to the other sacraments.

Though united in their opposition to Catholic baptismal theology, the three Protestant streams were equally vociferous towards each other. While Lutherans believed that one finds salvation in the waters of baptism because the Word is "in" the water (just as Christ is "in, with and under" the bread in the Lord's Supper), Reformed theologians objected to this literal understanding of the relationship of water and salvation. While Calvin used instrumental language ("through") just as he did regarding the Lord's Supper as well (there is a genuine spiritual communion with Christ through eating and drinking at the Lord's table), Zwingli objected to any language implying something beyond mere symbolism (as he did regarding the Lord's Supper). The Anabaptists adopted Zwingli's symbolic understanding of baptism but only baptized adult believers. These three streams (Lutheran, Reformed and Anabaptist) crashed against each other and created a whirlpool of controversy and acrimony. They went down to the river and not only drew lines in the sand but drew their swords against each other and Catholics.

The Lutheran Stream

The reformation of baptismal theology began with Martin Luther's *Babylonian Captivity of the Church* (1520).[2] Luther redefined baptismal theology in the light of the word "promise." Sacraments are "those promises which have signs attached to them."[3] These are effective signs for Luther. The Word of God contains the promise and attaches the promise to particular signs. The promise in relation to baptism is, according to Luther's *Small Catechism*, that "the power, effect, benefit, fruit, and purpose of Baptism is to save."[4] As the *Augsburg Confession* (1530) affirms, baptism is no mere "profession among men," but it is a sign and testimony of the will of God toward us so that faith "believes the promises that are set forth and offered."[5] Baptism, according to Luther, "effects the forgiveness of sins" (*Small Catechism*). Consequently, the *Augsburg Confession* (article 9) continues the tradition of the church from the earliest times with the affirmation that "baptism is necessary for salvation."

This high view of baptism may seem inconsistent with Luther's understanding of faith alone (*sola fide*). But it is precisely his understanding of faith that gives baptism such importance. Faith grasps the gospel promise of the dying and rising Christ in baptism. Baptism is the means by which we enter a "baptismal covenant" where the promise is assured to us. God promises the forgiveness of sins and promises not to impute the sins that are committed after baptism. As a result, believers are prepared to live out of the promise of God and to mortify sin in their lives by the exercise of good works.

The means by which we receive this promise in baptism is faith or trust (*fiducia*). Despite the reality of sin, faith holds firm to God's mercy and his promise that he will hold believers guiltless. It is faith in the promise of God based upon his "baptismal covenant." Consequently, the sign of baptism, for Luther, is the "greatest comfort on earth." He writes:

> It is faith that is of all things the most necessary, for it is the ground of all comfort...For this reason we must boldly and without fear hold fast to our baptism and set it high against all sins and terrors of conscience...We must humbly admit, "I know full well that I cannot do a single thing that is pure, but I am baptized and through my baptism God, who cannot lie, has bound himself in a covenant

with me. He will not count my sin against me, but will slay it and blot it out."[6]

Baptism is the divine promise of forgiveness. It is not simply an historical event that lies in the past. It covers the whole of life. The Christian life begins in baptism, but it also entails the experience of a "daily baptism." Everyone, according to Luther, should "regard his baptism as the daily garment which he is to wear all the time."[7] Penance is a daily return to the gift of baptism which has bestowed salvation to all those who have received it by faith. The certainty of baptism lies in God who has promised to work in it. Even the form of baptism has significance for Luther in this respect. He describes baptism as that "act or observance [which] consists in being dipped into the water, which covers us completely, and being drawn out again. These two parts, being dipped under the water and emerging from it, indicate the power and effect of baptism" which is dying and rising with Christ (*Large Catechism*).

According to Luther, God connects the water, Word of God, and name of God in such a way that it is an event in which God bestows his blessings. The Word of God is not only a promise attached to the water, but the presence of God (the name of God) in the water. It is "divine" water (not "mere" water) because God is present in the water as he does his work of salvation for us. Luther writes in his *Large Catechism*:

> For mere water could not do such a thing, but the Word does it, and (as said above) the fact that the name of God is comprehended therein. But where the name of God is, there must be also life and salvation, that it may indeed be called a divine, blessed, fruitful, and gracious water; for by the Word such power is imparted to Baptism that it is a laver of regeneration. For the kernel in the water is God's Word or command and the name of God which is a treasure greater and nobler than heaven and earth.

By this understanding of water comprehended in the Word, Luther intended to counter several contrary positions. Baptism is not about water alone, nor is it anthropocentrically based upon human faith, and neither is it obscured by subsequent acts of penance. Luther simply affirmed that where the name of God is, God is present. Where God is present, there is life and salvation. The name of God is attached to baptism and is present in the water, and therefore salvation is there. But "it is not the water that produces these effects, but the Word of God connected with the water, and our faith which relies on the Word of God connected with the water" (*Small Catechism*).

The Word qualifies baptism as the element of salvation: it is a word of command and promise. The command identifies baptism as God's work. The word of promise proclaims it as God's gift. In the external act of baptism God is actively present. Baptism, then, does not take place in our subjective self. It is a work external to us; a work of God delivered through external means. "Thus faith clings to the water," Luther writes in the *Large Catechism*, "and believes that it is Baptism, in which there is pure salvation and life" because as an external element "it can be perceived and grasped by the senses and thus brought into the heart, just as the entire Gospel is an external, oral proclamation. In short, whatever God effects in us he does through such external ordinances."

Faith rests on God's external work of baptism, and not baptism on God's work of faith. Baptism is not an anthropocentric act. For whatever is in the human self will necessarily fluctuate, including faith. But when one turns from experience and human faith to the divine command and promise, that is, the external Word and work of God, this fluctuation ceases. Assurance has its sole basis in what God has done rather than in the maturity of our faith.

> I myself also, and all who are baptized, must speak thus before God: I come hither in my faith and in that of others, yet I cannot rest in this, that I believe, and that any people pray for me; but in this I rest, that it is Thy Word and command. Just as I go to the Sacrament trusting not in my faith, but in the Word of Christ. (*Large Catechism*)

To base baptism on human faith would therefore place baptism on an uncertain foundation since faith always lacks something. Rather, the role of faith is to receive baptism, not create it. Faith looks to baptism, grasps it, and clings to it. It clings to the promise of God in baptism; it grasps the work of God in baptism. "Baptism is not a work which we do," Luther writes, "but is a treasure which God gives us and faith grasps, just as the Lord Christ upon the cross is not a work but a treasure comprehended and offered to us in the Word and received by faith" (*Large Catechism*).

Luther's emphasis on faith, though consistent with his theology of justification by faith alone, seems inconsistent with his practice of infant baptism. For Luther faith is necessary for the effectiveness of baptism since "where faith is lacking, it remains a mere unfruitful sign" and "without faith Baptism is of no use" (*Large Catechism*). However, Luther never questioned the practice of infant baptism because he had seen the fruit of the Spirit in the lives of people so baptized ("That the Baptism of infants is pleasing to Christ is sufficiently proved from his own work. God has sanctified many who have been thus baptized and has given them the Holy Spirit"). But, more importantly, his theocentric understanding of baptism attributes salvation in infants to the work of God rather than to the faith within in the individual. God pours faith into the infant[8] and accepts the faith of the parents and church that present the child as the context for his work. The church prays to "God to grant him faith" (*Large Catechism*). God answers the prayer by pouring faith into the infant and granting the forgiveness of sins through baptism. Baptism is God's work, and he graciously works in infants through the faith of the church.

The Reformed Stream

In addition to the German Lutheran response to Roman Catholicism, another Protestant tradition with a variant baptismal theology arose out of the Swiss Reformation. Though they shared Luther's understanding of justification, Reformed theologians believed that Luther too closely identified baptism and salvation. Reformed theology resisted any close identification between justification and baptism, especially when grace was conceived as "in" the water.

Reformed theology emphasized the distinction between the sign (water) and the thing signified (grace).[9] The water is an outward sign of an inward grace. However, Reformed theologians have disagreed about the exact relationship between the sign and the thing signified. Two major perspectives have emerged. One tradition emphasizes the symbolic character of the relationship, but the other tradition emphasizes instrumentality. For one, baptism symbolizes the inward grace of the Spirit, while for the other baptism is the means by which the Spirit works his grace. Thus the question is whether baptism only symbolizes God's gracious work or whether it is also a means of God's gracious work? The Zurich Reformer Hulydrych Zwingli championed the former while John Calvin of Geneva affirmed the latter. The former view has now become enshrined in contemporary American Evangelicalism (e.g., "Baptism is, then, a symbolic act, by which an individual expresses his conviction that God has already performed the substantial work of grace in the soul"[10]) but the latter is often present in the Reformed creeds (e.g., the *Belgic Confession* [1566]: "For they are visible signs and seals of something internal and invisible, by means of which God works in us through the power of the Holy Spirit. So they are not empty and hollow signs to fool and deceive us, for their truth is Jesus Christ, without whom they would be nothing"[11]).

Huldrych Zwingli (d. 1531)

The Zurich Reformer rejected any idea that either baptism or the Lord's Supper could confer, convey or otherwise function instrumentally in the distribution of divine grace.[12] "External things are nothing," Zwingli writes. "They avail nothing for salvation."[13] Externals are material objects that cannot affect spiritual reality or effect spiritual blessings. "Material water cannot contribute in any way to the cleansing of the soul" (*On Baptism*, 154). Only faith, as an internal spiritual experience, can function as an instrument of grace. Zwingli, in contrast to Luther, radicalized the Protestant understanding of *sola fide* as he set faith in contrast to the external act of baptism. Whereas Luther believed that faith grasps the salvation that God gives in baptism, Zwingli believed that faith experiences salvation prior to baptism. By faith one already possesses what baptism symbolizes. "The one necessary thing which saves those of us who hear the Gospel," according to Zwingli, "is faith" (*On Baptism*, 137).

Zwingli recognizes that his perspective is new and breaks with the consensus of the church from the earliest times: "In this matter of baptism all the doctors have been in error from the time of the apostles...For all the doctors have ascribed to the water a power which it did not have and the holy apostles did not teach" (*On Baptism*, 130). The church has erred "because they thought that the water itself effects cleansing and salvation" (*On Baptism*, 156). Of course, no theologian ever believed that water alone or water as a material reality effected salvation. But the consensus of the church was that baptism and salvation are connected by God's command. Zwingli, however, rejected any such connection since "Christ himself did not connect salvation with baptism: it is always by faith alone" (*On Baptism*, 136).

Theologically, Zwingli roots this disconnection in John 6:63, "the flesh profits nothing." The flesh, or material reality or externals, is worthless in relation to salvation. The flesh, or any external, cannot cleanse the conscience. Rather, the Spirit of God is the sole agent of salvation. Zwingli contrasts the "Spirit" of John 3:8 with the "flesh" of John 6:63. God saves according to his own will and sends the Spirit to whomever he wants, whenever he wants. "Therefore," Zwingli writes, "the Spirit of grace is conveyed not by this immersion...For if it were thus, it would be known how, where, whence and whither the Spirit is borne."[14] The baptismal waters do not bind God's freedom. Rather, God gives grace through faith as the effect of divine election rather than through faith as expressed in baptism. Zwingli's Augustinian theology meant that God cannot be bound in his actions by externals. God cannot be put into the position of waiting for some human act or decision as a precondition for his own work, nor can he be required to act just because somebody somewhere decides to be baptized. Rather, God freely elects without any human acts, much less external acts. People believe because they are elect. They are not elect because they believe or because they have been baptized.

Zwingli's focus, then, was on the work of God through his Spirit in the heart rather than any work of God through baptism. As "God moves inwardly according to his own sovereign choice" (*On Baptism*, 163), God baptizes the elect in his Spirit and effects their salvation. God gives faith through this inner spiritual baptism.

External water baptism is unrelated to God's sovereign action. While "none can be saved" without Spirit baptism, "it is quite possible to be saved without the baptism of external teaching and immersion" (*On Baptism*, 137).

What, then, is the function of water baptism for Zwingli? Essentially, it is an ecclesial event that is for the benefit "of fellow-believers," and not so much "for a supposed effect in those who receive it" (*On Baptism*, 136). Since it is not connected to salvation (and therefore unrelated to faith) and it is for the benefit of the church (congregation), the baptism of infants is a proper act of the church. Baptism is not primarily an assurance or seal of faith since if one's faith is so insufficient as to need a sign then "it is not faith."[15] Baptism is a sign for other believers. "Immersion in water is simply a ceremony by which they testify that they are of the number of those who repent" (*On Baptism*, 147). "Baptism is an initiatory sign or pledge," Zwingli writes, "with which we bind ourselves to God, testifying the same to our neighbor by means of the external sign" (*On Baptism*, 148). Baptism is a public act of allegiance, an external sign of membership and commitment. Infants, therefore, are baptized in order to bear witness to their membership in the visible church. It does not guarantee salvation though it confirms membership in the visible church (which is not necessarily identical to the saved, invisible church).

Zwingli's baptismal theology has an anthropocentric impulse. Instead of viewing baptism as God's faith-strengthening pledge to the believer, he primarily described baptism as the Christian's pledge to his fellow believers. Consequently, baptism is more about what we do than what God does. Baptism became a human work which testifies to God's work and no longer the work of God. For Zwingli, then, baptism is a part of the church's confession and is not an instrument of God's activity among his people. It is more about what we pledge to do or what we do than it is about what God has done for us or in us.

John Calvin (d. 1564)

While sharing many perspectives with Zwingli, the Geneva Reformer believed the Zurich Reformer went too far. Calvin does not locate the chief or fundamental purpose of baptism in its public profession. On the contrary, he believes its primary significance is its correlation to saving faith. In other words, baptism is more about what God does in relation to our faith than about what we do in our profession of faith. Much of what Calvin writes about the sacraments in general and baptism in particular in his *Institutes of Christian Religion* (1559) is directed against those who would reduce the sacraments, including baptism, to some kind of anthropocentrism or mere public human profession. He writes: "but we do not tolerate that what is secondary in the sacraments be regarded by them as the first and even the only point. Now, the first point is that the sacraments should serve our faith before God; after this, that they should attest our confession before men" (*Institutes*, 4.14.13).[16]

While there is some scholarly debate about the exact correlation Calvin envisioned between baptism (sign) and the forgiveness of sins (the thing signified), it is clear that he does not follow Zwingli. The essential difference is that Calvin understands baptism as an effective sign. God works efficaciously through this sign in the power of the Spirit by faith. The sign and the thing signified have a real, spiritual connection through faith and the Spirit. Calvin summarized his thinking in a comment on Ezekiel 9:14:

> We must hold, therefore, that there is a mutual relation between faith and the sacraments, and hence, that the sacraments are effective through faith. Man's unworthiness does not detract anything from them, for they always retain their nature. Baptism is the laver of regeneration, although the whole world should be incredulous (Titus 3:5): the Supper of Christ is the communication of his body and blood (1 Corinthians 10:16), although there were not a spark of faith in the world: but we do not perceive the grace which is offered to us; and although spiritual things always remain the same, yet we do not obtain their effect nor perceive their value, unless we are cautious that our want of faith should not profane what God has consecrated our salvation [*sic*].[17]

Calvin is concerned about two things. First, the sacraments have no effective function apart from faith. Without faith, baptism has no meaning or significance. Second, the sacraments have genuine spiritual significance through faith. Baptism is no mere sign or symbol. Rather, it is the "laver of regeneration" and grace is actually received through baptism.

Baptism is "appointed to elevate, nourish, and confirm our faith," so that God "speaks to us by means of the sign" in that he "washes and purifies us" so that we participate in all the benefits of union with Christ. "These things I say," Calvin continues, "we ought to feel as truly and certainly in our mind as we see our body washed, immersed, and surrounded with water. For this analogy or similitude furnishes the surest rule in the sacraments" which is "that in corporeal things we are to see spiritual, just as if they were actually exhibited to our eye." However, Calvin wants to situate us between two extremes. On the one hand, we must not think that "such graces are included and bound in the sacrament, so as to be conferred by its efficacy," but on the other hand, "nor does he merely feed our eyes with bare show," but rather God "leads us to the actual object, and effectually performs what he figures" (*Institutes*, 4.15.14). The sign conveys the "substance and reality, inasmuch as God works by external means" but only "in so far as we receive [it] in faith" (*Institutes*, 4.15.1). "God, therefore, truly performs whatever he promises and figures by signs; nor are the signs without effect, for they prove that he is their true and faithful author" (*Institutes*, 4.14.17).

Calvin, then, polemicizes against two extremes. He rejects Zwingli's anthropocentric and merely symbolic understanding of baptism, but he also rejects any kind of sacramentalism that locates the virtue of baptism in the water. Against Zwingli, Calvin affirms the effective character of the sign and trusts the promise of God that the sign and the thing signified are genuinely connected by the power of the Spirit. Against Roman Catholic sacramentalism, he affirms the necessity of faith as the means by which the effectiveness of baptism is received. Fundamentally, Calvin believes baptism is a genuine means of grace that is effective through faith and the internal working of the Spirit. God performs what the sign promises. Concerning the sacraments in general, Calvin writes: "God...performs by the secret virtue of his Spirit that which he figures by external signs, and, accordingly, that on the part of God himself, not empty signs are set before us, but the reality and efficacy at the same time conjoined with them."[18]

But what does the sign represent and effect? Calvin summarizes the relationship of baptism and its effects (through faith) with three ideas. First, baptism is "a sign and evidence of our purification, or (better to explain my meaning) it is a kind of sealed instrument by which he assures us that all our sins are so deleted, covered, and effaced, that they will never come into his sight, never be mentioned, never imputed" (*Institutes*, 4.15.1). This encompasses the past, present and future. Baptism testifies to the reality of our forgiveness in such a way that "we are washed and purified once for the whole of life," and as we sin in the future we remember our baptism as a testimony of our forgiveness (*Institutes*, 4.15.3). This is not, of course, a license to sin, but it is a comfort to those who despair over their sin. Baptism is God's sure testimony to us that we are forgiven.

Second, baptism "shows us our mortification in Christ and new life in him." This is no mere testimony of a life we should live, but in reality a grafting into Jesus' death and resurrection that empowers our life and transformation. "As the twig derives substance and nourishment from the root to which it is attached, so those who receive baptism with true faith truly feel the efficacy of Christ's death in the mortification of their flesh, and the efficacy of his resurrection in the quickening of the Spirit (Rom. 6:8)." Consequently, "we are promised, first, the free pardon of sins and imputation of righteousness; and, secondly, the grace of the Holy Spirit, to form us again to newness of life" (*Institutes*, 4.15.5).

Third, baptism unites us with Christ so that we are "partakers of all his blessings." Just as Christ himself was baptized and united himself to baptism, so "all the divine gifts held forth in baptism are found in Christ alone" (*Institutes*, 4.15.6). We participate in the divine community through baptism and thus baptism "is the initiatory sign by which we are admitted to the fellowship of the Church, that being engrafted into Christ we may be accounted children of God" (*Institutes*, 4.15.1).

These benefits are given to believers through baptism by the power of the Spirit as they receive it in faith. This means-of-grace understanding of baptism is reflected in several Reformed creeds.

For example, article 24 in the *French Confession of Faith* (1559) reads: "We believe that the sacraments are added to the Word for more ample confirmation, that they may be to us pledges and seals of the grace of God, and by this means aid and comfort our faith, because of the infirmity which is in us, and that they are outward signs through which God operates by his Spirit, so that he may not signify any thing to us in vain."[19] Even the *Consensus Tigurinus* (1549), which attempts to unite Zurich and Geneva Reformers, affirms that the sacraments "are indeed instruments by which God acts efficaciously when he pleases, yet so that the whole work of our salvation must be ascribed to him alone." Further, the 25th article of the Anglican *Thirty-Nine Articles* (which influenced Wesley and Methodism) affirms: "Sacraments ordained of Christ be not only badges or tokens of Christian men's profession, but rather they be certain sure witnesses, and effectual signs of grace, and God's good will towards us, by the which he doth work invisibly in us, and doth not only quicken, but also strengthen and confirm our Faith in him."[20] The Presbyterian *Westminster Confession of Faith* (1644), article 38.6, affirms that "the efficacy of Baptism," though not tied to the moment of baptism in an absolute sense, is "not only offered, but really exhibited, and conferred, by the Holy Ghost."

However, we would misread Calvin if we concluded that he believed baptism was necessary for salvation in the same way that Luther argued or even that the church throughout history believed.[21] While Calvin believed that baptism was the normal or ordinary means by which God worked to save, baptism is not absolutely necessary to salvation. Indeed, faith is more important than baptism, and baptism is an "inferior mean" (*sic*) though it is a confirmation of forgiveness through faith.[22] He rejects the idea that "all are lost who happen not to be dipped in water" and thus rejects the rationale for "emergency baptisms" (*Institutes*, 4.15.20). Calvin believed that infants of believers are born "holy" and thus part of the redeemed through participation in the covenant family, though he is uncertain about infants who are not part of a believing family. He concludes: "Now, then, when they make baptism to be so necessary that they exclude all who have not been dipped with it from the hope of salvation, they both insult God."[23]

The Believers' Church Stream

Contemporary with Luther and Reformed theology, another Protestant tradition emerged in the early sixteenth century. Anabaptists (pejoratively named by their enemies as "those who baptize again") arose first in the environs of Zwingli's Zurich. The radical character of Zwingli's reformation, which was much more thorough (according to primitivist standards) than Luther's, lent itself to increasingly progressive changes. This included the abolition of infant baptism. While Zwingli appears to have entertained the idea in 1523,[24] he quickly dismissed it and opposed the Anabaptist movement when it arose in 1525.

The Anabaptist tradition began on January 21, 1525 when fifteen people were "rebaptized," as recounted at the beginning of this chapter. On Easter of that same year, Balthasar Hubmaier baptized (by affusion) over three hundred adults in the southern German town of Waldshut. Zwingli immediately opposed this trend and by 1527 Anabaptists were drowned for their faith.

Balthasar Hubmaier (d. 1528)

Though a practicing Anabaptist for only three years (he was burned at the stake in Vienna and his wife was drowned), he was the chief architect of Anabaptist baptismal theology for the Swiss Brethren and through them influenced the whole "baptist" tradition. The most educated of the early Anabaptists (he received his doctorate in theology from Ingolstadt University in 1512), he became the theologian of the Anabaptist movement, along with Michael Sattler who authored the *Schleitheim Confession* (1527). Upon his move to Waldshut in 1520, Hubmaier came under the influence of Zwingli's reformatory movement.

Hubmaier applied the principle of *sola Scriptura* (Scripture alone) in a radical manner. Instead of sophisticated arguments for and against infant baptism, Hubmaier repeatedly asked for the "clear Scripture" where God instituted infant baptism: "Either you must point out with a clear Scripture where God has instituted infant baptism or it must be rooted out."[25] For Hubmaier a "clear Scripture" was either an explicit command or an approved example. If there are no such texts, then infant baptism must be rejected since only what God authorizes is acceptable. "Here you must point out clearly the institution of infant baptism in the Scriptures," he challenges his opponents, "or it must be uprooted... If, however, you want to practice infant baptism and do not prove the same as an institution of God, then you and not we are adding to the Word of God" (Hubmaier, 184).

Moreover, when Scripture only models the baptism of believers (e.g., in Acts) and only commands the baptism of believers (e.g., Matt. 28:19-20), this excludes the baptism of those who do not believe (including infants). Hubmaier writes: "As soon as Christ commanded baptizing believers in water, from that hour on all people were already excluded who were not yet instructed in faith" (Hubmaier, 205). From the Great Commission "one clearly and certainly understands that this sending of the apostles consists of three points or commands: first, preaching; second, faith; and third, outward baptism" (Hubmaier, 115).

Hubmaier understands that he is working against several centuries of tradition. But only the Bible should be regarded as an authority in matters of faith. In his responses to reformers, he repeatedly denounces appeals to tradition and early Christian authorities such as Cyprian, Augustine, etc. "I will trust Cyprian, councils, and other teachings just as far as they use the Holy Scripture, and not more" (Hubmaier, 280). He was willing to go against the whole history of Christian tradition as it was known to him: "Even if it had always been like that, it would still not be right, because a wrong is always a wrong" (Hubmaier, 137). However, he published a book (*Old and New Teachers on Baptism*) arguing that infant baptism had not always been a universal practice nor was it the most ancient practice.

He believed he was taking Zwingli's understanding of baptism to its logical conclusion—to the conclusion that is "clearly" present in the New Testament. Baptism is fundamentally an outward testimony of an inward faith. Through baptism "we publicly testify outwardly before the people that we already inwardly believe and trust in Christ" (Hubmaier, 158). Since baptism is an outward expression of faith, only believers can express the meaning of baptism. Consequently, "even if there were no Scripture on earth which states that faith should precede water baptism, its meaning and understanding would still be enough" (Hubmaier, 134-135).

The inner baptism of the Spirit occurs through faith. Water baptism is an external testimony of that work. "Faith alone makes us righteous before God" (Hubmaier, 32). Regeneration has nothing to do with baptism. "No element or outward thing in this world can cleanse the soul. Only faith purifies the hearts of people" (Hubmaier, 227). Consequently, salvation is through faith alone and is not connected with baptism. "We know well," Hubmaier writes, "that salvation is bound neither to baptism nor to works of mercy. Being unbaptized does not condemn us, nor do evil works, but only unfaith. However, whoever is believing lets himself be baptized and brings forth good fruits" (Hubmaier, 191).

Baptism, then, does not effect, convey or mediate the forgiveness of sins. Rather, "the baptized testify to the forgiveness of their sins, which remission had already taken place in faith before one has come to water baptism" (Hubmaier, 189-190). Nevertheless, as believers come to baptism, they (1) confess their sin and guilt; (2) affirm their faith in the forgiveness of sins through Jesus; and (3) commit to live according to the "Rule of Christ" (Hubmaier, 142). Believers enter the visible community through baptism.

Thus, while Hubmaier always distinguished regeneration by faith from entrance into the visible community, the fullness of redemption is only received in the church where the Holy Spirit performs his full communal work. Baptism, though unnecessary for forgiveness and regeneration, is necessary ecclesiologically. "This outward confession is what makes a church, and not faith alone; for the church that has the power to bind and loose is outward and corporeal, not theoretical" (Hubmaier, 352). There is no church without baptism. Without baptism, "it is impossible to know who is in the church or who is outside, whom we have authority to admonish or not, who are brothers or sisters" (Hubmaier, 420).

The church, then, consists of baptized believers. The community lives under the "Rule of Christ." While there is salvation within the invisible church through faith, there is no salvation in the visible church without baptism and the Lord's Supper because these are visible, communal acts of faith that bind the community together. "For through" baptism, "as through a visible door, by the public confession of faith we must enter into the general Christian church, outside of which there is no salvation. For in water baptism the church uses the key of admitting and loosing, but in the Supper the key of excluding, binding, and locking away, as Christ promises and gives to it the power of the forgiveness of sins" (Hubmaier, 175).

Hubmaier's baptismal theology is essentially that of every "baptistic" movement that followed in subsequent centuries (from Dutch Mennonites[26] to American Baptists[27]). It is enshrined in the Anabaptist *Schleitheim Confession of Faith* (1527) which affirms: "Baptism shall be given to all those who have learned repentance and amendment of life, and who believe truly that their sins are taken away by Christ."[28] Baptism is a visible entry into the visible church, but it is neither a means of grace nor necessary for salvation. Baptism has an ecclesiological but not a soteriological function. It identifies members of the faith community, but it does not define the invisible church. Baptism, in good Zwinglian fashion, is a profession of faith but not a means of grace. What Zwingli began, baptists—in whatever stripe or form—have continued.

English Baptists

Though the Swiss Anabaptists were the fountainhead of the modern believer's baptism movement, they regularly poured water on adult believers rather than immersing them. Hubmaier used a milk pail in Waldshut. While immersion was recognized as an appropriate mode—indeed Luther, Calvin and Zwingli regularly referred to baptism as a dipping or an immersion though they each recognized a variety of modes[29]—the Swiss Anabaptists followed the general practice of continental Western Europe by pouring water on the heads of baptismal recipients.[30]

Immersion as a peculiar practice of the baptistic movement is the work of English Baptists in the mid-seventeenth century and other continental groups followed suit in the early eighteenth century (e.g., the German Brethren or Dunkards). Apart from some conservative regions of Germany (particularly where Luther was personally influential) and eastern Europe (where, for example, immersion was the primary mode in Poland as well as in Eastern Orthodox circles), only England maintained the tradition of immersion from its earliest times into the seventeenth century. A council in Chelsea, England, for example, asserted the necessity of immersion as opposed to pouring or affusion as early as 816. The 1549 *Book of Common Prayer* for the Church of England says that the minister will "dyppe [the child] in the water thryse."[31] The 1552 and 1559 prayer books, however, provide for the pouring of water on a child if the child was weak.[32] But immersion remained the norm.

English Baptists originated with the work of John Smythe (1565-1612), a dissident who fled to Holland in 1608 and through the influence of Mennonites adopted believer's baptism by pouring. Ultimately Smythe united with the Mennonites, but Thomas Helwys, who had worked with Smythe, led a group back to England in 1612 that initiated the Baptist movement in England. Roger Williams (1603-1683), part of the Puritan migration to America, led the beginnings of the Baptist movement in America. By 1641 some Baptists groups, particularly the Calvinist Baptists (the "Particular Baptists" in distinction from the "General Baptists") began to practice immersion exclusively and by 1644 the Calvinist *London Baptist Confession of Faith* prescribed baptism in the following manner:

> The way and manner of the dispensing of this Ordinance the Scripture holds out to be dipping or plunging the whole body under water: it being a sign, must answer the thing signified, which are these: first, the washing the whole soul in the blood of Christ: secondly, that interest the Saints have in the death, burial, and resurrection; thirdly, together with a confirmation of our faith, that as certainly as the body is buried under water, and riseth again, so certainly shall the bodies of the Saints be raised by the power of Christ in the day of the resurrection, to reign with Christ.[33]

The mid seventeenth century was a turbulent time of debate. The Baptist movement was emerging as a significant group in England and both the Anglican establishment as well as Presbyterianism opposed this and Catholic interests.[34] Ultimately, Baptists became exclusively immersionist while other traditions preferred pouring or affusion, though some maintained a strong immersionist perspective (such as in the *Book of Common Prayer*). But this affusionist consensus in the Presbyterian tradition was hard won. The *Westminster Confession of Faith* (1648), article 38.3, states, "dipping of the person into the water is not necessary; but baptism is rightly administered by pouring, or sprinkling water upon the person."[35] This creedal decision, however, was not without controversy. On August 7, 1644 there was a heated discussion about the necessity of immersion among the Presbyterians, and whether the *Westminster Directory of Public Worship* ought to require immersion. Dipping was excluded altogether by a vote of 25 to 24. In this context many begin to defend sprinkling as a Biblical method rather than simply a traditional option. According to the *Directory*, sprinkling or pouring was not only sufficient and expedient, but also "lawful."[36]

Conclusion

The history of baptismal theology and practice is vast and complicated. The river diverges deeply and radically during the Reformation. The water is far from calm. Indeed, it churns with conflict and division—and death. A single, brief chapter cannot do justice to the great diversity of practices nor to the finely nuanced understandings of various representatives of the Reformation. Nevertheless, in this brief survey, three Protestant streams diverged from the Catholic predecessor. Each one gathers at the river rather differently.

Lutherans go down in the river to baptize their children. In this moment God gives them the seed of faith, forgives their Adamic sin and incorporates them into the divine community. They believe something actually happens in water by virtue of the Word of God. Reformed (Calvinian) believers also go down in the river to baptize their children. In this moment God seals his covenantal promises and assures his people of their union with Christ. God confirms the presence of his Spirit who has planted the seed of transformation in the heart of the infant. They believe God's Spirit acts through the sign to seal, confirm and effect union with Christ. Anabaptists (Zwinglians in regard to the meaning of baptism) go down in the river to baptize believers. These believers testify to the work of God in their hearts, profess their faith in Jesus and enter the visible church as members of a community of faith. They make a public confession of what God has already done through faith.

****

Principle

The relationship between the water—what it signifies or symbolizes and what God is doing in or through it—was a major point of discussion in the Reformation and has been ever since. The Reformation witnessed, for the first time in Christian history, the legitimacy of infant baptism hotly contested and the soteriological significance of baptism questioned.

Prayer

Father, as we have conflict at the river with others who claim allegiance to your Son just as we do, help us to understand each other and acknowledge each other's faith in you. Give us love for each other as we dialogue. Give us wisdom to discern your will in everything. Give us, Lord, the insight to fully appreciate your work for us through your gift of baptism. Amen.

Questions

1. Identify the essential difference between Luther, Calvin, Zwingli, and Hubmaier. With what baptismal theology do you more closely identify? Why?

2. What most surprised you about the historical journey in this chapter? Why is this significant for you?

3. Why do you suppose the conflict was so sharp regarding Anabaptism that the death penalty was imposed? What does this say about the importance of baptismal theology that some would kill and some would die for it?

7 / White Water: The Stone-Campbell Movement

I had read the 2d of the Acts when I expressed myself to my wife as follows: "Oh, this is the gospel—this is the thing we wish—the remission of sins! Oh, that I could hear the gospel in these same words—as Peter preached it! I hope I shall some day hear it; and the first man I meet who will preach the gospel thus, with him will I go." So, my brother, on the day you saw me come into the meeting house, my heart was open to receive the Word of God, and when you cried, "The Scriptures no longer shall be a sealed book. God means what he says. Is there a man present who will take God at his word, and be baptized for the remission of sins?"—at that moment my feelings were such that I could have cried out, "Glory to God! I have found the man whom I have long sought for." So I entered the kingdom where I readily laid hold of the hope set before me.[1]

—William Amend to Walter Scott

Walter Scott was appointed the preaching evangelist for the Mahoning Baptist Association in southeastern Ohio in August 1827. There was a dire need for revival since the churches in the Association had only grown by a total of 34 members in the previous two years.

Scott met with limited success in his first few months, but on November 18, 1827, he changed the nature of his exhortation at the end of his sermon. Instead of inviting people to the mourning bench so that they could "pray through" to assurance, he invited them to baptism in order to receive the remission of sins with full assurance of God's promises. William Amend was the first to respond.

In the next six months, Scott and his associates baptized 800 persons. Within that same time period, preaching the same message, John Secrest baptized 530, Jeremiah Vardeman 550, and within three months John Smith baptized 339. A new "Reformation" was exploding with the proclamation of "baptism for the remission of sins."

In response to this evangelistic explosion, Alexander Campbell began a series of ten articles in the *Christian Baptist* on January 7, 1828, entitled, "The Restoration of the Ancient Gospel." Its theology became the standard understanding of baptism in the Stone-Campbell Movement.

****

The English Baptist churches, as well as continental Brethren churches, emerged out of the stream of Anabaptist or Mennonite theology described in the previous chapter. They affirmed the necessity of personal faith, and thus regeneration, prior to baptism. Baptism was a public testimony of a grace already received and a public entrance into the visible church. Baptism was not a means of grace, but a sign of grace previously received. In other words, the English Baptist movement was thoroughly Zwinglian in its understanding of the meaning of baptism. Baptist baptismal theology, then, reflected a relatively new understanding of the meaning of baptism in contrast to Catholic, Lutheran and Calvinian theologies as well as earliest Christianity.

However, a few Baptists dissented from the broader consensus. For example, influential English Baptist Thomas Grantham (1634-1692) argued that baptism was "the means for remission of sins" and a "condition whereupon one shall receive the gift of the

Holy Spirit" as well as "the way of incorporating persons into the church of Christ," though baptism was not absolutely necessary for salvation and unnecessary for admittance to communion.[2] But probably the most significant movement toward a more instrumental understanding of baptism in baptistic theology was among the Scottish Baptists of the late eighteenth century.

Archibald McLean (1733-1812), the father of Scottish Baptists, "concluded from the New Testament that baptism was for the remission of sins."[3] Generally, Scottish Baptists were more Calvinian than Zwinglian in their baptismal theology, which is understandable since the Scottish Baptist movement arose in the context of a Scottish Presbyterian (Calvinian) understanding of baptism. According to Torrance, Scottish theology regarded baptism as the "sacrament of justification by grace."[4] Indeed, the 1560 *Scottish Confession of Faith* affirms: "we utterly damn the vanity of those that affirm sacraments to be nothing else but naked and bare signs. No, we assuredly believe that by baptism we are engrafted in Christ Jesus, to be made partakers of his justice [righteousness], by which our sins are covered and remitted." The Scottish Baptists claimed that they arrived at their understanding of believer's baptism by studying the Bible alone and appear to have had no explicit connections with the English Baptists and thus continental Anabaptism. The Scottish Baptists generally, and McLean in particular, practiced closed communion—only immersed believers are members of the visible church.[5]

The Stone-Campbell Movement (also known as the American Restoration Movement) emerged from Scottish Presbyterian and Baptist roots.[6] Thomas Campbell (1763-1854) and his son Alexander Campbell (1788-1866), in particular, were Scottish Presbyterians who were strongly influenced by Scottish Baptists. They were familiar with their leaders, particularly Archibald McLean and the Haldane brothers (James and Robert). These influences came to the forefront when the Campbells moved from Presby-terian to Baptists circles.

Ultimately, Alexander Campbell merged the Calvinian meaning of baptism as a means of grace with the Anabaptist practice of believer's baptism.[7] Some of Campbell's followers would radicalize this merger so that immersion for the explicit purpose of the remission of sins would become a line in the sand dividing the saved from the lost, which channeled the waters of baptism into a divisive and sectarian course. Troubled water became white water. Baptism became a human act of loyalty in compliance with a divine plan rather than a divine means of transformation.

Alexander Campbell's "Rediscovery" of the Ancient Gospel

Though Scottish Presbyterians when they arrived in America from Northern Ireland (Thomas in 1807 and Alexander in 1809), they soon rejected infant baptism. This was occasioned by the birth of Alexander's first child, Jane, on March 13, 1812. Instead of baptizing his daughter, Alexander—along with his father, mother, wife and several others—went down in the river to be immersed by the Baptist minister Matthias Luce on June 12, 1812.

Throughout these early years, Campbell adopted a Zwinglian understanding of baptism. Baptism was an emblem or sign of something that had already taken place. This is most evident during his 1821 debate with the Presbyterian John Walker. Campbell rejects any "means" language and relegates the relationship of baptism to salvation as merely "figurative" or "emblematic."[8] While baptism is "an ordinance by which we formally profess Christianity," the internal seal of the Spirit is all that is necessary for assurance and does not require "any external ordinance to perfect it." Indeed, many throughout Christian history have "had all the blessings of redemption as fully bestowed upon them, as any who have been baptized."[9] In fact, Campbell explicitly rejects any instrumental language. When one of his Presbyterian opponents argued that infants are regenerated "through Baptism as the appointed mean," Campbell accused him of Catholicism. Baptism, according to Campbell's early thought, is not a converting ordinance.[10]

However, late in 1821 Walter Scott gave Campbell a tract written by the Scottish Baptist Henry Errett that adjusted his thinking.[11] Errett, in line with good Scottish Calvinian theology, argued that baptism was "connected" with "salvation" and the "forgiveness of sins." Errett rejected any "literal" understanding of the language, but also rejected any perspective that sees baptism "merely as an ordinance" or "only as an ordinance."

This tract, along with a second debate on infant baptism with the Presbyterian W. L. McCalla, had a profound impact on the Campbells as they now consistently referred to baptism rather than Christian experience as God's testimony of forgiveness and regeneration. Thomas Campbell was the first to articulate this understanding in September 1823:

> Such being the gospel testimony concerning the love of God, the atonement of Christ, and the import of baptism for the remission of sins: all, therefore, that believed it, and were baptized for the remission of their sins, were as fully persuaded of their pardon and acceptance with God, through the atonement of Christ, and for his sake, as they were of any other article of the gospel testimony....Or why could he have received baptism, the import of which to the believer was the remission of sins, had he not believed the divine attestation to him in that ordinance, concerning the pardoning of his sins upon his believing and being baptized? Every one, then, from the very commencement of Christianity, who felt convinced of the truth of the gospel testimony, and was baptized, was as fully persuaded of the remission of his sins, as he was of the truth of the testimony itself.[12]

A month later Alexander made this a major plank in his debate with McCalla. He argued that the "nature and design of baptism is suited to believers only." In particular, the remission of sins is only applicable to adults, not infants (who, at most, are only guilty of one sin). Baptism "in some sense" washes away "sins." The blood of Christ "really cleanses us who believe from all sin," but the "formal proof and token of it" is a "baptism expressly 'for the remission of sins!'" Baptism, then, "formally washes away our sins" so that though our sins are "really pardoned" when we believe, we have "no solemn pledge of that fact, no formal acquittal, no formal purgation" until we "washed them away in the water of baptism."[13]

Campbell understood that this was a significant shift from his previous baptistic (Zwinglian) theology. In fact, he directly addressed his Baptist friends on this point during the debate:

> Tell them you make nothing essential to salvation but the blood of Christ, but that God has made baptism essential to their formal forgiveness in this life, to their admission into his kingdom on earth. Tell them that God had made it essential to their happiness that they should have a pledge on his part in this life, an assurance in the name of the Father and of the Son, and of the Holy Spirit, of their actual pardon, of the remission of all their sins, and that this assurance is baptism. Tell the disciples to rise in haste and be baptized and wash away their sins, calling on the name of the Lord.[14]

Campbell believed that some Baptists reduced baptism "to the level of a moral example, or a moral precept." But Campbell invested theological significance in baptism. It is God's "formal pledge on his part" of the believer's "personal acquittal or pardon."[15] Baptism was no longer a mere symbol for Campbell.

Campbell applied the Scottish Presbyterian (Calvinian) understanding of baptism to adult immersion. Indeed, Campbell, whether knowingly or unknowingly, alludes to Calvin's own words by referring to baptism as a "proof and token" of the remission of sins. Baptism is God's "sensible pledge" of forgiveness, salvation and regeneration.[16] Campbell, then, found assurance in God's baptismal promise rather than in a subjective experience.

As significant as the move from padeobaptism (infant baptism) to credobaptism (believer's baptism) was, this reinterpretation of the nature of assurance was equally important. Previously Campbell had sought assurance in a subjective religious experience. In line with seventeenth and eighteenth century Puritanism, Campbell had been taught to expect a conversion experience that would give evidence of his regeneration. Without such an "interposition" of divine aid he "could derive no assurance of the favor of God."[17] Thus believers were taught to look within themselves for the "true signs of regeneration."[18]

Campbell's baptismal theology shifted radically during his lifetime. It was not simply that Campbell was now a baptist rather than a paedobaptist, but that he had also rejected the conversion narrative of his earlier training. He no longer sought a subjective religious experience to confirm his regeneration and assure him of the remission of sins. On the contrary, he now regarded immersion as that objective moment which assured him of God's forgiveness. Campbell found the answer to his struggles with special grace in the gracious promises that God had attached to baptism. Baptism, as an expression of obedient faith in Jesus Christ, offered him the assurance of God's forgiveness.

But Alexander Campbell's baptismal theology had not yet reached its zenith. In the wake of Walter Scott's successful revivalistic preaching of baptism for the remission of sins, Campbell began a series of essays entitled "Restoration of the Ancient Gospel."[19] In this series Campbell begins to use the language of means or instrumentality: "forgiveness is through immersion"[20] or baptism is "a certain act by, or in which their sins are forgiven."[21] Baptism is a "medium through which the forgiveness of sins is imparted."[22] Campbell is quite adamant about this point: "I do earnestly contend that God, through the blood of Christ, forgives our sins through immersion—through the very act, and in the very instant."[23] Clearly, Campbell has moved well beyond Zwinglianism and embraced a high Calvinian understanding of the instrumentality of baptism as a means of grace.

This was clarified as Campbell responded to his critics. For example, the Virginia Baptist Andrew Broaddus believed that Campbell ascribed to external water what belonged only to the instrumentality of faith. It is a "living faith (not immersion nor any outward or bodily act)...by which we pass from a state of condemnation, into a state of favor and acceptance with God." For Broaddus, baptism functions as a "declarative justification" in that it is an "outward sign and declaration that the believer has experienced" the blessing of remission of sins. Only faith functions instrumentally.[24] But Campbell complained that Broaddus reduced baptism to a "mere external bodily act" or a simple "mutual pledge" by which people are received into the visible church. Broaddus's problem is that he "gives to baptism no instrumentality at all in the work of salvation."[25] In other words, Broaddus is too Zwinglian and Campbell was Calvinian. Whereas for Broaddus the "exercise of faith" is wholly "internal" and a matter of the heart alone, Campbell believed that faith is exercised through "trusting in Christ, coming to him and receiving him" in the act of immersion.[26]

The development of Campbell's baptismal theology ultimately reflects his Scottish roots. When he moved from paedobaptism to credobaptism in 1812, he adopted a Zwinglian understanding of baptism's design. In 1823, however, he moved away from Zwinglianism though he did not fully embrace an instrumental understanding of baptism. However, he rejected the conversion narrative of his contemporaries. Instead of seeking the assurance of divine grace through an existential experience at the "mourner's bench" (where penitent believers sought to "pray through"), he urged his Baptist colleagues to call people to baptism for their assurance rather than to prayer as God's appointed moment of formal forgiveness.[27] Baptism, for Campbell, was the "sinner's prayer." By 1828 Campbell had adopted an instrumental understanding of baptism's function. Baptism was the concrete moment through which God acted to apply the blood of Christ and forgive sin.

Baptismal Controversies

Campbell recognized that his position was rather "bold" since for him "immersion, next to faith, is a *sine qua non*, without which" no worship is acceptable to God.[28] If baptism has an instrumental function as the moment of forgiveness through faith, then it locates the experience of salvation in the act of believer's immersion. Campbell, then, affirmed a position rather unique in Baptist thought, that is, only immersed believers fully experience salvation and have the full assurance of the remission of their sins.

The Rebaptism Controversy

Many enthusiastically received Campbell's strong connection between baptism and the remission of sins. In theological terms, many rejoiced in the promise of forgiveness attached to baptism because they had for months or years sought that assurance through a mourning bench experience. However, in practical terms, some so linked baptism and the remission of sins that they decided that those who were baptized without recognition of this link were not properly baptized and thus needed rebaptism.[29] Where the Anabaptists were accused of "rebaptizing" those who had been "baptized" as infants, some followers of Campbell began to "rebaptize" those who had been "baptized" as Baptists.

The first to press this understanding of "rebaptism" was John Thomas (1805-1871) of Richmond, Virginia, who later founded the Christadelphians.[30] Thomas was immersed "for the remission of sins" by Walter Scott in 1832. Thomas began teaching his form of "rebaptism" in the fall of 1834, and some were reimmersed in 1835. Thomas argued that only those who are immersed with the "eye of faith [that] can see those waters dyed around him with the blood of Jesus" are truly baptized. If the recipient does not "believe or confess for himself" then "his dipping will be mere immersion and not baptism."[31] Anyone who misunderstands the meaning and nature of baptism should be reimmersed, and Baptist immersion immerses people into a "declaration of falsehoods" because they are immersed believing they are already saved rather than saved through baptism.[32] If one does not understand the biblical meaning of baptism, then one cannot be properly baptized.

Alexander Campbell, of course, was immersed long before he came to his instrumental understanding of believer's baptism. Immersed in 1812, he did not connect baptism and the remission of sins until 1823, and then did not view it as the precise moment of forgiveness until 1828. However, Campbell himself was never re-immersed. His reaction to Thomas was negative. He regarded Thomas's views as analogous to the legalism of the Pharisees who demanded circumcision "according to the manner of Moses." He strenuously objected:

> Why on all your definitions of the kingdom, supposing, as you do, that he that is not formally and understandingly immersed for the remission of his sins cannot enter into his kingdom; and it being a fact that before the year 1823, since the fifth century, baptism for the remission of sins was not preached, and not until the year 1827 were many immersed with this apprehension of the subject...either the promises of God have failed, or such persons as were baptized as you were the first time, are in the kingdom![33]

Campbell argued that all that was necessary for baptism was faith in Jesus as the Messianic Savior of the world. Everyone immersed upon a simple confession of trust in Jesus receives all the blessings that God has attached to baptism regardless of whether they are aware of those blessings or not.

Though a minority position early in the Stone-Campbell Movement, Thomas's position simmered in many quarters throughout the mid-nineteenth century until it fully erupted in 1884 when Austin McGary began publication of the *Firm Foundation* in Austin, Texas. McGary founded his journal to attack the position of the Nashville-based *Gospel Advocate* and its editor, David Lipscomb, on the rebaptism question. McGary regarded the acceptance of "Baptists" into the church without rebaptism as "shaking in the Baptists." Lipscomb, along with James A. Harding, believed that those who were immersed upon a confession of faith in Jesus in obedience to the divine command were biblically immersed whether or not they were aware that baptism was the moment of forgiveness.[34]

The Churches of Christ, in particular, have discussed this problem throughout the twentieth century. Though Campbell and Lipscomb's position dominated the late nineteenth and early twentieth centuries, McGary's position ultimately became the position of the *Gospel Advocate* by the mid-twentieth century and dominated the Churches of Christ in the last half of the twentieth century. However, Lipscomb's position on rebaptism did not die and was represented by various thought leaders among churches, including all the presidents of Harding University.[35]

The Problem of the Unimmersed

In the midst of Campbell's controversy with John Thomas during 1835-1838, a woman from Lunnenberg, Virginia, whose sympathies were with Thomas, wrote a letter that was intended to put Campbell on the defensive. Her letter asked Campbell "how any one becomes a Christian" and "at what time did [he] become a Christian."[36] Her question raised the issue of whether there were Christians among the "sects," particularly among the Baptists. But it also raised the larger issue of whether unimmersed believers were Christians as well, since she wanted to pinpoint the exact moment a believer became a Christian.

Campbell's basic response was that "everyone that believes in his heart that Jesus of Nazareth is the Messiah, the Son of God; repents of his sins, and obeys him in all things according to his measure of knowledge of his will" is a Christian.[37] Campbell compares one who is unimmersed to an imperfect Christian. He cannot bring himself to deny that any person who "is acting up to the full measure of his knowledge," and has not been "negligent, according to his opportunities, to ascertain the will of his Master" is a Christian. He feels that if he were to paganize all the unimmersed simply because they have never had an opportunity to learn about immersion, he would be "a pure sectarian, a Pharisee among Christians." Therefore, he cannot regard all the unimmersed as "aliens from Christ and the well-grounded hope of heaven."[38]

Campbell insists that anyone who was sprinkled in his infancy ought to be immersed. Since sprinkling is "at best only the fallible inference or opinion of man," the unimmersed ought to be immersed because in it "we have the sure and unerring promise of our Savior and Judge." On this ground, "the present salvation can never be so fully enjoyed, all things else being equal, by the unimmersed as by the immersed."[39] But Campbell refuses to make immersion absolutely essential to salvation, though it is absolutely necessary to the full enjoyment of assurance. According to Campbell, all who have "obeyed according to their knowledge" and are not "willingly" ignorant of the will of heaven, "although debarred from the full enjoyment of the kingdom of grace here, may be admitted into the kingdom of glory hereafter."[40]

Campbell did not make immersion a *sine qua non* of eternal salvation. Everyone will be judged according to their opportunities or circumstances. Anyone who has had no opportunity to be immersed is not subject to the divine command, and consequently he would not affirm that "remission is absolutely suspended upon being baptized in water."[41] The God who has "always enjoined upon man 'mercy, rather than sacrifice'" has "never demanded" baptism "as [an] indispensable condition of salvation."[42] Thus, Campbell "cannot make literal immersion in water, in all cases, essential to admission into the kingdom of eternal glory."[43] Campbell believed this even while he was unfolding his understanding of baptism in his "ancient gospel" series. For example, in

1829 he wrote: "I doubt not but many Paidobaptists of all sects will be admitted into the kingdom of glory. Indeed all they who obey Jesus Christ, through faith in his blood, according to their knowledge, I am of opinion will be introduced into that kingdom."[44] It was not a new point in Campbell's theology.

Campbell's argument, however, is not simply about voluntary ignorance and opportunity. Rather, it is rooted in a theological perspective that perceives the heart of God and the nature of Christianity in a certain way. Thus, he alludes to God's preference of mercy over sacrifice as well as God's desire for character over ritual. He asks: "We have, in Paul's style, the inward and the outward Jews; and may we not have the inward and the outward Christians?"[45] Campbell recognized this "inward" baptism in the holy lives of the unimmersed:

> The case is this: When I see a person who would die for Christ whose brotherly kindness, sympathy, and active benevolence know no bounds but his circumstances; whose seat in the Christian assembly is never empty; whose inward piety and devotion are attested by punctual obedience to every known duty; whose family is educated in the fear of the Lord; whose constant companion is the Bible: I say, when I see such a one ranked among the heathen men and publicans, because he never happened to inquire, but always took it for granted that he had been scripturally baptized; and that, too, by one greatly destitute of all these public and private virtues, whose chief or exclusive recommendation is that he has been immersed, and that he holds a scriptural theory of the gospel: I feel no disposition to flatter such a one; but rather to disabuse him of his error. And while I would not lead the most excellent professor in any sect to disparage the least of all the commandments of Jesus, I would say to my immersed brother as Paul said to his Jewish brother who gloried in a system which he did not adorn: "Sir, will not his uncircumcision, or unbaptism, be counted to him for baptism? and will he not condemn you, who, though having the literal and true baptism, yet dost transgress or neglect the statutes of your King?"[46]

Another extended statement by Campbell is worth careful reflection:

> I cannot, therefore, make any one duty the standard of Christian state or character, not even immersion into the name of the father, of the Son, and of the Holy Spirit, and in my heart regard all that have been sprinkled in infancy without their own knowledge and consent, as aliens from Christ and the well-grounded hope of heaven. "Salvation was of the Jews," acknowledged the Messiah; and yet he said of a foreigner, an alien from the commonwealth of Israel, a Syro-Phenician, "I have not found so great faith—no, not in Israel."
>
> Should I find a Pedobaptist more intelligent in the Christian Scriptures, more spiritually-minded and more devoted to the Lord than a Baptist, or one immersed on a profession of the ancient faith, I could not hesitate a moment in giving the preference of my heart to him that loveth most. Did I act otherwise, I would be a pure sectarian, a Pharisee among Christians. Still I will be asked, How do I know that any one loves my Master but by his obedience to his commandments? I answer, In no other way. But mark, I do not substitute obedience to one commandment, for universal or even for general obedience. And should I see a sectarian Baptist or a Pedobaptist more spiritually-minded, more generally conformed to the requisitions of the Messiah, than one who precisely acquiesces with me in the theory or practice of immersion as I teach, doubtless the former rather than the latter, would have my cordial approbation and love as a Christian. So I judge, and so I feel. It is the image of Christ the Christian looks for and loves; and this does not consist in being exact in a few items, but in general devotion to the whole truth as far as known.[47]

Fundamentally, Campbell argues that obedient transformation into the image of Christ is more important than any particular divine command. A transformed life is more important than a misperception of God's will regarding baptism. Baptism is not a watershed command in the sense that one's misunderstanding of it negates God's grace in a life transformed by faith in Christ.

But Campbell's qualifications of his baptismal teaching were not well received by many. His remarks created a firestorm within his own ranks, and his words in the "Lunnenberg Letter" have been debated ever since.[48] The letter evidenced a disagreement within the movement over the state of the pious unimmersed. While in the nineteenth century most everyone agreed that only the immersed were members of the visible church, there was disagreement regarding Campbell's Lunnenberg letter and it is difficult to discern whose opinion held sway in various quarters. For example, Moses Lard, certainly one of the more conservative leaders in the Stone-Campbell Movement in the mid-nineteenth century, rejected open communion but believed that the pious unimmersed would still be saved. Though "God may esteem [the pious unimmersed] very highly, much more so than many of the immersed, and even very certainly save" them, Lard argues, they are not members of the visible church and therefore cannot be called "Christian." Lard said that "with our brethren these positions are postulates and not matters of controversy."[49] J. W. McGarvey reflected a common perspective in this letter to an inquirer:

> I have no doubt there are pious unimmersed persons who have never been immersed. It would be absurd and ridiculous to deny it in the face of what we see and know of thousands of persons living and dead who have exhibited self-sacrificing love of God and man, which puts to shame all common disciples. I have as little doubt that many unimmersed persons will be saved in the final day. It is not necessary in order to contend for scripture teaching on the subject of baptism to take the ground that God has tied his hands and put it out of his power to grant mercy to any who have been misled in regard to that ordinance. He has bound us, but he has not bound himself; except that he is bound to do what he has promised. Don't injure the cause of truth by taking positions that rob God of the power to be merciful.[50]

At the beginning of the twentieth century, however, some churches in the Stone-Campbell Movement began to admit unimmersed persons to their membership.[51] Ultimately, this segment of the movement became the Disciples of Christ (Christian Church) who now generally "recognize that both infant and believer's baptism can be authentic practices in the one church of Jesus Christ."[52] However, Independent Christian Churches/Churches of Christ and the Churches of Christ (a cappella) generally practice closed membership and do not recognize infant baptisms as authentic baptisms. Yet, there are on-going discussions of the state of the unimmersed within these segments of the Stone-Campbell Movement.[53]

Baptismal Consensus Among Churches of Christ

Between the 1930s and 1950s a consensus emerged in Churches of Christ both east (*Gospel Advocate* in Tennessee) and west (*Firm Foundation* in Texas) of the Mississippi River. During this period the two previous controversies, with the exception of a few peripheral figures, were concluded. The Churches of Christ generally rebaptized those who had not been previously immersed "for the remission of sins" and viewed the unimmersed as having little, if any, hope of salvation.

What theological perspectives grounded this consensus? Social factors influenced it. The Churches of Christ were staking out their identity in the early twentieth century over against other Free Church movements in the South, particularly the Baptists. Consequently, representatives of Baptist Churches and Churches of Christ battled each other in numerous debates across the south. Whatever the sociological influences, however, the fundamental root was theological.

Alexander Campbell's baptismal theology articulated an instrumental understanding of baptismal grace but at the same time valued character more than ritual and mercy more than sacrifice. A living faith that exhibited a transformed character was more important than a correct understanding of baptism. However, few in mid-twentieth-century Churches of Christ believed that faith without baptism was transformative. Baptism was regarded more like a line in the sand or, to mix the metaphor, a watershed. Baptismal water became an absolute distinction between the lost and the saved.

Campbell had more of a relational understanding of baptism, while the baptismal consensus of the twentieth century held more of legal understanding of baptism. Henry Webb has described the difference in terms of covenantal (relational) versus contractual (legal) frameworks.[54] A relational or covenantal perspective highlights transformation as the goal of God's work and how baptism serves that goal. But a contractual or legal perspective highlights obedience as a test of loyalty and how baptism functions as the primary test of obedience.

James A. Harding (1848-1922), a foundational thinker among Churches of Christ, illustrates the significance of this distinction. Harding, among others,[55] classified baptism as a "positive" ordinance in conformity to "positive law" which is different from "moral law."[56] A "positive" law is a command whose only basis of obligation is the fact that God commanded it while a "moral" law is rooted in the moral character of God. Moral law is obligatory in its own right, but positive laws are obligatory solely by the explicit command of God. For example, the command "You shall not commit adultery" is rooted in God's own sense of faithfulness, but the command "Do not eat of that tree" is a test of strict obedience. Moral obligations have crutches. There are inducements, inclinations, and natural propensities. But a positive law is an absolute test of loyalty. The significance of the positive command, then, is that it is unencumbered by the crutches of moral obligations and it gives a clear indication of the loyalty of the person involved.

The Indiana editor of the *American Christian Review*, Benjamin Franklin, whom Harding regarded as one of his mentors, applied this distinction to baptism. Positive law is "the highest test of respect for divine authority" since it "tests" the condition of the "heart" as it penetrates "deep down into the inmost depths of the soul." Obedience to positive law "rises above mere morality…into the pure region of faith." Disobedience to positive law reveals the "spirit of disobedience."[57] Therefore, it is a damning disobedience. Examples of positive law include blood on the door-posts (Ex. 12:1-13), touching the ark (1 Chron. 13:11), Abraham sacrificing Isaac (Gen. 22), Naaman immersing himself in the Jordan (2 Kings 5), the ritual for tumbling the walls of Jericho (Josh. 2), and immersion in water for the remission of sins (Mark 16:16).[58] "Baptism," writes Franklin, "is the test of his belief in Christ—the trial of his loyalty to the King" and if one neglects or fails to understand this command which is intended to "develop the spirit of obedience in him," then "what ground have we for expecting obedience of him in the future."[59]

Harding followed Franklin's lead. Harding was involved in a rather lengthy give-and-take on the question of the unimmersed in the pages of the 1883 *Gospel Advocate*. Harding offered no biblical hope to the unimmersed. "That these people," he wrote, "are not in the kingdom is evident to us."[60] "Doubtless," Harding said in his debate with the Methodist Nichols, "there are immersed Methodists who are entitled to the name Christian. No matter how excellent and amiable a man may be, he is not entitled to the name Christ until he has been properly initiated into the church of Christ. Unimmersed people have not been so initiated."[61]

Harding believed that the clarity of this command was unavoidable. "If a man does not understand the baptismal question, in this country," he argued, "it is because he will not, not because he cannot understand. It is not the Lord's fault; he made the matter plain enough."[62] As a clear positive command, it demands obedience rather than debating. Ignorance is no excuse.[63]

The positive command of God provides a definitive line of demarcation between those in Christ and those outside of Christ. According to Harding, the problem here is not baptism, but the heart: "Now let it be understood I do not find fault with these people because they have not been baptized. That is not the disease; it is only a symptom; unbelief is the disease; their hearts are not right."[64] Because the command is so clear and so simple, according to Harding, a refusal to obey or a failure to understand must reflect an unbelieving heart.

The New Testament, according to Harding, is "divine law" and the "rule of doctrine, faith and practice."[65] "Legal power" applies when a New Testament text authorizes the practice. The search for "legal power" means that the New Testament must be scanned as a legal document that authorizes only what it contains. Consequently, Harding could read the New Testament like a legal brief. Baptism is a positive command within this perfect law. Thus, God commands immersion as a loyalty test.

> Baptism and the Lord's Supper under the new covenant, and the ceremonial law of the Jews under the old covenant, are illustrations of positive law…Positive law differs from moral law in that it can be obeyed perfectly. Positive law is therefore a more perfect test of faith and love, a more perfect test of allegiance to God, than moral law….For these two reasons, doubtless, God has ever been more ready to overlook the infractions of moral, than of positive law; and for the same reasons the positive is peculiarly adapted to the expression and the perfection of faith. I would not have you suppose that I think God would for a moment tolerate a willful violation of moral law. No, no; I simply mean that God, who knows so well our inherited weakness, is patient and gentle with us in our imperfect obedience to this law, and in our many backslidings from it. But positive law we can obey perfectly, and he is strict and stern in demanding that we shall do it.[66]

The application is apparent. God is gracious toward our moral failings because he understands our weaknesses and our inability to obey moral law perfectly. He understands our sanctification will be slow and progressive due to our weaknesses. However, God is stern and unyielding in his insistence on obedience to positive law because we can obey it perfectly. Positive law has such clarity that there is no misunderstanding it. The command to be immersed must be obeyed or else.

This is how Harding explains why God can act with such grace and forgiveness toward the moral failings of David, but at the same time remove Saul from his kingship and instantly kill Uzzah. Saul and Uzzah "violated a positive law."[67] God can bear with the moral failings of his people because of their weaknesses, but God will not tolerate the violation of his explicit positive laws.

This legal understanding elevates obedience in baptism above moral transformation. Baptism, then, is more important than transformation. Indeed, moral transformation is meaningless without baptism. Failure to be properly baptized, then, is as culpable, perhaps more so, than moral failure, even if it is due to ignorance or mistaken understanding. Churches of Christ, therefore, generally concluded that baptismal error was a sign of willful ignorance, stubborn pride or pernicious disloyalty to God. Consequently, the unimmersed failed the test of positive law and thus evidenced their rebellion, just as Adam did in the Garden. Thus, according to this view, the unimmersed have no hope because they are overtly disobedient.

Conclusion

The fundamental impulse of Alexander Campbell's baptismal theology was the assurance of the forgiveness of sins. He rejected the frontier search for assurance through a subjective conversion experience. Instead of calling the sinner to "pray through" at the mourner's bench, the early Stone-Campbell Movement called sinners to Jesus through "washing away their sins" in the river. Baptism was God's "sensible pledge" by which he assured believers of his gracious forgiveness. It was an objective moment of assurance and a means of grace. Campbell, in essence, adopted a Calvinian understanding of the meaning of baptism, and he recognized this in an extended quote from Calvin at the conclusion of which he wondered whether his opponents would now call Calvin a "Campbellite."[68]

Campbell framed this understanding of baptism in a covenantal or relational context where God's main interest was not baptism but transformation. The "inward" Christian is more important than the "outward" Christian, and the "image of Christ" is more important than exact obedience in every detail. Consequently, while Campbell articulated a "high" view of baptism, he also understood that transformation was more important than obedience to that single command.

But Campbell's perspective was soon overshadowed by, first, a veiled hope for the unimmersed (as in Lard and McGarvey) and, then, by a technical exaltation of baptism over moral transformation. The veiled hope would appear occasionally, but it was left undeveloped for fear of devaluing baptism. But, then, the veiled hope was lost because baptism assumed the status of a technicality as positive law where obedience to positive law was more a test of faith than conformity to moral law. Whereas Campbell valued the "image of Christ" more than technical obedience to a single command, the Churches of Christ, in general, valued immersion more than the "image of Christ" in that they would not recognize the "image of Christ" in some solely because they were unimmersed.[69]

Campbell leads believers down in the river to experience the assurance of God's gracious forgiveness as part of God's transforming work in them, but some of his theological descendents went down to the river to draw a line in the sand. They turned baptism into a legal technicality rather than a divine work of transformation. They separated themselves from others and condemned them because they did not share the same understanding of baptism. Even in his own day Campbell felt that some had "given to baptism an undue eminence—a sort of pardon-procuring, rather than a pardon-certifying and enjoying efficacy."[70] On the other hand, some, put off by the sectarian application of a Calvinian understanding of baptism, have returned to a more Zwinglian perspective.[71] We think the swing to Zwingli's symbolic view is unnecessary and anthropocentric.

****

Principle

Campbell recovered a Calvinian baptismal theology while adopting the Anabaptist practice of believer's baptism. In so doing, Campbell did not devalue the faith of the unimmersed, but called the unimmersed to the assurance that God gives through a more biblical practice of baptism.

Prayer

Father, we thank you for those who have gone before us. Give us the humility to learn from them—from their mistakes as well as their insights. We acknowledge that you have placed each of us within our own history—we are not orphans. We are grateful for our forebears and give you glory for their work that has benefited us so greatly. Give us the courage to follow you as your word directs just as they did according to their understanding. Amen.

Questions

1. How does Campbell model a willingness to change one's understanding of baptism as the word convicts? How many changes do you recognize?

2. Why does Campbell object to re-immersing those who had been previously immersed on a confession of faith in Christ? Has this discussion arisen in your experience or in the context of your congregation?

3. Campbell resisted exalting the command to be immersed above the "image of Christ." How do you evaluate his resistance? Is one a Christian when through faith in Christ they do the will of God as far as they know it?

4. What is the effect of viewing baptism as a positive law and then giving positive law a greater theological significance than moral law? Explain that rationale and assess it.

8 / *Drowned in the River: Baptism and Justification*

Rock of Ages, cleft for me,
let me hide myself in Thee;
let the water and the blood,
from thy riven side which flowed,
be of sin the double cure;
cleanse me from its guilt and power.

Nothing in my hand I bring,
Simply to Thy cross I cling;
Naked, come to Thee for dress,
Helpless, look to Thee for grace;
Foul, I to the fountain fly;
Wash me, Saviour, or I die.

—Augustus Toplady, 1776[1]

****

When we go down in the river to pray, what happens? Do we come up out of the water doubly cured?

New Testament language says that through baptism we are forgiven of our sins and given the Holy Spirit (Acts 2:38), our sins are washed away (Acts 22:16), we are united with Christ (Gal. 3:27; Rom. 6:3), we are saved (1 Pet. 3:21), we are regenerated (Titus 3:5), and cleansed (Eph. 5:26) among other redemptive themes. This is the language of conversion, justification, sanctification, glorification and salvation.

In this chapter and the next we will talk about justification and sanctification, the past and present dimensions of our salvation, as it relates to our journey down into the river. Humanity needs a "double cure," as the classic hymn "Rock of Ages" reminds us. We need freedom from both the guilt and the power of sin. We need both justification and sanctification; forgiveness and transformation; salvation from wrath and purification. What is the relationship between baptism and the "double cure"?

Grace, Faith and Works

> For it is by grace you have been saved, through faith—and this is not from yourselves, it is the gift of God—not by works, so that no one can boast. For we are God's workmanship, created in Christ Jesus to do good works, which God prepared in advance for us to do (Eph. 2:8-10).

Ephesians 2:8-10 is one of the clearest, yet one of the most disputed, texts on grace. It is clear because it declares that we are saved "by grace through faith." It is disputed because it demands interpretation. It is rarely sufficient to quote the text of Ephesians 2:8-9. Everyone wants to know what you mean when you quote it.

Ephesians 2:1-7, as a single Greek sentence, sets the motive and nature of God's actions in the context of God's mercy, kindness and grace. It describes our sinful condition before God, God's act in Christ to save us according to his mercy and grace, and his goal of glorifying us along with his Son. We were dead in sin, so God raised us with Christ so that he might pour out his riches upon us. God's act in Christ made us alive with him, raised up with him and seated us in heavenly places with him. Our actions did not move God to grace, but God's grace moved him to act on our behalf. His work is a gracious work for sinners who did not deserve it.

Ephesians 2:1-7 is grounded in the principle of Ephesians 2:8: "For it is by grace you have been saved, through faith." The term "for" has explanatory force. The principle of verse 8 explains in summary fashion what was described in verses 1-7. In fact, verses 8-10 summarizes God's saving work.

First, grace is the ground of our salvation. Salvation is God's work, not ours. This is the plain meaning of the word "grace"—it is unmerited favor; it is God's disposition of saving love toward undeserving sinners. Wrath is what is owed, but grace is bestowed. The central assertion of the doctrine of grace is that salvation is God's work.

God is the subject of the verbs relating to salvation in verses 1-7. He is the active worker here. Further, Paul explicitly clarifies this point by excluding works from the ground of salvation. Salvation is "not from yourselves, it is the gift of God." Salvation does not arise out of our own goodness. Salvation arises out of God's gracious heart. We are not saved from within but from without. We do not save ourselves but God saves us.

Paul underlines this point by offering a further contrast. Not only is salvation "not from yourselves," it is also "not by [literally, out of] works." Salvation does not arise from the works that we do. Our works do not contribute to our salvation—they are not the source or ground of our salvation. Salvation is fundamentally a gift of God and anything that undermines that principle is legalism and denies the gospel. In this sense, there is nothing we can do to effect our justification and there is nothing we can do to contribute to our salvation.

Paul does not qualify the kind of works he is talking about here. He does not say "works of merit" or "works of the law of Moses." Rather, he simply says "works." He does, however, provide a motive for why works are excluded as the source of salvation: "so that no one can boast." Paul excludes all boasting from salvation except the boasting that is in Christ. If we boast in any work, human effort, or obedience to law, then we exclude Christ.

Second, salvation is by faith. We are saved through the instrumentality of faith. Faith is the means by which we receive God's grace. Through faith we have access to God's grace, and by faith we continue to stand in his grace (Rom. 5:1-2). Faith is the human response to God's gracious offer of salvation. Faith receives what God is willing to give. God saves by grace, but through faith.

Human response is required for salvation. No one is saved without faith. Faith is the means of salvation, and faith is a human response to God's gracious offer. God's grace is offered to everyone, but is only applied to those who receive it through faith. Consequently, there is a sense in which we must do something to receive salvation—we must "do faith" or we must trust in Jesus as our Savior. Yet, even this faith arises out of God's grace that took the initiative to redeem us. God gives us grace to have faith in order that we might have a transformed life in his presence and service.

What "works" are excluded from the means of salvation? Are the works of Ephesians 2:10 included or excluded by 2:8-9? Some believe the works excluded by 2:8-9 are the works of the Mosaic Law and the works of 2:10 are part of the concept of "faith" in 2:8. The works included are the divine requirements contained in the faith system. But there is nothing about the Mosaic Law in Ephesians 2:1-10 that would contextually qualify "works." Rather, 2:8-9 is categorical, that is, it excludes all good works, including the works of 2:10. Paul uses the same word for works in 2:9 that he uses in 2:10. The works of 2:10 follow salvation and therefore are excluded from the "means" of salvation.

Third, good works are the result of salvation. They are not the basis or ground of salvation. We are not saved because we work, but we work because we are already saved. Ephesians 2:10 clarifies the relationship between works and salvation, as if Paul wishes to head off any misunderstanding. We are saved by grace through faith—not out of our works. We are saved in such a way that no one can boast in the good works they have done. This is true because, as verse 10 says, we are created for good works, and not because we do good works. Rather, we are God's work—we are God's doing, his creation. We work the works of God because we are God's work of salvation—new creatures in Christ.

Ephesians 2 distinguishes between the ground of salvation and the means by which we appropriate it. The ground of our salvation is the merit by which we stand before God. God's work in Christ earns the righteousness (salvation) that is given to us in justification. The means by which we are saved is the method of appropriation. It is the way we receive the divine gift of righteousness—a righteous, justified standing before God. We are saved through faith.

The ground of our salvation is wholly outside of us. Titus 3:5 explicitly denies that we are saved by "works of righteousness," that is, works which earn righteousness (cf. 2 Tim. 1:9). We are not saved on the ground that we are good enough. Rather, we are saved by the merits of Christ's work. The righteousness of God is imputed to us as a gift that saves us (Rom. 1:16-17; 4:1-8; 5:17-19). The ground of our salvation, then, is the grace of God alone as it is offered to us in Christ Jesus.

Faith, not works, is the means of justification. The gift of righteousness is given to believers. Without faith no one can please God or enter into his presence since it is through faith that God gives his gift of righteousness. As a means, faith does not contribute to the merit of our righteous standing, but it is the instrument by which the righteousness from God is received. Faith, as Luther put it, is the "beggar's hand."

Baptism and Justification

All theological thought must begin with God's gracious initiative in creation and redemption. A theology of grace must saturate all our thinking. God's goal is to redeem and transform all that is fallen and to have a people for himself. The history of redemption is a history of God's relentless pursuit of this goal.

Faith trusts in and depends on God's saving work in Christ. Faith submits to God's will in all that it knows. We are saved by faith only in the sense that faith is the only principle by which we are saved. As Cottrell comments, "we should acknowledge that faith is the sole means of receiving salvation, and in this sense agree that people are justified by (that is, by means of) faith alone."[2]

Martin Luther was, of course, a formative advocate of justification by faith alone (*sola fide*). Yet, his baptismal theology was so "high" that the Lutheran theologian Paul Althaus described it as "basically nothing else than his doctrine of justification in concrete form."[3] Luther reacted strongly against those who interpreted *sola fide* in a way that excluded baptism from a role in the justification of the sinner.[4]

> But as our would-be wise, new spirits assert that faith alone saves, and that works and external things avail nothing, we

> answer: It is true, indeed, that nothing in us is of any avail but faith, as we shall hear still further. But these blind guides are unwilling to see this, namely, that faith must have something that it believes, that is, of which it takes hold, and upon which it stands and rests. Thus faith clings to the water, and believes that it is Baptism, in which there is pure salvation and life.

Faith saves, according to Luther, but it saves as God works through the external gift of baptism. For Luther, baptism is a "sacrament" of justification. We are justified by faith through baptism. Sola fide does not exclude the grace of baptism. On the contrary, faith grasps God's justifying grace through baptism.

But what is the biblical basis for such a conclusion?

Baptism and Ephesians 2

If all works are excluded, as Ephesians 2 teaches, what does this say about baptism? Does this mean that faith alone saves without the instrumentality of baptism? We must remember that in verse 8 Paul is summarizing verses 1-7. We are saved by God's act, not ours. When we were dead, God made us alive with Christ, raised us up with Christ, and sat us in the heavenly places with him. God raised us from the spiritual grave and made us alive through his work in Christ. We who were once dead in sin were made alive in Christ through our death and resurrection with him.

To participate in the death and resurrection of Jesus is baptismal language in Romans 6 and Colossians 2. God circumcised our hearts, made us alive with Christ and forgave us our sins when we were "buried with him in baptism and raised with him through faith in the power of God, who raised him from the dead" (Col. 2:12). When Paul says that God "raised us up with Christ" (Eph. 2:6), the total framework of his thought (e.g., Rom. 6) and the parallel with Colossians imply a baptismal context.

Colossians 2:11-3:4 and Ephesians 2:1-10 have conceptual and verbal parallels. Both describe sinners as dead in sin and uncircumcised, and both describe salvation in terms of circumcision, resurrection and life with Christ. Both texts affirm that salvation is God's work through faith. In other words, they both breathe the same theological atmosphere and complement each other (see the chart below).[5] In this framework, Paul's teaching concerning baptism in Colossians 2:12-13 illuminates his language in Ephesians 2:5-6.

Concept/Word	**Ephesians**	**Colossians**
Sinner's Lost Condition		
Dead in Sin	2:1, 5	2:13
Uncircumcised	2:11	2:13
Christian's Saved Condition		
Made Alive	2:5	2:13
Raised with Christ	2:6	3:1-3
Circumcised	2:11	2:11, 13
Transition		
God's Work	2:10	2:12
By Grace	2:8	No Reference
Through Faith	2:8	2:12
In Baptism	No Reference	2:12

Colossians 2:11-15 gives concrete expression to our salvation by grace through faith. The theme of Colossians 2:1-10 is incorporation into Christ (2:2, 6, 7, 9). In Christ, Paul writes, "you were circumcised" by the circumcision of Christ that is not accomplished by human hands, but by the Spirit of God (2:11). But Paul immediately provides a baptismal context for understanding this spiritual circumcision. Paul's point is that spiritual circumcision has come in the place of fleshly circumcision. Baptism is the occasion or means by which God circumcises the heart by his Spirit.

The present participle "having been buried with him" in Colossians 2:12 modifies the past tense verb in Colossians 2:11 "you were circumcised." The grammar indicates that the circumcision took place at the moment of burial. In other words, when they were buried with Christ and raised with him, they experienced the circumcision of Christ. As the text states, "you were circumcised...when you were buried with him in baptism."

But this baptism was effectual only through faith in the power (or, more literally, the working) of God. Baptism is not effectual because of what we believe about baptism or because we believe in baptism. Rather, baptism is effectual through our faith in the work of God in Christ. The gospel grounds the efficacy of baptism and it is effectual only through faith. This is the problem we see with infant baptism. If faith renders baptism effectual, then baptism without faith is ineffectual. Just as by grace through faith we are saved, so in baptism we die and rise with Christ through faith.

Our participation in the death and resurrection of Jesus in baptism through faith means that while we were once dead in sin, we are now alive to God (Col. 2:13). This entails the forgiveness of our trespasses and the cancellation of our debt of sin (Col. 2:14). This is the language of justification in a baptismal context. Those who have been raised with Christ have experienced justification (cf. Rom. 4:25), and we were raised with Christ in baptism through faith in God's work.

Baptism is fundamentally God's work—he forgives, he raises up, he makes alive. We simply entrust ourselves through faith in his power. In baptism, we do not "do," accomplish or effect anything but receive everything. Baptism does not belong in the category of "work" but in the category of "faith." It is a human response that arises out of faith, expresses faith, and receives God's gracious salvation as a gift. Baptism participates in the instrumentality of faith and therefore is not excluded from the means of grace. Baptism, just like faith, is the beggar's hand that receives what God gives.

The following chart summarizes our theological perspective.

Grace, Faith and Works

Text	*Ground*	*Included Means*	*Excluded Means*	*Blessing*	*Effect*
Eph. 2 Col. 2	Divine Grace	Faith-Baptism	Not Works	Salvation	Good Works
Tit. 3:3-8	Divine Mercy	Washing of Rebirth and Renewal of Holy Spirit	Not Works of Righteousness	Justified	Good Works

Grace is the ground of our salvation, but faith is the means. Baptism participates in the instrumentality of faith. It is not, and never is classified as, a "work" in Biblical theology. Rather, it shares the instrumental function of faith and thus is pictured in Scripture as part of the saving faith that justifies because of God's grace. Baptism, then, is both a sign and means of justification because it serves and participates in the role of faith in justification.

Baptism as a Means of Receiving Grace

Even the casual reader of Paul's letter to the Romans recognizes that justification by faith is one of the letter's major themes. The terms "justify," "justification," "righteous," or "righteousness," all derived from the same Greek root, are prominent in Romans 3-5. As a reminder, here are a few:

> 3:24—[we] are *justified* freely by his grace
> 3:28—man is *justified* by faith apart from observing the law
> 4:6—God credits *righteousness* apart from works
> 4:13—*righteousness* that comes by faith
> 4:25—[Jesus] was raised to life for our *justification*
> 5:1—we have been *justified* through faith
> 5:9—we have now been *justified* by his blood
> 5:17—God's abundant provision of grace and of the gift of *righteousness*
> 5:19—through the obedience of the one man the many will be made *righteous*

Righteousness is a free gift. No one earns it; it does not come through works, but by faith. We are justified by what Jesus has done rather than because of what we have done.

Romans 3-5, however, is followed by the longest discussion of baptism in Paul's letters. The close proximity of baptism and justification is not only spatial, but conceptual. Paul links baptism and justification as well as baptism and sanctification (holiness) in Romans 6. Through baptism we participate in the death (blood) and resurrection (life) of Jesus that is the justifying work of God for our salvation. The death and resurrection of Jesus is the act of obedience that justifies us, and baptism is our moment of union with that act. As a result, Paul closely associates baptism and our justification.

Paul's language is telling. First, we are "buried with [Jesus] through baptism into death" (Rom. 6:4). The term "through" is the

Greek term *dia*, which denotes agency or instrumentality. In other words, we are buried with Jesus by means of baptism. The same word is used in Titus 3:5 when Paul affirms that God "saved us through (*dia*) the washing of rebirth and renewal by the Holy Spirit." Ephesians 5:26 expresses the same idea as Paul writes that we are cleansed "by the washing of the water through the word." This is the language of means or instrumentality. Baptism is the means by which we are united with the death of Christ. This does not mean, of course, that the water unites us, but that God unites us to the death of his Son by the power of his Spirit in baptism. God acts through baptism. Paul's language is instrumental in character.

Second, through baptism we are united with the death of Christ. We die to sin when we are united with Christ's death. "Don't you know," Paul asks in Romans 6:3, "that all of us who were baptized into Christ Jesus were baptized into his death?" We die to sin when we are united with Christ's death; Christ's death is the death of sin. This is justification—to die to sin is to be separated from sin. Romans 6:7 declares: "anyone who has died has been freed from sin." We die to sin through baptism and the one who has died to sin has been "freed from sin." Significantly, the term "freed" is the word Paul uses so often in Romans 3-5 that is translated "justify." Whoever has died with Christ and thus experienced a death to sin has also been declared righteous (justified).

But who has "died" to sin? The context identifies the one who has been buried with Christ in baptism as the one who has been united with Christ's death and thus dead to sin. Baptism is connected to justification as a means rather than a mere sign. This is consistent with Paul's summary declaration in 1 Corinthians 6:11. Though we were once sinners deserving of God's wrath, now we have been "washed," "sanctified," and "justified in the name of the Lord Jesus Christ and by the Spirit of our God." Washing, sanctification and justification are correlate occasions—the people of God are cleansed, justified and sanctified through baptism in the name of Jesus and by the power of the Spirit.

Paul and James

Paul consistently excludes works from justifying faith (Rom. 4:5-6; Titus 3:5). The righteousness of justification does not arise out of the works we do. Our righteousness in Christ is from God (external to us) instead of from within ourselves (internal to us). This is the theological principle by which works are excluded, since works can always give rise to boasting. However, Paul is not indifferent to works for he sees faith as living and active. Paul's definition of saving faith is "faith working through love" (Gal. 5:6; cf. 1 Thess. 1:3). Further, he encourages believers to excel in good works. God has called us for this purpose (Eph. 2:10; Titus 3:8). But these good works follow justification and are not part of it.

At this point our minds inevitably turn to James and his discussion of faith and works. In particular, many Christians categorize baptism as a "work" and invariably appeal to James to help explain the meaning of baptism. On the one hand, some categorize baptism as a work in James' frame of reference and thus exclude baptism from the means of justification and only give it a demonstrative function. Baptism, then, demonstrates one's justification just as Abraham demonstrated his faith through offering Isaac, though he was saved years prior. On the other hand, some categorize baptism as a work in James' frame of reference and conclude that justification is not through faith alone but is through faith and works (where baptism is the first "work"). Thus, we are justified when our faith works through baptism just as Abraham was justified when he offered Isaac.

But baptism is alien to James' purpose. Instead he presses the point that a living faith will demonstrate itself in good works. James identifies these "works" as a benevolent lifestyle (2:15—food and clothes; 1:27—religion defined in relation to orphans and widows; 1:22ff—being doers of the word and not hearers only; 4:18—to "do good" is benevolent ministry). "Works" in James functions as a plural of category for obedience to God, that is, transformed living. One cannot be a hearer only. That is a false or spurious faith. It cannot save. That faith is dead, barren, and fruitless (2:14).

The notion of justification in James is demonstrative rather than declarative. Works demonstrate or evidence one's justification. Abraham was justified long before he offered Isaac (cf. Gen. 15:6). His offering of Isaac demonstrated a living faith that evidenced his justification (Gen. 22). James ties justification to works in this sense: no one can claim to be justified who does not show evidence of transformed living because this is the means by which living faith is evidenced.

Works "complete" or "perfect" faith (James 2:22). A tree is made perfect by its fruits in that it attains its legitimate development in bearing of fruits, which shows that it is a living tree. Faith expresses itself in appropriate actions by which the integrity of faith is demonstrated. Faith constitutes the foundation that reaches fruition in works.

Thus, the principle of faith is the means of justification. This principle receives the righteousness of God as a gift without works, but that faith will necessarily and inevitably express itself in transformed living if it is genuine. In this sense, good works demonstrate our justification, but they are not the means of our justification in the same sense that faith is. Good works are the proof of faith. The principle of faith always includes within itself the willingness to obey God's commands and do his works. A faith that refuses to obey is a dead faith that cannot save.

Baptism and faith are never categorized as "works" in biblical theology. Rather, baptism is closely coordinated with faith and shares the instrumentality of faith as the means by which we receive God's gift of justification. Baptism is a human response, just like faith, but it is also a means of grace, just like faith. Through faith, we grasp God's gift of justification when we are united with Christ in his death and resurrection through baptism. Baptism is the "sacrament" of justification.

Conclusion

The sole ground of salvation is the death and resurrection of Christ. Grace alone (*sola gratia*) provides the ground of our salvation. This grace is appropriated through faith. The human response of faith is the means by which we accept the grace God offers in his Son. Gospel obedience includes submission to Christ through baptism as an expression of faith. Baptism without faith is ineffectual and faith without baptism does not comply with what God commands. Baptism, then, is the particular embodiment of faith by which God seals the remission of our sins. It is part of the conversion narrative. Through baptism, we express our trust in Jesus' saving work. Baptism participates in the instrumentality of faith.

Baptism is a concrete expression of the gospel: death and resurrection of Christ (Rom. 6:3-5). It is no mere symbol, but an effective sign of justification. It is an objective moment of assurance and our passive reception of God's gift of righteousness. Baptism is our objective connection with Christ's own history in our personal histories: it links the story of redemption with our own personal stories.

God calls us to the river, and when we go down in the river to pray, God encounters us. He washes us, cleanses us, justifies us and sanctifies us. He makes us one of his own and gives us what his Son has earned for us. He not only gives us "right standing" (justification) in his Son, but he empowers and transforms us by the power of his Spirit. We go down into the river to receive the "double cure"—to be saved from wrath (justification) and made pure (sanctification), to be cleansed from both the guilt and power of sin.

****

Principle

We are saved by grace—nothing we do contributes to the righteousness of our standing before God. We are saved through faith—we bring nothing to God but a "beggar's hand." Baptism is the concrete moment of faith, the performative symbolic act, by which we participate in the death, burial and resurrection of Christ—we die with him and are raised with him. Just as in his death he delivered us from our sins and by his resurrection we were justified, so baptism is that ritual, overt, "sensible" moment where we experience that death and resurrection through faith.

Prayer

Father, we thank you that you have redeemed us in your Son. We glory in the cross and boast in his resurrection. Thank you, Lord, for the gift of baptism wherein we experience that death and resurrection in our own lives. Thank you for the assurance of forgiveness, the presence of your Spirit, and the renewal that you give us through that gift. We confess that you have put to death sin in our lives, freed us from its guilt and raised us to walk a new life. We praise you because you have redeemed us through your Son and by your Spirit. Amen.

Questions

1. Why does such a simple sentence as "you are saved by grace through faith" spark such controversy? How do we complicate Paul's brief summary of salvation?

2. Would you agree with Luther that baptism is the doctrine of justification in concrete form? What is the relationship between baptism and justification?

3. How helpful is the distinction that grace is the ground, faith is the means and works are the effect of salvation? Where would you place baptism? Is it part of the ground, means or effect of salvation? What biblical texts would you use to support your answer?

4. What is the significance of the point that the New Testament never calls baptism a "good work," but always connects it to faith? What do people mean when they say baptism is a "work"?

5. How would you recommend we use the language of faith and works in relation to baptism?

9 / Seeking the Kingdom: Baptism and Sanctification

"Going under symbolizes the end of everything about your life that is less than human. Coming up again symbolizes the beginning in you of something strange and new and hopeful. You can breathe again."[1]

****

In the previous chapter we recalled the double cure of God's redemption. After justification the second part of that cure is the sanctifying power of the Holy Spirit that continues the process of transformation in our lives. In the last chapter we concluded that baptism is an effective sign of our justification. But the saving work of God in us does not end with justifying us and converting us. The ongoing role of the Holy Spirit is to conform us into the image of Christ so that we reflect his character and his glory. Baptism, therefore, is about more than justification. This chapter focuses on sanctification. The Holy Spirit also uses baptism as a means of empowering every believer for discipleship.

Through the Spirit's role of sanctification we are transformed in order to conform to the image of Christ. Hence, we are image bearers. We are a community conformed to God's image so that

Christ may be exalted above all of us (Rom. 8:29). As Paul says (2 Cor. 3:17-18),

> Now the Lord is the Spirit, and where the Spirit of the Lord is, there is freedom. And all of us, with unveiled faces, seeing the glory of the Lord as though reflected in a mirror, are being transformed into the same image from one degree of glory to another; for this comes from the Lord, the Spirit.

Baptism is a sign and means of receiving the Holy Spirit, whose primary role is to sanctify us for God's presence, his service, and his glory. Through baptism we are transformed for relationship with God, called to be disciples, and empowered by the Holy Spirit. After sin has been drowned in us, we come up for air. We have been justified. We're relieved beyond belief. We do not want to return to the depths. Our response might be, "I'm thankful to be saved. I'm glad it's over. I want to rest." The Holy Spirit, however, leads us beyond these primary responses toward sanctification in the following ways:

We are the temple of the Holy Spirit. Baptism prepares us for the presence of God's Spirit in our lives. God cleanses the temple and dwells in it. We are that temple. Baptism, then, is a means through which God pours out his Spirit and grace through the faith of the one submitting to baptism.

Discipleship is our role in the covenant. Baptism signals transformation, but God's work in us is far from complete. Though discipleship begins before baptism, the event of immersion marks a new identity, ethic, and world view that defines discipleship.

The Holy Spirit empowers us for holy and hopeful living. Baptism marks a lifetime process of dying to sin and renewing our appeal to God for new life. The Holy Spirit empowers us to live holy and hopeful lives through union with Christ by producing fruit in our lives.

Sanctification takes us beyond gratitude to a relationship with God, beyond relief to discipleship, beyond rest to empowerment by the Holy Spirit to die daily to sin and live in Christ. One role of the Spirit is to regenerate us—give us new life daily. Our role is to respond in discipleship. The joint venture between the Holy Spirit and us we call a "transformational covenant." We are empowered, and we in turn offer ourselves as living sacrifices (Rom. 12:1-2; 5:11).

Sanctification is a word derived from Scripture. New Testament writers use the word "holy" (*hagios*) in various forms in referring to sanctifying, making holy, consecrating. For example, God himself is holy (1 John 2:20; Rev. 6:10) and God's people are to be holy (1 Cor. 6:11; Acts 20:32; Heb. 10:10). The major difference between the Old and the New Testament in regard to "setting apart as holy" is the work of the Holy Spirit and Christlikeness in the lives of believers. For instance, Peter says to set apart (or make holy) Christ in our hearts (1 Pet. 3:15). Paul contrasts the past life of the Corinthians with their washed and sanctified lives in Christ (1 Cor. 6:11).[2]

The Father, Son, and Holy Spirit are each involved in the lives of believers through sanctifying acts. We too are called to act in the process of sanctification, to keep in step with the Spirit (Gal. 5:25), to offer ourselves as living sacrifices (Rom. 12:1). We are called to be holy just as God is holy (1 Pet. 1:16). We do not believe we save ourselves in these acts, nor are we able to attain perfection, nor is that the goal. The goal is Christlikeness—being formed in the image of Christ. This process of being transformed, sanctified, and conformed into Christ's image is a covenant between God and us.

A Temple of the Holy Spirit

God desires to live in us as his temple of the Holy Spirit. When the Holy Spirit takes up residence in our lives, all competing loves must come into submission or be cast out of the Spirit's home—our bodies. God's Spirit presence in our lives leads to a greater sense of calling and discipleship. Paul links casting out sin and uniting with Christ to the presence of the Holy Spirit in our lives. Paul asks the rhetorical question to the Corinthians, "Do you not know that wrongdoers will not inherit the kingdom of God?" (1 Cor. 6:9a). He continues by saying, "Do not be deceived! Fornicators, idolaters, adulterers, male prostitutes, sodomites, thieves, the greedy, drunkards, revilers, robbers—none of these will inherit the kingdom of God" (1 Cor. 6:9b-10).

The important transition comes in the next sentence, where Paul says simply, "And this is what some of you used to be" (1 Cor.

6:11a). Moreover, Paul does not leave them hanging with the negative picture of their past and the failure to inherit the kingdom of God. He continues with what amounts to the double cure: "But you were washed, you were sanctified, you were justified in the name of the Lord Jesus Christ and in the Spirit of our God" (v. 11b).

Paul points back to what the Corinthians once were and contrasts their past sin with, "you were washed." They were blessed with a two-part gift of being justified and sanctified. This washing, for Paul, served the purpose of transforming the Corinthians from adulterers to doubly-cured Christians, justified and sanctified. Through this washing, the Corinthians were cleansed from the guilt and power of sin.

Paul ends this section of his letter with a connector to verse 11b. Being washed, justified, and sanctified, says Paul, creates a union with Christ that leads to a radically different lifestyle. The new resident in our lives—the Holy Spirit—demands a new ethic. We cannot honor the presence of evil and the presence of God in our bodies at the same time:

> Do you not know that your bodies are members of Christ? Should I therefore take the members of Christ and make them members of a prostitute? Never! . . . Shun fornication! Every sin that a person commits is outside the body; but the fornicator sins against the body itself. Or do you not know that your body is a temple of the Holy Spirit within you, which you have from God, and that you are not your own? For you were bought with a price; therefore glorify God in your body. (1 Cor. 6:15-20)

This new world view may have perplexed some of the Corinthians, because few if any pagan religions they had practiced made claims that any god or spirit lived in them and demanded a new ethic. Certainly Corinthians could identify with temple structures, but Paul used the metaphor of a temple to describe the Holy Spirit's dwelling in the body (1 Cor. 6:19). Against a backdrop of pervasive temple worship and the idea that the body was not holy, Paul's rhetorical questions about the Spirit living in the body were even more profound. A new owner had taken up residence in their lives—one who had paid a dear price for the temple of their bodies. They were, therefore, to honor and glorify God not simply as assent, belief, or in some mystical or spiritual sense but in their bodies. We, too, are not our own. Christ paid a dear price to free us, and in his death we unite with him. "And God raised the Lord and will also raise us by his power" (1 Cor. 6:14).

When we are washed in the name of Jesus and in the Spirit, God communes with us through his presence. The gift of the Holy Spirit is God's presence in our lives. God has always wanted to dwell among his people in order to experience relationship with them. God created us to share life with us. And even though we rejected his communion in the Garden, God continued to pursue a relationship with us. In Israel, he dwelt among his people in a tabernacle (Lev. 26:11-12) and in a temple (2 Chron. 6:41-7:2). Now, however, God dwells in us through his Spirit (2 Cor. 6:16). Yet, we anticipate a day when God will fully dwell with his people in a new heaven and new earth (Rev. 21:1-4). Divine presence means communion and relationship.

Baptism prepares us for God's presence. Baptism is a means through which God pours out his Spirit and grace through the faith of the one submitting to baptism. Ceremonial washings prepared Israel for God's presence. For example, Israel was baptized in the cloud and in the sea in preparation for God's holy presence at Mt. Sinai (1 Cor. 10:1-4). Priests prepared for God's presence by ceremonial washings (Ex. 29:4; Ps. 26:6; Heb. 10:22; Num. 8:6f). They were purified by water before entering the tabernacle or temple. The priests were cleansed in "The Sea," a 17,500-gallon cast iron bath in the temple courts (1 Chron. 4:1-6). Levitical cleansing was a preparation for God's presence (cf. Heb. 10:22). Levites were not ceremonially washed simply so they could be cleansed. They were being prepared so they could enter the presence of Almighty God.

In a similar way, our baptism is a washing, not the removal of dirt from our bodies (1 Pet. 3:21), but the means through which God prepares us, sanctifies us to be in his presence. We are God's temple. Baptism is a means of God's grace, but the gift is not an end in itself. By God's grace through faith we are justified and brought into a relationship. In baptism we are sanctified for service to God (Eph. 1:11-12; cf. Eph. 2:8-10). Our baptism prepares us for the daily presence of God's Spirit in our lives. We do not enter the temple. Rather, God has entered us and called us his temple. Through cleansing our sinful lives we enter the presence of our holy God. But we are called into his presence for a covenantal relationship, for discipleship.

Discipleship Covenant

In order to renew the discipleship dimension of baptism, we view baptism as part of Christ's missional imperative to make disciples. The command to "make disciples" is for the church, though individuals follow that command. The burden, however, should not simply be on individuals to make decisions for Christ. The church has a burden to make disciples, empowering them through the washing of rebirth, teaching them about the cross and resurrection, about God's redemptive work in us from the beginning. Jesus said to his disciples,

> All authority in heaven and on earth has been given to me. Go therefore and make disciples of all nations, baptizing them in the name of the Father and of the Son and of the Holy Spirit, and teaching them to obey everything that I have commanded you. And remember, I am with you always, to the end of the age. (Matt. 28:18-20)

Christ's call indicates that baptism is vital in the process of making disciples.

Faith leads us to the river and to discipleship. Faith does not stand on the bank and wish to dive in the water. Faith takes the plunge and drowns the old person of sin in the water. Plunging into the divine community of God means we experience a radical shift of identity, lifestyle, and world view. In baptism we appeal to the grace of God and plunge into a journey of following Christ. God enacts a life-changing discipleship bond with us through faith, by means of immersion's connection with the Christ-event, and by the power of the Holy Spirit.

The context of Peter's reference to baptism in 1 Peter 3:21 is his call to arms in the journey of faith. His call is to live for God in the face of great suffering. They have not plunged into the flood of dissipation (1 Pet. 4:4) but in the flood of Noah, that symbolizes their baptism (1 Pet. 3:21). Peter connects the resurrection of Christ with coming through the flood. The promise of Christ's resurrection, the fact that Christ is at God's right hand with angels and all authorities in submission to him, is the basis of Peter's call to arm ourselves with the same attitude of Christ, who suffered in his body. If we suffer for good—with Christ—we also will live, not for evil human desires, but for the will of God (4:2). The one who goes down into "the river of pain" with Christ will be overjoyed when his glory is revealed (4:13). The promise of making it through the flood comes through the resurrection of Christ.

This discipleship covenant concept has shaped our understanding of the reciprocal relationship between the Spirit and us. My (Greg) wife, Jill, and our three children lived in Uganda and ministered there with a mission team of rural and urban church planters and nurturers. Through the gift of discernment of both Ugandans and my fellow mission teammates, we developed a redemptive analogy for baptism. In the Soga region of Uganda, Churches of Christ refer to baptism as "Mukago" (cutting a covenant with Jesus, hereafter covenant). Soga adults universally understand this covenant as a ceremony through which two close friends become siblings by cutting their arms and tasting one another's blood. Through the eyes of their own cultural rite of covenant, baptism into Christ made sense as a relationship bond. In baptism they understood that they were entering a relationship that would bestow blessings but also require covenant faithfulness.

Such a redemptive analogy binds together the ceremony and doctrine of baptism. God wants a covenant with us. On the cross, Christ shed his blood for us. He was the first to draw blood from his own veins in order to cut a covenant with us. We cut a covenant with Jesus Christ. Baptism is not taught in those Ugandan churches as a work but as a covenant—which implies that the response is not only ours but God's. The first cut of the covenant has been done. Our response is the grateful "Yes" to Jesus' covenant already accomplished for us at the cross. Through baptism, God mediates this covenant of grace to us. Karl Barth says the beginning of the Christian life involves "the grateful Yes of man to God's grace."[3] We view baptism as the work of God rather than merely the action of humans—it is primarily a transformational covenant through which God mediates his grace. Baptism is a discipleship covenant.

Empowered by the Spirit

One role of the Holy Spirit is to facilitate the continuing process of sanctification. We are empowered by the Spirit for daily living. The Spirit's work includes regenerating us with new life by the power of Christ's resurrection. We are continually cleansed of sin's guilt by the power of Christ's sacrifice. The Spirit also empowers us with God's strength for the daily journey of dying to self. For that is our life—to die daily to sin and live daily in step with the Spirit (Gal. 5:25). Salvation is both a past action—we are justified—but also a present reality and future hope. It is both a past and future event as well as an ongoing process. The work of God in the past to justify us is continued in the present to mark and seal and give us an inheritance (Eph. 1:13-14). Paul here focuses on the present aspect of salvation—our sanctification by the power of God's Spirit that he poured out on us (cf. Titus 3:6). God has already raised us in the sense that we have been justified and seated with him in heavenly realms. We are transformed by the overwhelming flood of God's mercy, and the present reality is that we are empowered to die daily and live daily.

We cannot live unless we die. In Christ, by faith, we are empowered and continually regenerated by the Spirit. Out of Christ, without faith, we are not empowered and regenerated. We are dead in sin and transgressions (Eph. 2:1f). In Galatians, Paul frames this discussion in terms of a promised inheritance given to the heirs who belong to Christ (Gal. 3:29). All who are children of God through faith, all who are baptized as if putting on Christ, have become heirs according to the promise (Gal. 3:26-29). We are no longer slaves to sin. Instead, God continually bathes us as a parent does a child. The rivers of forgiveness, justification, cleansing, and healing continue to flow. We live by faith as children. Paul says, "And because you are children, God has sent the Spirit of his Son into our hearts, crying, 'Abba! Father!' So you are no longer a slave but a child, and if a child then also an heir, through God" (Gal. 4:6-7). We are not abandoned children but adopted heirs according to the promises of God. And God has always and will always keep his promises. He said he would empower us by his Spirit. Meanwhile, we keep in step. Empowerment means something is demanded. Yet we are not saved to luxuriate in our salvation but are transformed for relationship and service to the one who called us his craftsmanship (Eph. 2:8-10).

Empowered by the Spirit, we are heirs and called to a life worthy of an heir of the Kingdom (cf. Eph. 4:1-3; Phil. 1:27). Those who chose to continue living by the acts of the sinful nature, forfeit the inheritance (Gal. 5:16-21). The Spirit, however, wars with the sinful nature. The one who by faith is made right by God is transformed, given a new identity, new ethic, and new world view, but also empowered by the Spirit to walk in this new kingdom relationship with Christ and the Father. We die daily. The Spirit regenerates us, thus producing fruit in us—our empowerment to keep in step with the Spirit.

> By contrast, the fruit of the Spirit is love, joy, peace, patience, kindness, generosity, faithfulness, gentleness, and self-control. There is no law against such things. And those who belong to Christ Jesus have crucified the flesh with its passions and desires. If we live by the Spirit, let us also be guided by the Spirit. (Gal. 5:22-25)

The fruit of the Spirit has often been described as something we produce, but this is not the picture painted by Paul in Galatians. We do not produce the fruit but the fruit is produced in us. Those who by faith live not under the pedagogue of the law but the Spirit will from our new teacher receive the fruit of the Spirit. We, like students of the Spirit, keep in step with the Spirit. The Spirit is the one who intercedes for us, makes footprints in strides our feeble legs can reach. The Spirit produces fruit in us.

The work of God to justify us is being completed by the sanctifying role of the Holy Spirit. Paul says it is only by the grace of God that "I am what I am" (1 Cor. 15:10). He was motivated by this grace to work hard in service to God—yet he stops in the middle of his sentence to qualify work, "—though it was not I, but the grace of God that is with me" (1 Cor. 15:10). The grace of God motivates us to work, but the work does not save us. The power to will and to act according to God's good purpose comes from the Holy Spirit in us. God empowers us to "work out our salvation with fear and trembling" (Phil. 2:12-13). The phrase, "work out your salvation" is misleading. The verse may appear to contradict Paul's own teaching of grace and salvation but is made more clear by reading it in light of what it follows—the section on imitating Christ's humility (Phil. 2:1-11)—and the continuing phrase, "…for it is God who is at work in you, enabling you both to will and to work for his good pleasure." This is God's activity in us by his Spirit. Paul's language of working out our salvation, then, would read more clearly in light of the context before and after the phrase, as "continue to bring the deliverance of God to completion." God's deliverance grounds sanctification, the Spirit's work in progress. This is the ongoing role of the Holy Spirit, the continual deliverance that God seeks to bring to completion in the end times. So we live in hopeful expectation of this final completion. This expectant living is connected to our deliverance in Christ. For example, Paul repeats the imagery of being raised with Christ in reference to baptism (2:12) to call for holy living:

> So if you have been raised with Christ, seek the things that are above, where Christ is, seated at the right hand of God. Set your minds on things that are above, not on things that are on earth, for you have died, and your life is hidden with Christ in God. When Christ who is your life is revealed, then you also will be revealed with him in glory. (Col. 3:1-4)

Therefore, we are empowered to live the holy life by union with Christ both in death and in his resurrection, and this forms the basis for our new identity, lifestyle, and world view. Our minds, then, are set not on earthly things but on things above.

Conclusion

"Baptism," says William Willimon, "is a lifetime process of God's work in us."[4] Dramatic events such as faith and baptism as well as ordinary daily steps of faith are the road markers of this process of God's work in us. Baptism is an empowering event that embodies in us God's work in Christ. Baptism is not a disjointed command that is held out as separate from the theological truths of the gospel. As such, we risk focusing too much on the external act of baptism and too little on the work of God's Spirit downriver from our baptism. There is power in the blood, power in dying with Christ, power in the initial cleansing in the river. Yet there is also power in the rising that transforms our lives. By faith in Christ we are washed. And God's Spirit continuously renews us. The power of baptism, through faith and the work of God in Christ and the Spirit, is for death and life—death to sin and life for God. We have been justified by God's grace, and the Spirit is poured out on us richly through Jesus Christ our Savior, so that we might become heirs according to the hope of eternal life (Titus 3:7).

So the Holy Spirit leads as children walking with the Father. As God's Spirit led Christ to the wilderness, so the Spirit leads us to a daily death to self. Because of the justifying death of Christ, the power of the resurrection of Christ and his subsequent pouring out of the Spirit of God, we are continuously washed and clothed and seated where we do not deserve to sit—as adopted children. We do not deserve to be the temple of God's Spirit. But if we are cleansed of guilt by faith in Christ, washed and renewed as a priest preparing for entrance into the temple. We are God's temple. The Holy Spirit dwells in us. The transformational covenant is our partnership with God's Spirit: we live by the Spirit, so we keep in step with the Spirit. We are disciples empowered by God's Spirit to walk, die, and live daily in hope. Jesus told his disciples, "I will not leave you orphaned; I am coming to you" (John 14:18). Christ would send the Counselor—the one whose patience is like that of a mother with a suffering child. The Spirit leads us from the banks of the river of pain to live in hope. Those who by faith dive in will also live.

****

Principle

God transforms us to be his temple. His Spirit lives in us, leads us in discipleship, and empowers us to produce Spiritual fruit. This is the transformational covenant, our partnership with God's Spirit. By the power of the Spirit we die and live daily under the new way of the Spirit.

Prayer

Father, how can we keep in step with your Spirit? Are your steps not too far apart for us? Are we not like little children behind you? Carry us. Teach us your ways and empower us to live in the covenant with you. Produce fruit in us in keeping with repentance. We submit to your leadership. Show us how powerless we are to produce that fruit. Then teach us to walk in that new awareness in your steps. Amen.

Questions

1. What is sanctification?

2. How can we focus more on sanctification?

3. How does the Holy Spirit sanctify us?

4. What is the purpose of this sanctification?

5. What is a transformative covenant as defined in this chapter?

6. How does the Holy Spirit help us keep this covenant?

7. If the Holy Spirit has a role in our salvation, what is it?

8. Describe the Holy Spirit's role in empowering us daily?

10 / *Transformed Unimmersed Believers?*

While, then, baptism is ordained for remission of sins, and for no other specific purpose, it is not as a procuring cause, as a meritorious or efficient cause, but as an instrumental cause, in which faith and repentance are developed and made fruitful and effectual in the changing of our state and spiritual relations to the Divine Persons whose names are put upon us in the very act.[1]

—Alexander Campbell

How do I know that any one loves my Master but by his obedience to his commandments? I answer, In no other way. But mark, I do not substitute obedience to one commandment, for universal or even for general obedience...It is the image of Christ the Christian looks for and loves; and this does not consist in being exact in a few items, but in general devotion to the whole truth as far as known.[2]

—Alexander Campbell

Is it possible that the same person could write both of these statements? While "restoring the ancient gospel" with a "high" view of baptism, Campbell also recognized that it was not *the* divine command. The general obedience of faith through transformed living in conformity to the image of Christ was more important than the misunderstanding, misapplication and misappropriation of the single command to be immersed.

****

We have articulated a "high" view of immersion. Does this mean that transformed unimmersed believers are excluded from divine grace? Is immersion a line in the sand? Is it a watershed that divides heaven and hell?

In our view baptism is deeply connected with the nature of faith. Faith is the instrument by which we receive God's grace, and baptism participates in that instrumentality. Baptism, as a means of grace through faith, is theocentric rather than anthropocentric. God works through baptism and his saving work is associated with baptism: forgiveness, justification, sanctification, transformation, resurrection, purification, and the gift of the Spirit. Through faith baptism is God's transforming work.

We have attempted to articulate a biblical understanding of baptism as a converting and transforming moment. In Luke-Acts, baptism is part of the conversion narrative where people turn to God in faith and repentance. The Spirit is poured out upon new converts in connection with baptism. Faith, repentance, baptism and the filling with the Spirit form a narrative event through which God initiates people into his community. In Paul, baptism is a reference point for union with Christ, in whom are all the benefits of redemption and salvation. It is a transition, through faith, from death to life. Through baptism we die to sin and are made alive in Christ.

The New Testament does not know any "unbaptized" Christians. The consensus of the church for the first fifteen hundred years was that baptism was necessary for salvation, though there were exceptions (e.g., the martyrdom of catechumens). Despite the fact that an anthropocentric, symbolic understanding of baptism emerged in the sixteenth century (Zwingli), it was not until the rise of revivalism in the eighteenth and nineteenth centuries that the exclusion of baptism from conversion narratives became prominent. In particular, American revivalistic Christianity portrayed "conversion" as something that happened before baptism through religious experience (e.g., the Methodist revivalist Charles Finney) or the "sinner's prayer" (e.g., R. A. Torrey).[3] Nevertheless, even American revivalism urged new believers to be baptized and every Christian group, with few exceptions (e.g., Quakers), practices some form of baptism.

Consequently, we find several competing conversion narratives on the contemporary landscape. One conversion narrative begins with infant baptism. Baptism admits them into the church and they become part of a nurturing community of faith. Conversion is thus understood as divine initiation into the community, subsequent confirmation and a life-long maturation. Another conversion narrative focuses on the "born again" experience through the "sinner's prayer." This is the dominant Evangelical model that has its roots in Puritanism and revivalism. Baptism is not part of the conversion narrative but is a symbolic testimony to the saving experience of faith. In this narrative believers are saved before they are baptized, though rarely do any remain "unbaptized." Another conversion narrative, the one articulated in this book, includes both faith and baptism. Baptism participates in the function of faith as a means of grace and is part of the conversion narrative. The conversion experience is incomplete without baptism.

The first two narratives stand in tension with the biblical picture as we have drawn it. On the one hand, we believe faith is necessary to the function and meaning of baptism. Consequently, infant baptism has no place in the conversion narrative. As a result, in our view, many in contemporary Christian communities—as well as the church as a whole since the fifth century—have not fully participated in the biblical conversion narrative. On the other hand, we also believe that baptism is part of the conversion narrative. Consequently, in our view, those who believe that the conversion narrative is complete without baptism do not fully articulate a biblical conversion narrative. Tension clearly exists among professing Christians—between those baptized as infants, those who articulate a conversion narrative without baptism though they are subsequently baptized, and those who see faith-baptism as their conversion narrative. All agree, however, that baptism is part of the Christian faith, though there is disagreement about its role in the conversion narrative.[4]

In this chapter we consider the question of how we should view those on either side of this tension. As advocates of faith-baptism in the conversion narrative, how should we treat those who see the conversion narrative differently? If faith-baptism is part of the conversion narrative, should we regard those who were baptized without faith or those whose do not understand baptism to be part of the conversion narrative as authentic believers and fellow travelers on the path of Christ? Does our "high" view of faith-baptism mean we regard others who disagree with our understanding of baptism's role in the conversion narrative as excluded from the grace of God?

At root, we believe this is a hermeneutical discussion, not a heart problem. The present tension is the result of centuries of tradition and debate over particular texts in Scripture. We must approach the discussion with hermeneutical humility, recognizing that not only are we influenced by those centuries but also that our conclusions are open to criticism and subject to Scripture. But while the form, subject and meaning of baptism is debated among professing Christians, in the light of Scripture and historic Christian tradition none should be considered disciples of Christ who refuse to be baptized and reject baptism as God's command.

We understand that ultimately this is God's judgment. God decides who are his. God will include whomever he wants. However, this does not address how we should treat believers who do not share our conversion narrative but affirm baptism differently. Do we treat them as genuine or false believers? How should they treat us, especially if they view our perspectives as legalistic and sectarian? While we cannot make God's decision for him, we do have to decide how we treat each other as fellow believers in Christ. For that reason we believe this chapter is necessary.

The Process of Transformation

While our question is how those who believe faith-baptism is part of the conversion narrative should treat those who do not, the answer to that question is not found in a narrow treatment of the biblical texts regarding baptism. We need to place the question in the larger narrative of God's redemptive story. Ultimately, the answer must arise out of the heart, intent and goal of God. The broad strokes of God's story provide the context for understanding and applying the particulars. The broader story should shape any particular understanding of God's demands or commands.

While we cannot rehearse the full dimensions of God's story in this brief chapter, we must understand God's goal. God created humanity to share his loving communion. He created us to share his fellowship and enjoy his life. But humanity rejected this offer. Instead of joining God in his story, we created our own stories and sought our own interests. We degenerated. Instead of reflecting God's glory, we fell short of it (Rom. 3:23). We failed to image God's life in our own lives. Nevertheless, God still yearns for us and pursues us with an unrelenting love. He still wants to share his life with us. Consequently, throughout history God has acted and continues to act redemptively. He called Abraham, created Israel, sent his Son and poured out his Spirit. God seeks a people for himself among whom he can dwell in holy fellowship.[5]

God's goal, then, is to dwell with his people (cf. Rev. 21:3). To this end God works to transform fallen humanity into his image. Just as God created us in his image, so now he seeks to restore that image. Paul succinctly summarizes God's intent in Romans 8:29, "For those whom he foreknew he also predestined to be conformed to the image of his Son." God desires the full conformity of his people to his image. In the end God will conform us to the image of his Son in both body and spirit (cf. Phil. 3:21), but even now we "are being transformed into the same image from one degree of glory to another" by his Spirit (2 Cor. 3:18). By the power of God we pursue and are engaged in the process of transformation into the image of Christ.

Salvation, then, is not simply about the forgiveness of sins but about formation into the image of God. Forgiveness is a means toward the end of transformation. God forgives so that we may share God's holy life. Salvation is not fundamentally about crossing a line in the sand marked "saved," but about the process of being conformed to the image of Christ.

This perspective is important because it shapes how we read Scripture. In particular, it shapes how we read "commands" in

Scripture. Are "commands" fundamentally legal tests of loyalty or are they modes of transformation? When we read biblical "commands" as legal tests of loyalty irrespective of faith and moral transformation, then we reduce obedience in God's redemptive story to "crossing lines in the sand." For example, Michael Hughes defended the following proposition in an online debate: "If a repentant, confessing believer in Jesus Christ has fully committed himself/herself to being obedient to Christ Jesus in baptism, but dies unexpectedly prior to actually complying with that command (due to circumstances beyond his/her control), that person will be condemned to eternal punishment in hell."[6] Obedience viewed in this way becomes a mechanical "jumping through the hoops" by which we comply with the command's legalities. In this instance, obedience becomes a "check list" of requirements. But when we read "commands" as modes of transformation, obedience is part of God's transformation of character by the mediation of his presence. Obedience becomes identification with God's values and community. In this understanding, obedience has relational meaning. It is about shared life with God. The former approach understands "command" as a legal technicality, but the latter understands it as a mode of relational transformation.

Baptism should be understood as a mode of relational transformation. When baptism becomes a "line in the sand," then we have transformed it into something God never intended. We reduce his transforming work to a legal detail as if the whole of God's work in a person's life stands or falls on this one command. Indeed, when baptism becomes a legal watershed that divides the world between those who can go to heaven and those who cannot, we exalt baptism over transformation. When we exalt the means over the end we turn baptism into a legal technicality rather than a mode of divine transformation.

This way of reading Scripture misconstrues the heart of God. It pictures God as the judge of legal technicalities rather than the parental mentor who transforms us through loving guidance. God is not the God of technicalities, but the Father who lovingly pursues us and is gracious with our mistakes. This is the theological trajectory found within the biblical narrative to which we now turn our attention.

Theological Trajectories in Scripture

The relationship between transformation by faith and baptism is part of the broad relationship between faith and ritual in Scripture. "Ritual" is not necessarily negative. We have used the term "ritual" throughout this book to describe how God mediates his grace through concrete, external ordinances. We have used it in a fundamentally positive sense. Unfortunately, the word has come to mean something merely formal, external and rote. This negative connotation projects staleness, boredom and meaninglessness. This association misses the fuller, fundamentally positive notion of ritual. Ritual mediates the presence of God. It is not a lifeless, dead custom, but a divinely prescribed concrete moment through which God works his redemptive presence among his people.

Sacrifice, for example, was a ritual in Israel. But it was neither lifeless nor meaningless. On the contrary, it mediated God's reconciling presence among his people. Through sacrifice God's people entered into covenant with him, experienced forgiveness through the atoning blood, and enjoyed God's fellowship.

The Sabbath was another ritual in Israel. It was a day of rest that participated in God's own rest on the seventh day. This holy day mediated God's presence as God's people rested in God's redemptive blessings and enjoyed his peace. The Sabbath command was important in Israel as a "holy convocation" (Lev. 23:3), and the penalty for its violation was severe (e.g., Ex. 31:15).

In this sense baptism is also a ritual. It is an external sign through which God mediates his presence. The water of baptism is an effective sign of God's redemptive work in the death and resurrection of Christ. Through baptism we experience God's forgiveness and sanctifying presence. Baptism is connected with God's saving work in Christ.

But ritual is only important as it relates to God's ultimate goal and intent. Ritual serves the goal rather than *vice versa*. It participates in the journey toward the goal and thus is a means to an end. And the end is more important than the means. Several exemplary narratives in Scripture underscore the importance of this principle. They illustrate the principle that God values a seeker's heart and benevolent mercy more than ritual.

Heart Over Ritual—The Case of Hezekiah's Passover

The Passover was one of the most important festivals in Israel's worship. It celebrated Israel's redemption from Egyptian slavery. As a ritual, it was central to Israel's identity. The Exodus marked off Israel as a nation redeemed by God. As they crossed the Red Sea on dry ground, they were "baptized into Moses" (1 Cor. 10:1).

When Hezekiah began his reign as King of Judah, the temple had been closed for several years (2 Chron. 29:7). When the temple was cleansed, Hezekiah invited "all Israel and Judah" to celebrate the Passover at the newly rededicated temple (2 Chron. 30:1).[7] However, Hezekiah celebrated the Passover in the wrong month. Though the Law prescribed the first month, Hezekiah celebrated it in the "second month" (2 Chron. 30:2). While many think Hezekiah is following the "Second Passover" law of Numbers 9:2-14 which permits those who are unclean at the time of the first month to celebrate the Passover in the second month once they are clean, the text of Chronicles does not explain the rationale in this light. Hezekiah recognizes that his plan is irregular but he justifies it because "priests had not sanctified themselves in sufficient number" for the celebration in the first month and the people were not yet "assembled in Jerusalem" (2 Chron. 30:3). Chronicles' rationale for the irregularity does not invoke Numbers 9 and the rationale includes more than Numbers 9 permits. Numbers 9 permits a second Passover but it does not permit a wholesale abrogation of the first. Thus, grace took precedence over prescribed dates.

But may unclean people eat the Passover? Unclean people ate what was clean. This was a clear violation of the Law. Chronicles clearly states that they "ate the Passover contrary to what was written" (2 Chron. 30:18, NIV).

Some have invoked Numbers 9 as a specific authorization for this irregularity, but it does not address this situation. The presumption of Numbers 9 is that those who eat a "second Passover" will be clean when they eat it. Numbers 9 does not authorize unclean people to eat the Passover. Hezekiah's celebration not only violates Numbers 9, but also Leviticus 7:19-21 regarding sacrificial meals. The penalty for such a violation was death.

But Hezekiah prays for the people. The prayer appeals to the gracious promise of God in 2 Chronicles 6-7 (especially 7:14).

God accepts anyone who seeks him "even though" they do not seek him "in accordance with the sanctuary's rules of cleanness." The critical point is orientation—those "who set their hearts to seek God" (2 Chron. 30:19). This phrase combines two important words in Chronicles: "heart" and "seeking." The two terms are linked in 1 Chronicles 16:10; 22:19; 28:9; 2 Chronicles 11:16; 12:14; 15:12,15; 19:3; 22:9; 30:19 and 31:21. "Seek" (translating two Hebrew synonyms) appears fifty-four times in Chronicles and "heart" (translating two Hebrew synonyms) appears sixty-four times. God seeks hearts that seek him. God takes the initiative and seeks out those hearts that yearn for him and trust him (cf. Heb. 11:6; Matt. 6:33; John 4:23-24).

Hezekiah prays for the forgiveness of those who violated the divine ritual out of a heart that sought God. The guiding principles of the prayer are two: (1) the goodness of God who seeks a people for himself (1 Chron. 28:9; 29:14-17) and (2) the orientation of the heart toward God. Hezekiah roots his prayer in God's forgiving nature. Those whose hearts seek God are received, even though they transgress his ritual prescriptions, because God is "good."

God accepted unclean worshippers because they had a heart to seek him. The text explicitly records, as if to emphasize the legitimacy of Hezekiah's request, that "the Lord heard Hezekiah and healed the people" (the promise of 2 Chron. 7:14). Significantly, Chronicles commends Hezekiah's Passover renewal in 2 Chronicles 31:21: "every work that he undertook…to seek his God, he did with all his heart." Even though he admitted ritually unclean people to the Passover, his Passover is described as wholehearted because he sought God in everything.

Why would Hezekiah expect God to forgive this? Was it not clear in the Law that unclean people who eat sacrificial meals should be punished? Did not God forbid unclean people to eat the Passover? Perhaps even some of Hezekiah's priests could have objected that if they permitted unclean people to eat the Passover that God would judge them and reject their Passover. But Hezekiah knew his God. He knew God's compassion, grace and goodness toward those who seek him out of a genuine heart of faith. Hezekiah knew that faith was more important than the rules of the ritual. God accepted the heart rather than the ritual because the heart is more important than the ritual. A faith that seeks God is more important than technical obedience to ritual. The process of transformation is more important than a particular ritualistic act. Mercy has always been more important than sacrifice (Hos. 6:6).

Mercy Over Sacrifice—the Sabbath Controversy in Matthew

The importance of Sabbath in Israel can hardly be questioned. Indeed, the Law prescribed severe penalties for those who violated it (Ex. 31:15). Consequently, Sabbath-keeping was serious business in Israel. As a ritual, it mediated God's own Sabbath. Israel rested with God on that day. To violate the Sabbath was to reject God's gracious gift of his own rest.

Unfortunately, some in Jesus' day viewed the Sabbath through legal lenses rather than relational ones.[8] They regarded the Sabbath as a technical legality rather than a relational enjoyment of God's presence. While they may have valued the relational dimension, when they prioritized the legality, they denied the relationality. The Pharisees in Matthew 12:1-14 subjected Jesus and his disciples to this technical critique and Jesus rebuked them. Indeed, he sought to re-orient their reading of the Sabbath institution. He pointed to the relational function of the Sabbath rather than its legal technicality.

As the disciples passed through a field, they plucked some heads of grain and ate them. The Pharisees pointed out that what they were doing was unlawful on the Sabbath (Matt. 12:2). The disciples were in legal violation of the Sabbath, even though they did this because they "were hungry" (Matt. 12:1). The disciples, apparently, were not presumptuously breaking the Sabbath, but acting out of human need.

Jesus does not dispute the illegality of the violation. Indeed, Jesus compares the disciples' actions with David's in 1 Samuel 21:1-6. Just as the disciples ate what was "unlawful" because they were "hungry," David also ate what was "unlawful" because he was "hungry" (Matt. 12:2-4). Jesus justifies his disciples on the same principle that justified David's eating the bread that only priests should eat.[9] David violated a ritual technicality by eating the bread of presence in the tabernacle. Nevertheless, David was justified because he was hungry. Human need was more important than ritual technicality. Human life (and thus transformation) is more important than ritual. One cannot use the Sabbath to deny mercy or doing good (Matt. 12:7, 12).

Jesus' fundamental justification is found in Matthew 12:7. Quoting Hosea 6:6, "I desire mercy not sacrifice," Jesus appeals to the underlying principle by which to judge what is lawful and unlawful on the Sabbath. This hermeneutical principle should govern the use and misuse of ritual. Basically Jesus rebukes the Pharisees for even needing the example he offered them. If they had understood that God desires "mercy, and not sacrifice," they never would have accused the disciples of doing anything unlawful.

Several points reveal the significance of this quotation. First, Jesus has previously quoted Hosea 6:6 in Matthew's account (9:13). Jesus justified eating with Matthew's unclean friends by an appeal to Hosea 6:6. Second, the word "mercy" also occurs in Matthew 23:23 when Jesus identifies it as one of the "weightier matters" of the Law. "Mercy" is more important than Pharisaic strictures on tithing. Third, "mercy" is identified as more important than both "sacrifice" and Sabbath. Fourth, Jesus applies this principle to the Sabbath. He concludes that it is lawful "to do good" on the Sabbath as a function of mercy (Matt. 12:12). "To do good" in Jewish literature is an act of benevolence or mercy (cf. Gal. 6:10; James 4:17). One may violate (desecrate) the Sabbath in order to show mercy; benevolence takes precedence over the rituals of the Sabbath. When the Pharisees objected that the disciples should not eat on the Sabbath, they exalted the Sabbath over mercy and thus turned the Sabbath into a legal technicality that denied mercy.

Sacrifice and Sabbath were essential and necessary rituals in the faith of Israel. They were neither unimportant nor optional. But both are subordinate to the principle of mercy. The rituals serve the goal of transformation. They serve mercy rather than vice versa.

The ritual is not the most important thing. The Sabbath was made for humanity, not humanity for the Sabbath (cf. Mark 2:23-3:6). Ritual is made for humanity, not humanity for ritual. Rituals serve the ends for which God has designed them. They were not designed to deny mercy to the heart that seeks God.

Transformation Over Technicalities

God's goal is transformation into the image of Christ. Everything else serves that end. Rituals teach us something about God and mediate the divine presence in ways that shape the character and community of God's people. They are positive, helpful and healthy dimensions of our life with God. Baptism as an immersion ritual of death and life roots believers in the death and resurrection of Christ and empowers their transformation into new life.

Hence, ritual prescriptions must remain in a subservient role. They must serve God's goal. When some asked Jesus what the greatest commands were, Jesus quoted Deuteronomy 6:4 and Leviticus 19:18 (Mark 12:29-31). The greatest command was to love God with all your heart and the second was to love your neighbor as yourself. When the inquirer heard this, he answered Jesus approvingly: "'To love him with all the heart, with all the understanding and with all the strength,' and to 'love one's neighbor as oneself'—this is much more important than all whole burnt offerings and sacrifices" (Mark 12:33).

To love God and your neighbor is more important than ritual. It is more important than sacrifice, Sabbath or baptism. We must place these in the right order or else we will exalt baptism over love for God and neighbor. If we reverse the order or even coordinate them so that they are equivalents, we will deny mercy while affirming sacrifice. We deny a person's love for God when we make baptism more important than a transformed life.

But if we love God, will we not keep his commandments (cf. John 15:9-17; Deut. 10:12-13)? Absolutely! Whoever loves God will seek to obey him in everything. But in the context of John 15 and Deuteronomy 10 we need to remember that the fundamental command is to love God and love each other (John 15:17). We love God when we love each other. Obedience is the fruit of loving God and that fruit is transformed living. Rituals are part of obedience, but they are secondary to transformation.

God seeks hearts that seek him, and God transforms people who seek him. God is not the supervisor of technicalities who denies mercy to those who seek him but have mistaken his rituals through ignorance, weakness or other non-rebellious circumstances. God values the transformed life above all else. We must not deny mercy to those whose transformed lives God values simply because they have not conformed to our understanding of a divine ritual.

Therefore, God values a transformed life more than he values baptism. This does not render baptism unimportant, unnecessary or meaningless. Baptism is God's transforming work, but God values the goal of baptism more than baptism itself. God will work toward the goal even when baptism is misunderstood and misapplied as long as the heart seeks God and does not neglect or rebel against what one believes God requires.

Common Questions

Those of us in the Stone-Campbell tradition who hold a high view of baptism are passionate about our understanding. We believe it is biblical and we resist any deflation of baptism's significance because we believe it is so devalued in much of contemporary Evangelicalism. It is understandable, then, that when we have presented the views in this chapter on various occasions some common and persistent questions are raised. These questions are legitimate and deserve attention.

1. Doesn't your position deny the plain teaching of Scripture that baptism is a means of salvation and thus undermines the importance of baptism so as to render it unnecessary?

Was sacrifice unnecessary just because it was less important than mercy? Was the Sabbath unimportant just because human needs took precedence over it? Were the purity rules of the Passover unimportant just because the heart took precedence over them?

We affirm that baptism is a means of grace and that its importance is connected to salvation and transformation. The biblical conversion narrative involved faith, baptism, the forgiveness of sins and the gift of the Spirit. We affirm and teach this.

But we recognize that faith and mercy are more important than baptism. We affirm Jesus' point that God values mercy more than sacrifice. God chose the faith of those who sought him over their uncleanness at the Passover. In the same way, God chooses faith over baptism in those whose hearts seek him though they misunderstand or misapply baptismal teaching. Indeed, recognizing the relationship between faith and ritual means that we place baptism in its intended role rather than assigning it a significance that outweighs faith and transformation.

Baptism is no less important than sacrifice and Sabbath in Israel's faith. But it is no more necessary than sacrifice and Sabbath were in Israel's faith. Jesus teaches us to choose mercy over sacrifice without devaluing the significance of sacrifice. Consequently, we acknowledge that faith is more important than baptism without devaluing the significance of baptism.

2. Isn't your analogy misguided because faith and baptism are so inextricably connected unlike the rituals of the Old Testament? In other words, is baptism legitimately categorized as a ritual in the same sense that sacrifices and Sabbath are?

Faith and baptism are deeply related to each other. They are connected at every level so that even what is assigned to faith (e.g., remission of sins in Acts 10:43) is connected to baptism (e.g., remission of sins in Acts 2:38). They are united in their meaning and significance. However, one is more foundational or fundamental than the other. Faith renders baptism effective (cf. Col. 2:12) and baptism participates in the instrumentality of faith as the means of grace. Baptism serves faith. Faith does not serve baptism. Baptism was made for faith rather than faith for baptism. Consequently, faith must have priority and so we value faith more than baptism. This does not devalue baptism because its value derives from God's work through faith.

The rituals of Israel mediated the presence of God among them. They were externals but they were no mere symbols. Through the Sabbath, the people enjoyed the rest of God. Through sacrifice, they experienced divine forgiveness. But the effectiveness of these rituals was rooted in faith. Sacrifice without faith was meaningless. Faith was as necessary to these rituals in Israel as it is to baptism.

Nevertheless, when circumstances dictated, faith was accepted even when the ritual was not perfectly performed. The heart that seeks God is more important than eating the Passover clean. Mercy was more important than sacrifice and the Sabbath. God accepted faith even when it did not rigidly or technically comply with the rituals. We believe God calls us to view baptism the same way.

3. If the Holy Spirit is given in the context of or in connection with baptism, how can we speak of unimmersed transformed people without the Holy Spirit?

We affirm a strong connection between baptism and the reception of the indwelling Spirit of God. The baptism of Jesus is paradigmatic. Just as Jesus received the Spirit as he came up out of the water, so God gives the Spirit to the baptized. In Luke-Acts the Spirit is given in the context of baptism. When the Spirit is given before baptism, then it is expected that those who so received the Spirit will be baptized (Acts 10). When the Spirit is not given at baptism, it is expected that they should receive the Spirit to confirm their incorporation into the community of faith (Acts 8). Baptism and the gift of the Spirit are part of a single conversion narrative (Acts 2:38; 5:32). We are baptized in the Spirit (1 Cor. 6:11; 12:13), renewed by the Spirit in the washing of regeneration (Titus 3:5-6) and born of water and the Spirit (John 3:5).

While we affirm this strong connection, we do not limit the work of God's transforming Spirit. While we affirm the unity of a birth of water and the Spirit in God's intention (John 3:5), we also affirm that the Spirit is free to blow wherever God wills (John 3:8). Jesus teaches that the Spirit of God is free to transform and give birth, as he desires. Just as God was not limited by ritual to work his saving will in the Old Testament, he is not limited to baptism in his transforming work. The Spirit may transform whomever he desires whenever he desires through faith. Just as God normally gave his presence to the ritually clean at Passover, God is not limited to the ritually clean. God may work through faith, through hearts that seek him, for transformation.

We rejoice in the promise of God that those who are baptized receive the indwelling Spirit. By that promise we are assured that God is at work in our hearts by his Spirit to transform us into the image of Jesus. We are grateful for the word of promise that is attached to baptism, just as Israel was grateful to the word of promise attached to sacrifice and Sabbath. But we must not limit God's work to a ritual when a fundamental hermeneutical principle in the story of God exalts faith over ritual and mercy over sacrifice.

When people confess faith in Christ, seek God with their whole heart and exhibit transformed lives, we recognize the fruit of the Spirit in them. God is glorified by their lives because they reflect the transformation that is God's goal. We cannot judge the heart, but we can see the fruits. God is more interested in the process and goal of transformation than in technical obedience to one of his prescribed rituals.

4. Doesn't God's call for strict obedience and his punishment of people for their disobedience undermine your position? If God calls for obedience (cf. Matt. 7:21), is he not concerned about strict conformity to his laws?

Is "obedience" equivalent to "technical, perfectionistic, ritual observance"? Certainly, to conduct a ritual as prescribed is obedience. To be immersed for the remission of sins upon a confession of faith is obedience. But is the significance of obedience technical in character or relational?

God desires obedience. He demands it. When Saul returned with animals to sacrifice after failing to comply with God's command in 1 Samuel 15, his intent to sacrifice was not accepted because he was disobedient. Samuel rebuked Saul: "to obey is better than sacrifice and to heed than the fat of rams" (1 Sam.15:22). God will not accept sacrifice without obedience. But Samuel's point was not about the technicalities of ritual. Rather, it concerned Saul's heart and intent. Saul overtly rejected the Lord's word to him and refused to comply with what he knew was the clear word of God. Saul's problem was a lack of transformation. His disobedience arose out of a rebellious heart of unbelief. He deliberately disobeyed what he knew to be God's command.

Matthew 7:21 calls for obedience. We cannot call Jesus "Lord" and yet refuse to do the will of the Father. Some claimed that they had done wonderful things in the name of the Lord (prophecy, exorcisms, healing). Though they had acknowledged God in their gifts, they had not done the will of the Father. Obedience in this context is submission to the kingdom ethics of the Sermon on the Mount. To do the will of the Father is to be like the Father (Matt. 6:48). Obedience in Matthew 7:21 is transformation into the image of the Father. God is more concerned about transformation than he is ritual.

But did not God reject people who violated the technicalities of ritual in their disobedience? Uzzah, Nadab and Abihu were struck dead, and Uzziah was afflicted with leprosy. But these incidents are no mere technical violations. These acts arose out of indifferent or rebellious hearts. Nadab and Abihu rebelliously contradicted the command of God by taking the fire from a place other than God prescribed and then offered God illegitimate fire while they were drunk (cf. Lev. 10:1-2, 9). Later that day, their family failed to follow the ritual prescriptions of the Law when they did not eat the sin offering. But Aaron explained to Moses that they could not eat because they were in mourning and this rationale was accepted. Mourning was more important than obedience to the prescribed ritual (Lev. 10:16-20). Rebellion was the reason for Nadab and Abihu's deaths rather than ritual perfectionism.

Uzziah arrogantly entered the temple to offer incense when only priests were permitted to do so. Uzziah's problem was not simply a matter of technical obedience. Uzziah disobeyed out of a prideful heart that did not heed the warning of the priests. The Hebrew text uses a succession of conjunctions (*waw*) to note the progression from pride to his arrogant act in the temple: "and his pride [literally, his heart was great]...and he was unfaithful...and he entered the temple" (2 Chron. 26:16, NIV). One led to the other. The technical violation in the temple was the result of previous pride and unfaithfulness. He was not punished for a mere technical violation. On the contrary, he was judged for the heart that exhibited this arrogant and rebellious disobedience.

Uzzah was part of an unholy convocation, and he dared to touch the presence of God. He died "before God" (1 Chron. 13:10). While we do not have any language in the text about Uzzah's heart or intention, when we read this narrative in the larger framework of the Chronicler's theology, Uzzah is not punished for a technicality. The Chronicler's theology is rooted in the idea that God accepts hearts that seek him and forsakes those who forsake him (e.g., 1 Chron. 28:9; 2 Chron. 15:2). God forsook Uzzah, but he did not forsake David. David and the priests also violated the technicalities of the Law, but they were not punished. David convened this assembly on the analogy of a pagan procession. The ark was put on a cart instead of carried with poles (cf. Num. 4:15). The Levites had not consecrated themselves according to the Law (cf. 1 Chron. 15:12-13). Indeed, David took responsibility for the whole fiasco (1 Chron. 15:13, NIV, "...the Lord our God broke out in anger against us. We did not inquire of him about how to do it in the prescribed way"). David was in technical violation of the Law. Nevertheless, neither David nor the Levites were struck down but only Uzzah. Why?

Presumably, Uzzah went too far as he treated something holy (the divine presence) with disrespect as part of an unholy procession. Uzzah touched what the Law specifically said he should not touch. And he acted, not on impulse, but in disrespect as part of a larger group that dishonored God. His act was the ultimate act of disrespect and God judged him in ways that he did not judge David or the Levites who also participated in the unholy procession. The heart rather than a technicality is the culprit. Within the theology of Chronicles, God forsook Uzzah because Uzzah had forsaken him (cf. 1 Chron. 28:9; 2 Chron. 15:2).[10] Apparently, this was not true of David or the Levites in the procession. They had not forsaken God even though they were also in technical violation of the Law.

Why was not Hezekiah's ritual violation punished with death, as in the case of Uzzah? Hezekiah's prayer (2 Chron. 30:18-20) answers the question and reveals the essence of the Chronicler's theology of worship. God, who is compassionate and good, receives those whose hearts seek him. The principle Hezekiah articulates in this prayer is that the heart makes the difference, not ritualistic technicalities. Uzzah's action arose out of a different motive than Hezekiah's, and thus God treated them differently.

When God is pictured as one who judges his people simply because they violate the technicalities of a ritual, the nature of God's holiness is seriously misunderstood. God is not searching for technical law-breakers; he is searching for hearts that seek him. He punishes those who rebelliously violate his commands but forgives those who seek him, even when they seek him in ritually imperfect ways. The heart is more important than ritual; obedience as transformation is more important than obedience as ritual.

5. How would you respond to people who ask what they must do to be saved?

The conversion narratives in Acts provide models for us. We would tell them to trust Jesus as their savior, repent of their sins and be immersed for the forgiveness of sins (Acts 2:38; 3:19;

16:13). We would not tell them to pray the "sinner's prayer." Rather, we would ask believers to call on the name of the Lord by being immersed in order to wash away their sins (Acts 22:16). Baptism is the sinner's prayer. It is the appeal of faith to God's promise of redemption through Jesus Christ. We go down in the river to pray as we call upon the name of the Lord who forgives our sins as we are immersed into Christ. This is, we believe, the normative or ideal picture of the New Testament, and this is what we teach people who seek Jesus.

But we do not think we can use this normative picture to deny mercy to those whose hearts seek God through Jesus and exhibit the fruits of the Spirit though they have misunderstood God's immersion ritual. We do not deny mercy to one whose life is transformed because this is God's ultimate interest. God chooses mercy over sacrifice, and he calls us to understand that principle as we continue the process of transformation together.

6. How do you relate to friends who were sprinkled as babies but yet appear to exhibit the fruits of the Spirit? What would you teach them about baptism?

We have many friends in this situation. Because of their profession of faith in Christ and because they manifest the divine work of transformation in their lives, we accept them as believers in the process of transformation. They are on a journey toward God. They experience God's transforming work by the Spirit and serve him in numerous ways.

Part of the process of transformation, however, is coming to a clearer understanding of God's work in our lives, including God's work through baptism. Consequently, we would gently but boldly teach them the view of baptism we have outlined in this book. We would affirm that baptism is God's transforming work and explain what we believe is the fuller significance of baptism for faith, discipleship and transformation. We would hope that we could persuade them to fully embrace a biblical theology of baptism and be immersed upon a confession of faith. However, their previous life of faith would not be de-legitimized by baptism. Rather, it is a fuller and more biblical expression of that faith.

We believe their situation is analogous to Apollos in Acts 18:24-26. He taught Jesus right, but baptism wrong. This did not de-legitimize his faith, but neither was he fully mature in his understanding of baptism. He was on a journey of faith and he grew in his understanding with the help of Priscilla and Aquila.

We also believe their situation is analogous to our own. We are not aware of all our sins and misunderstandings. Through faith we trust that God will forgive our ignorance, misunderstandings and misapplications. We also trust that God will forgive other believers of their ignorance as well, including their honest misunderstandings and misapplications of baptism. Since we are confident that God will accept the integrity of our hearts through faith in Christ, we believe God will also accept others with that same heart orientation. The grace God extends to us we should extend to others.

And we all need grace. While emphasizing the importance of baptism, some have failed to emphasize the significance of the Holy Spirit in transformation (and the Holy Spirit gets more "print" in Acts than does baptism). We need grace as we all struggle with significant theological and ethical issues such as pacifism or the meaning of "laying on of hands" in Hebrews 6:2 (which is part of the "ABCs" of the Christian faith). We need grace because we are not perfect and we receive grace from God through faith in Christ. In the same way we also extend grace to fellow believers in Christ whose lives manifest the fruit of transformed living though they have misunderstood or misapplied the Christian immersion ritual.

We are on the same journey with transformed, though unimmersed, believers. We both walk along the river. As we walk together, we can teach each other more about the path we walk. We would hope to teach the unimmersed to embrace the fullness of a biblical baptismal theology. They, we are sure, would hope to teach us a few things as well.

****

Principle

God alone knows the heart, but God has revealed that the heart is more important than ritual obedience. We value and give thanks to God for the transformed lives of those with whom we disagree on the topic of baptism, but at the same time we call all to a biblical understanding and practice of baptism.

Prayer

Father, truly you are the only one who knows the heart. We ask you, Lord, to search the heart of all who seek you and to hear the yearnings of their hearts and heal them. You alone are sovereign over salvation, and you will show mercy to whomever you desire. You are a gracious and compassionate God. We pray the prayer of Hezekiah for all those who seek you. We ask you to show your mercy to everyone who seeks you with their heart, just as we ask for mercy for ourselves despite all our misperceptions of your will. Give us the heart to show your mercy to others just as you have shown your mercy to us. Amen.

Questions

1. When we fail to value the transformed life of another because they are unimmersed, have we exalted immersion over the divine goal of transformation?

2. What do you think is the strongest point of this chapter and/or the weakest point in this chapter? Why?

3. How do you regard friends and family who disagree with you on the subject of baptism but evidence faith in Jesus in almost every other way?

4. Do you believe the ideas expressed in this chapter are a departure from or uphold ideals from the Stone-Campbell heritage? Why is that important or unimportant to you?

11 / Mixed Bathing: Baptism and the Church

The poor Negro folks who were to be baptized didn't have anything but a tent, and the white folks had the only available baptistry…The Lord had moved in the hearts of a few white Christians in such a powerful way that they said that their Negro friends would be more than welcome. Before the baptismal service was over, police came to put a stop to it…

The Lord's church was branded as a communist front organization where whites and Negroes socialized as brothers. The community systematically boycotted the business establishments of some of the Christians for months, nearly causing them to go bankrupt.

I grew up in that community. I saw firsthand the kind of social paranoia that caused the Jews to hate Jesus and nail Him to a tree.[1]

Carl Spain was a "rising star" of the Abilene Christian College faculty and a minister of the Hillcrest Church of Christ.[2] At a 1960 lectureship in Abilene, he spoke out against the college's anti-integration policy. "We are…suggesting that we offer Christian education to all Americans without respect of persons," he said. Education was not the only problem. In parts of the Southern United States in the mid-twentieth century, baptism of blacks and whites in the same baptistry was prohibited just as drinking from the same water fountain was. There was no mixed bathing—or baptizing. In this chapter we discern the church's commission to call disciples of Christ from a mixed-up world.

****

We go down in the river together: Jews and Gentiles, men and women, slaves and free, black and white, murderers and white liars. When we are baptized into Christ, the head of the church, we are also baptized into his body, the ragtag yet holy people of faith. We are included, says Paul, in the body of Christ when we are baptized (1 Cor. 12:13), added to the number of those who believe, says Luke (Acts 2:41). In baptism we are initiated into the kingdom of God and into the community of faith.

When we were born into this world we joined in solidarity with humanity. We were not born alone. The very act of conception, birth, and entrance into the world is impossible solo. Such is our entrance into the body of Christ. We were born again through faith in Christ and plunged into the waters in the name of the Father, Son, and the Holy Spirit. Graciously God brings us into fellowship with the greater body of Christ. We are not baptized alone. We are led before a congregation and the throne of God from which living water flows. In front of witnesses we get scrubbed of the sin that comes through solidarity with Adam and our stubborn will to go solo in this world. We were meant to walk together. Like Adam we cannot make it alone. We need one another. We need fellowship.

In our faith and through our baptism, we are adopted as children into the body of Christ. Entrance into the community was an important issue in Galatia. Paul mentions baptism in Galatians in the context of his defense of faith in Christ against those who would enforce the rituals of the Jewish law on new Christians, Gentiles in particular.[3] Rather, Paul says we are baptized into this family of faith. In Christ Gentiles are no less justified or sanctified; the Jews have no special status over the Greeks in the family of believers. Men are no more justified before God than women, freedmen no more than slaves. Paul's ideal of Jews and Gentiles joining one body is entirely consistent with Christ's teaching to make disciples, not of the Jews only, but of all nations.

Members of a specific church have no special status in the body of Christ, as if owning influence or righteousness worldwide, because of external laws or by being born into a certain social, economic or religious situation.[4] All enter the community through faith in Christ. All plunge in the common pool of union with Christ—even those, like the law-keeping Jews, who disapprove of mixed bathing. Paul explains that we are part of one family of faith:

> For in Christ Jesus you are all children of God through faith. As many of you as were baptized into Christ have clothed yourselves with Christ. There is no longer Jew or Greek, there is no longer slave or free, there is no longer male and female; for all of you are one in Christ Jesus. And if you belong to Christ, then you are Abraham's offspring, heirs according to the promise. (Gal. 3:26-29)

We who have faith are baptized into Christ and have clothed ourselves with Christ. We're all redeemed and adopted. We're all children who hear Christ's voice in our hearts, crying out to our Father. Paul's point was that under the law we are minors without full rights to the inheritance, but in Christ we are set free to receive the inheritance by faith in him:

> But when the fullness of time had come, God sent his Son, born of a woman, born under the law, in order to redeem those who were under the law, so that we might receive adoption as children. And because you are children, God has sent the Spirit of his Son into our hearts, crying, "Abba! Father!" So you are no longer a slave but a child, and if a child then also an heir, through God. (Gal. 3:4-7)

Baptism is mixed bathing, for we share the same water. Baptism is a means of uniting with Christ, the Spirit, and the Father, but also a means of joining the pool of believers who are children, adopted, and now crying the heart cry that Jesus put in our hearts, "Abba! Father!" Our baptism is an act of grace and unity. The waters unite, not divide.[5]

The Church's Role in Making Disciples

Christ commanded the church to make disciples. The command is the responsibility of the church, not simply a command for individuals. We must make disciples ranging from those within our own homes to those who are as different ethnically, socially, economically, and religiously as catfish and cats.

In this chapter we examine the church's role in initiating disciples into the kingdom. Out of the theological foundation of God's desire to share community, and out of the call by Christ to go and make disciples, we initiate disciples into the kingdom in these three ways: counter-culturally, cross-culturally, and intra-culturally. First, the Great Commission is counter-cultural. For instance, baptism and teaching everything the Lord commands will be counter-cultural in both secular societies and within Christian communities that do not encourage their members to go into the entire world and share their faith. God's story breaks into these communities, but the message counters many of their cultural practices. Second, following the commission to make disciples is cross-cultural—we are called to go out beyond Jerusalem, Judea, Samaria, to the ends of the earth (Acts 1:8). Third, the call to make disciples is intra-cultural. The church must intentionally seek, nurture, and make disciples of its children. Proclamation, faith, renewal by the Holy Spirit, baptism, and the call to discipleship are all included in each of these three categories.

Making Disciples Counter-Culturally: Baptizing by God's Authority

Changes and upheavals in North America are forcing us to think like missionaries in our own backyards, says C. Leonard Allen.

> When we are forced to think like missionaries, lots of exciting, often disorienting and scary things happen. You have to make sense of the faith in new and strange circumstances. Your theology gets tested. You find yourself having to revisit "the essentials." You find yourself having to sit more loosely with the cluster of traditions you've brought with you, some of which you may be seeing for the first time as your own local traditions that don't translate well (and shouldn't). We are being forced, perhaps kicking and

> screaming, to become missionaries. It's what should have been happening all along.[6]

Therefore, we respond to Christ's Great Commission as missionaries. The irony is that while we seek to be culturally appropriate missionaries, we are also proclaiming a message that is counter-cultural. When we call disciples to be baptized in the name of the Father, Son, and Holy Spirit, all other allegiances submit to God's new ownership. All other authority is laid on the chopping block. This is not to say that we rebel against parental authority or government authority, unless these directly oppose following the Lord. Yet, baptism is an act of initiation into a community that rejects an old way of life and longs for a new world.

"Any time the church takes baptism seriously, which is to say on its own terms, the surrounding society cannot help but see it as at least potentially politically threatening,"[7] Rodney Clapp said. The call to discipleship is unsettling and perhaps even subversive, says Clapp, because all other allegiances are called into question by the new life in Christ. Jesus said all authority in heaven and on earth has been given to him, and all other sources of authority must submit to him.

Baptism is particularly counter-cultural in places such as India, where the majority population follow another belief system. When an Islamic or Hindu family member is baptized into Christ, the act is not only an initiation into a community but a break from a former community. We are aware of new Christians in India who were ostracized because of their new faith. Their stores were boycotted, their children were mocked and families renounced them. In Muslim countries death is often a real prospect for new Christians from Muslim families. In any society conversion to Christ means a simultaneous joining of a new community and a breaking with the old.

The Great Commission was counter-cultural for the first disciples. When the Christian church began, Rome viewed Christian conversion as subversive. In other words, disciples who put their faith in Christ and were baptized were initiated into a counter-cultural community. When Christianity was legalized then later made the official religion of the Roman Empire, conversion was no longer counter-cultural but intra-cultural. This did not change its importance but changed the implications of the commission and conversion. In the United States, while most profess belief in God, many narratives compete against the conversion-to-Christ narrative. When our "Christian nation" too closely identifies Christianity and Americanism or capitalism, then our Christian identity is counter-cultural as we testify to the Lordship of Christ over America and our money. When an over-riding narrative of self-indulgence or staunch human independence pervades a culture such as ours, the commission to share faith and convert others is threatening and counter-cultural.

One great barrier to the counter-cultural nature of baptism is fear and doubt. Even until the end of Christ's ministry on earth, his disciples doubted: "When they saw him they worshiped him; but some doubted" (Matt. 28:17). How did this doubting crew take on the Great Commission? How could they initiate disciples into a counter-cultural community? Jesus addressed their doubts by saying, "All authority in heaven and earth has been given to me." The disciples, then, were empowered by the presence of God—the promised Holy Spirit. Christ added at the end of the commission, "Surely, I am with you always, to the very end of the age" (Matt. 28:20). The Spirit's presence would conquer their doubts when they received the baptism of the Holy Spirit days later. Peter and John would be empowered by the Spirit to say the counter-cultural and subversive words to the Sanhedrin: "Whether it is right in God's sight to listen to you rather than to God, you must judge; for we cannot keep from speaking about what we have seen and heard" (Acts 4:19-20).

Do we, like some of the disciples on that mountain, still doubt Christ's authority? Or do we have the boldness of Peter and John before the Sanhedrin to speak a counter-cultural message? Christ's command is to make disciples. The authority of Christ and the presence of the Spirit gave them the means of making disciples through baptism, pouring of the Holy Spirit on those who believed, and proclaiming everything Christ taught. After nearly three years with Jesus, some of the disciples still doubted him, but the Spirit confirmed his authority and gave them boldness. The presence of God is still with us, and God is calling churches to share the message of his Son by the power of the Holy Spirit. Jesus' promise to be with disciples till the end of the age still holds true today. God's

Spirit dwells in his church, in Christians. It is by the Spirit's power, not our own, that we hear and respond to the commission.

By the authority of Christ disciples are sent out to make disciples, baptizing them in the name of the Father, Son, and Holy Spirit, and teaching them everything Jesus has commanded. "Baptizing them" (*baptizontes*) is not in the imperative sense but modifies "make disciples." The disciples were called to replicate the discipleship Jesus had taught them, and the first call was to make disciples. The imperative "make disciples" is modified with "baptizing them," suggesting initiating disciples into the kingdom of God through baptism is an essential part of making disciples. Christ was transferring the authority to make disciples and empowering them by the Spirit's presence. He said, "I will be with you until the end of the age" (Matt. 28:20). We too are called and empowered by the Holy Spirit to do likewise.

Making Disciples Cross-Culturally: Going into all the World

The church is called not only to make disciples counter-culturally but also cross-culturally. The Great Commission is to "make disciples of all nations." This means we proclaim the gospel to those unlike ourselves in different cultures and socio-economic groups as well as those close to home. The imperative in Matthew 28:19 is to "make disciples" of the nations (*ethne*), a call to to go beyond Jerusalem, beyond their social and religious comfort zones to Samaria and to the ends of the earth (cf. Acts 1:8).

Christ's exhortation to make disciples of all nations remains an imperative today. The church is called to raise up disciples and send them out. When the church exhorts its members to share the gospel and make disciples, it is responding to the Great Commission. When new members are initiated into the kingdom through faith in Christ, baptizing them and teaching them everything the Lord commands, the church is fulfilling the Great Commission. One characteristic of Evangelical churches is that they encourage members to share their faith in Jesus Christ.[8]

The Churches of Christ generally encourage Christians to obey the Great Commission, but only a small percentage of members respond to the commission cross-culturally. The churches that nurtured my wife and me (Greg) also sent us out, prayed for us, gave us financial support, and visited us in Africa. They were part of the formation in us that led us to this decision, and when we asked them, they supported our cross-cultural response to the Great Commission. We joined a mission team in 1991, prepared for three years, and left in 1994 for Uganda. We spent the next seven years helping our mission team and Ugandans plant churches in rural Southeast Uganda. We told our Ugandan friends that this faith we profess is important enough to leave our American home to share. Few Ugandans had traveled far from home, and for them to see us come simply to tell them about Jesus was powerful.

Our Ugandan brothers and sisters are not only—in our American ethnocentric way of phrasing it—"part of us." When we went as missionaries, we joined them, becoming part of them. We tripped over our humanity in a strange culture. We confessed sins to our Ugandan fellowship as much as we did our own mission team. We sought to be human among them, to learn from them. One important thing we discovered is that individual Ugandans identify themselves through union with a clan. This means that Christians feel a profound interdependence with other churches, including our supporting churches in America. Over the years we discovered that we had grown to love one another as family. We had not forgotten our extended families in the United States, but we now had a new extended family in Uganda. And we were honored to introduce these extended families to one another on several occasions.

In cross-culturally expressing the Great Commission, we wanted God to enflesh himself and his ministry in us. We bear the image of God to Ugandans, and they bear the image of God to us and to their communities. Our mission was to plant churches and make disciples. Our strategy was patterned after Jesus' call to make disciples. We preached Christ and called for repentance of sins, deep reflection on life through Bible study and prayer, faith, discipleship, baptism, forgiveness of sins and renewal by the Holy Spirit. In baptism, we unite with Christ in his death and resurrection. And in following the Great Commission we unite, however imperfectly and awkwardly, with those baptized into union with Christ.

Nearly every cross-cultural expression of the gospel, however, takes place in settings that have been previously influenced by Christian ideas. We discovered, for instance, that in countries influenced by Catholic and Anglican movements, baptism is viewed as an initiatory rite that provides them several benefits: entrance into the church that in turn provides the further initiatory rites such as naming and baptizing children, marrying in the church, and last rites for burying the dead. Baptism in some of these churches is synonymous with having full rights to the rites. The final rite of burial, done by a priest, would ensure final initiation or entrance into our eternal home with God. The foregone conclusion in this setting is that baptism is the initiation rite that ensures this exit rite will be acceptable for spiritual well being after death.

Our purpose here is not to be specifically critical of Anglican or Catholic views. The purpose of explaining these views is to describe the context into which we introduced adult baptism for the remission of sins. We spoke of baptism as an entrance into a new life through a covenant with Jesus Christ (see chapter nine). Following Christ is more than getting a Christian name, attending church on Easter and Christmas, and having the right to rites. Baptism is a covenant that initiates us into the kingdom of God, defines our identity under the name of the Father, Son, and Spirit as disciples who follow everything that God commands and who share all things in Christ.

Initiation in the first-century church, pictured for us in the New Testament, particularly in Acts, was indeed spontaneous and urgent. After Peter's sermon on the day of Pentecost, the throngs came to be baptized, it seems, with little time elapsed. "So those who welcomed his message were baptized, and that day about three thousand persons were added" (Acts 2:41). The disciples also did not hesitate to baptize Lydia (16:14-15) and the Ethiopian (Acts 8:36-38). Those who heard and responded to the message of Christ crucified by and for the Jews and Gentiles (Acts 2) were immediately initiated.[9]

Baptism is urgent because Christ himself calls us to make disciples, to baptize them and teach them everything he commands. Baptism is urgent as it serves the goal of transformation and discipleship. When churches practice baptism as a technical command or primarily as a rite of naming and church status, they undermine the commission to make disciples. The church's role in making disciples is much more than that. Baptism is much more than that.

The kingdom life is an urgent and important call: to make disciples of all those who would have ears to hear the word of Christ.

Making Disciples Intra-Culturally: Baptizing our Children

The third way of making disciples is intra-culturally. As the church developed into the third century, lengthy instruction before baptism was introduced, and the time before baptism became longer. By some accounts in the third century, the catechesis or pre-baptismal instruction, could last up to three years. By the fourth century, and most probably before, this catechesis included the children of the church. This seems like a long time but consider that this instruction could be viewed as similar to what today's churches attempt to do through teaching Sunday school or extended Bible studies.

Our focus here is on our children, though this category may include God-fearing adults in our churches. How do we approach our children with our faith in Christ? We are called to nurture them in faith and lead them to discipleship in Christ, which includes baptism and receiving the Holy Spirit. How do we begin? Must we view our children as lost before they can be found? We do, in fact, nurture our children to honor God from the time they can sing, "Jesus loves me this I know," to the point when their faith leads them to baptism. But, are they converted, nurtured, or both? Certainly instruction and discipleship for our children precede baptism. As we nurture our children, their faith will bring them to the river. But what specifically is the church's role in leading them to the waters of baptism? How do we help our children discern their faith and come to baptism?[10]

A study of Southern Baptist methods of evangelizing their children helps to frame the discussion.[11] In the study, four ways emerged as the primary historic approaches of the church to sharing faith in Christ with their children. Over the years, children in Southern Baptist churches have been viewed in four ways:

- Non-members
- Prospects for evangelism
- Potential disciples
- Maturing participants in the faith community

First, early in the history of the Southern Baptist movement children were considered non-members. Though Baptist roots are found in English Puritanism, Thomas Halbrooks, author of the study, said that one major difference was the Baptists' insistence on adult baptism. Founder John Smyth said the church "is a company of the faithful: baptized after confession of sin and faith." Consequently, baptism "does not belong to infants."[12]

Second, children were also viewed as prospects for evangelism. Revivalists such as Charles G. Finney encouraged parents and teachers to instill Christian character and hope for traumatic conversion at "the earliest possible moment." Many revivalists did not baptize infants, but they did want to bring children into the fold as quickly as possible, viewing children as young as five years old as prospects for evangelism. By 1960, the normative age for responding to the gospel among Southern Baptists had dropped from "Juniors (ages nine to twelve) to Primaries (ages six to eight)."[13]

Third, in the mid-1900s, children were increasingly viewed as potential disciples. The revivalist's idea of children making decisions at such tender ages was called into question in light of developing ideas of educational psychology. Children in some churches were deferred until they reached the "age of disciple-ability." In 1963, Lewis Craig Ratliff wrote a doctoral thesis discussing the quest for "disciple-ability" in children, rather than "age of accountability." While accountability focuses on knowing right and wrong, disciple-ability requires the child to have an "ability to understand abstract ideas, the development of selfhood and independence from parents, and social maturity."[14] Ratliff pegged this range at somewhere between 13 and 15, and in this window of opportunity the child would be able to profess faith, follow Christ in baptism, and become a member of the church. Before this time the child is viewed as a potential disciple.

Fourth, Southern Baptists in the last several decades have begun to view children as maturing participants in the faith community, according to Halbrooks. This approach focuses more on nurturing children within the context of the church. William E. Hull, in a paper presented to the Baptist World Alliance in 1980, said Baptists need a theology of the child that recognizes and follows more of the Hebrew insights into the nurture of children. Three major stages of development, says Hull, are "infancy" (birth to 9 years) when children ought to be taught their religious heritage, "childhood" (9-12 years) when children ought to affirm this heritage and commit to faith, and "adolescence" (12 years and up), when children ought to take great responsibility in the life of the church and own their faith completely.

How do we view our children? Do we view them as non-members until they are baptized? Are they lost until they are baptized? Or do we view them as prospects for evangelism? Potential disciples? In a household with Christian parents, can we call this a Christian family when not all the children are baptized? What is the church's role in leading our children to faith?

This study of Southern Baptist views of children is significant because it describes four historic approaches to sharing faith with children in one denominational body. Most Evangelical churches today land near the maturing participants view. Stone-Campbell churches, on the other hand, come closer to the third view, though some churches and individuals seem to be moving toward the maturing participants view as well. Generally, however, most Churches of Christ view children as potential disciples until they reach an age where sin can be discerned and a decision to follow Christ can be made independently from parents.

To illustrate this range of views, we received a Christmas letter from close friends who are members of a Church of Christ, and they described how they are teaching their pre-school children the Ten Commandments and the books of the Bible. They also described ways in which the children participate in the life of their church. While they do not view their elementary school-aged children as Christians in the sense that they have decided to follow Christ on their own and have been baptized, they do view them as needing instruction and seek to bring them into the life of the church as nurtured participants. Our friends teach and nurture their children, yet they are viewed as too young to be baptized. They have not reached the age of accountability or disciple-ability. They would likely view their children in the third category: as potential disciples.

While views of children vary according to culture and churches worldwide, many parents and churches in the Stone-Campbell

Movement view their children as potential disciples. The closer a child comes to the age when she is convicted of sin and affirms Christ as her Savior and Lord, the more she is viewed as a prospect for evangelism. A Bible class full of children eleven and twelve years old is ripe with potential disciples in the typical understanding of Churches of Christ in the United States.

We have talked with conservative Baptists and Evangelicals who view five and six-year-old children as prospects for evangelism. As soon as the children are able to reason and know right from wrong, they move to convict their children of their sinfulness and their need for a personal Savior. For instance, we have Baptist friends who confessed Christ and were baptized at age five. Many in Churches of Christ would say this is too young. Catholics, meanwhile, baptize infants. For them, the process of maturing and confirmation begins as early as the child is able to comprehend the rites and teachings of the church.

How, then, do we approach our children with our faith in Christ? Do we view them simply as non-members until they come of age? Do we consider them prospects for evangelism as soon as they can reason and are able to say a prayer of repentance and submit to baptism? If we believe five or six years old is too young and we choose to wait and view our children as potential disciples, what age is right for disciple-ability or accountability? At what point do they become utterly sinful and ready for initiation or conversion? Or do we view our children as maturing participants in faith and nurture them? These are not easy questions, but there is more truth in the asking than in remaining quiet and continuing to allow these concerns to go unspoken. When we do not ask these difficult questions about our children's spiritual development, we fall back to the least common denominator within our particular tradition. The current least common denominator in Churches of Christ is the unwritten and rarely spoken idea of the "age of accountability."

A study by David Lewis, Carley Dodd, and Darryl Tippens revealed that twelve is the average age for baptism among children in Churches of Christ.[15] The goal of their study of coming to faith was not to pinpoint a particular age for baptism but to discern how to help shape young lives into the image of Christ. The 1995 report shows not only how adolescents view God but also proposes ways to build vital spiritual foundations in them through experience in the community of faith. In one chapter they explore the influences on baptism, reasons for baptism, life change at or after baptism, and ways to enrich the emotional and spiritual power of this ritual.

Are children in our churches really taking a U-turn in conversion, or are they instead coming to a signpost? Is conversion language of Scripture lost on our children? How can children developing faith in a Christian community identify with moving from darkness to light and condemned to justified? Adolescents, say the authors, "convert in a manner that is more appropriately 'Jewish' than 'pagan.' Most choose to be baptized after having been believers for years. Thus, the changes in belief and behavior are incremental, not radical."[16] They do not view baptism as a dramatic darkness to light experience because most were raised in a faith community. More than half of the adolescents surveyed, however, did say that baptism changed their lives by helping them display the fruit of the Spirit. So they view their baptism seriously but do not typically view their conversion experience in the same "dramatic terms our theological tradition holds up as normative."[17] The report points to a gap between the "theology of dramatic baptismal change, and the fact of change that is comparatively subdued, incremental, and colorless."

The significance they place on their baptism, however, grows in the late teen years. The language of Paul is applicable to the situation. Paul reflects on baptism as an event in the past that is continually significant. This reflection is vital to teens' understanding of their baptism. It becomes more and more important in hindsight. At the same time, the authors make it clear that nothing in their research would suggest that those baptized at age 12 are less likely to remain faithful than those baptized later. Those baptized in their late teens do show a more immediate response to the meaning of baptism. Among unbaptized 16-year-olds, however, only eight percent viewed God as important in their lives.

We must, therefore, prayerfully plan spiritual and faith formation in our children. When children can think independently, have a basic understanding of God's redemptive story and have faith in Christ, what prevents them from going down in the river to pray?

Faith in our God will bring our children to baptism when the time is right. The process of discipleship does not begin and end with a string of questions administered on a church pew the day of a child's baptism. While this call to count the cost is important, the church's role is deeper than simply discerning what a child knows before baptism. Our role is to nurture faith, to call our children to discipleship. Their faith will bring them to the river.

When we baptize our twelve-year-old believers, we do not baptize them believing that they were lost the day before because they were unbaptized. For instance, my (John Mark) daughter, Rachel, was baptized at the age of eleven. If for some reason she had died the night before, I would have "preached" her into heaven as though I had baptized her the day before. She did not move from lost to saved as much as she owned her faith and matured in her relationship with the faith community. When we baptize our children, we are initiating them into the full narrative of their faith and conversion over a long period of time.

Connectedness in the Church

Baptism is not a private event. At the Dewey, Oklahoma, Church of Christ, when a disciple is baptized, he or she is told that the circle of Christians holding hands around the auditorium symbolizes the circle of Christians worldwide. We are baptized into the body of Christ with everybody everywhere of every time who has also put on Christ.

We are not only united with Christ, the head of the church, but we are also united with the body of Christ. We plunge into the multi-ethnic, local, and worldwide community of Christians who call Christ their Lord. Speaking to the Corinthians, Paul says, "For in the one Spirit we were all baptized into one body—Jews or Greeks, slaves or free—and we were all made to drink of one Spirit" (1 Cor. 12:13).

The first Christians enjoyed this fellowship (*koinonia*) from the beginning of the church during Pentecost (Acts 2:42), having all things in common (*koina*) without regard to ethnic or social standing.

> Awe came upon everyone, because many wonders and signs were being done by the apostles. All who believed were together and had all things in common; they would sell

> their possessions and goods and distribute the proceeds to all, as any had need. Day by day, as they spent much time together in the temple, they broke bread at home and ate their food with glad and generous hearts, praising God and having the goodwill of all the people. And day by day the Lord added to their number those who were being saved. (Acts 2:43-47)

We who have faith in Christ, like the first Christians, enter into the divine community as children, adults, factory workers, fast food servers, doctors, lawyers, and teachers. We share community and seek the kingdom together.

As we live in this divine community and in our particular faith community, we share faith with a lost world. We join in communion with people unlike us. Yet we are appealing for the same cleansing, the same grace, in the same name. Christ has united himself in his death with all those murderers, adulterers, idolaters, molesters, and liars who receive him in faith. Our baptism is an appeal to be cleansed from all that. Ironically we find cleansing in a grave where we cast our old life into the grace of God, as if a burial at sea. There is no past life, no sin the water cannot swallow.

Ralph Wood told a story about joining a prison minister to help baptize an inmate. A guard escorted them past the razor wire into a room where a wooden coffin had been lined with plastic and filled with water. The guard watched curiously. "The barefoot prisoner stepped into the coffin like the one that would someday hold his lifeless body." The prison minister said to the prisoner, "George, I baptize you in the name of the Father and the Son and the Holy Spirit," then lowered him into the watery grave to be buried with Christ. Though the water was cold, writes Wood, the man sat in the coffin weeping. "I want to wear these clothes as long as I can," said the prisoner, "I am now a free man. I'm not impatient to leave prison because this wire can't shackle my soul. I know that I deserved to come here, to pay for what I did. But I also learned here that someone else paid for all my crimes." The man had molested his own 10-year-old daughter.[18]

We were united in Christ with a molester? Yes, a former one who repudiated that sin and has faith in Christ. The prisoner will continue to live with the consequences of his sin, and we also live with some consequences of ours. We too were once outside, uninitiated, in darkness, drowning in the depths. But Christ brought us near, into the light, into the divine community, and into his body of which he is head. We join the story of the first church. We are added to their number.

Conclusion

We are not baptized alone. We are baptized into a mixed community of believers, of fellow adopted children. A major work of the church, says William Willimon, "is the evangelistic business of claiming people for the kingdom and fitting them for life in that kingdom. Baptism is that rich, multi-faceted, complex way of engaging the body, head, and heart in that strange and glorious work of claiming, instructing, washing, anointing, blessing, and receiving people for the kingdom."[19]

Our fellowship is based in the knowledge that none of us dives into this mixed pool with special status. We were all slaves to sin but have been adopted in Christ. The call is for the church to take up its role in making disciples worldwide, next door, in the prisons, and in our own households. By the authority that the Father gave the Son, we're called to make disciples counter-culturally, cross-culturally, and intra-culturally, and the Spirit will be with us to the ends of the earth.

In the next chapter we discuss practical ways to reconnect baptism as a theological, symbolic, and powerful event of transformation in the church.

****

Principle

By viewing baptism as mixed bathing, we can begin to see the pool of believers with whom we share water, and this fact calls us to greater understanding of Christ's Great Commission to make disciples of all nations, to baptize and teach those who are willing to dive in with us, into the wonderful river of grace.

Prayer

Dear Lord, do you see us on the edge of the waters? We long to be unified, and this prayer came from your heart when you prayed that we would all be one. Make this oneness and unity a reality in our local churches, and help us not to become cynical of the slow pace of unity any more than we would be cynical of our own imperfection. Lord, please do as you promised and make unity an end times reality! We all long to be one in body, Spirit, and purpose. In the name of the Father, Son, and the Holy Spirit. Amen.

Questions

1. What is your baptismal story?
2. Have you shared your story with your children? Your church? A neighbor or friend?
3. How is baptism like mixed bathing?
4. Discuss two baptismal roles of the church.
5. How does baptism bring about fellowship? Unity?
6. When you were baptized, did you believe this connected you in relationship with God? To Christians in your church? Other Christians? Discuss.

12 / Navigating the River: Practicing Baptism Today

"Baptism should to be restored to its rightful place as a central liturgical act of Christian worship."[1]

—Timothy George

****

How can churches recapture baptism as a richly symbolic and communal moment of transformation? Practically, this has been done in churches by acknowledging and enriching the symbolism already embedded in the act of baptism through spoken words and rituals. The goal of this chapter is to tell stories of churches' baptismal practice. These will be used as models to help us develop our own baptismal rituals. While this is a practical endeavor, it must always remain theological as well.

We begin with four churches—vastly different places and times—that have done this. Yet they each developed their own practices of baptism enriched by spoken words and with attention to the symbol of baptism itself and surrounding rituals. By intentionally connecting the full biblical, symbolic, theological practice of baptism, these churches have experienced transforming moments together.

These models help us to think about how we too might connect our own baptismal story with the gospel narrative, how we might use spoken words and symbolism to more fully connect baptism to discipleship and community.

Four Church Baptism Stories

Easter Day, A.D. 259, Derbe in Asia Minor

Hermas received baptism today. For three years he sat at the feet of the church teachers. In the previous weeks he had fasted and prayed with the other baptismal candidates. They were expected to understand the nature of the work of God, the Father, the Son, and the Spirit and to prepare themselves to live within the ethical demands of the Christian faith. They repeated prayers of repentance, kneeled and kept vigil in the nights leading up to their baptism.

Hermas repented, mourned his past and longed to be free from the power of Satan. His mouth was dry and he could feel his heart pumping like a dove's breast pulses on the way to a sacrifice in the temple. He was conscious of his every footstep as he walked in the darkness of pre-dawn to the house of Phoebe, a wealthy widow on the edge of town. He didn't want to arouse suspicion from the neighbors and bring trouble on himself from the town council. The church had been meeting there since Phoebe herself had been baptized four years before. The house was dark except for oil lamps set on pedestals in the courtyard.

The candidates gathered in a room and greeted one another quietly. The first signs of light appeared in the eastern sky as Hermas crossed the courtyard toward the bath made from solid stone. The church leader blessed the water, which represented the sanctifying presence of the Holy Spirit. Standing in the water, Hermas denounced Satan and proclaimed his belief in Jesus Christ the Son of God. He removed his old garments and descended the stairs in nudity and full submission to God. He confessed belief in the Father and was immersed the first time. He confessed belief in the Son and was plunged in the water again. When he confessed belief in God, the Spirit, he was immersed a third and last time.

He ascended the stairs on the other side of the bath, and a brother in Christ wrapped him in a new white robe to symbolize his new life in Christ. Hermas joined the congregation in the courtyard, where each of the newly baptized was anointed with oil as the Levites of long ago were initiated into priesthood. Several leaders of the congregation laid hands on Hermas and blessed him. Every member greeted their new brother in Christ with a kiss on the cheek. Finally, they sat to eat the bread and wine as one body in Christ.

Hillsboro, Kansas (2001)

For Jessie and four other Mennonite Brethren teenagers, their baptism is a crossing over. An elder told them that they, like the Israelites, are crossing as through the Red Sea into a new community. They knelt as the congregation read these words to them from their hymnal: "We have pledged to renounce our sin of self-centered living and to bind ourselves under the authority of Jesus Christ to live in God's holy community, the Church, according to Christ's rule and kingdom." The minister asked, "Do you join with these believers gathered to witness your baptism into Christ's body in pledging to renounce your sin of self-centered living and to bind yourself under the authority of Jesus Christ to live in God's holy community, the Church, according to Christ's rule and kingdom?"[2] Jessie said, "I do," as did the others.

The congregation confessed God's work through Christ and proclaimed him Lord of Lords in a song. The elder asked Jessie, "Do you profess this faith to also be your faith, and do you pledge loyalty to Jesus Christ to live your life in this faith and hope with the power of the Holy Spirit?" Jessie said, "I do." The exchange sounded like sharing of vows in a wedding. And like a marriage, the candidates were not only publicly joining Christ but the Brethren as well. "Are you ready to submit to the regulations of the church?" the elder asked. After affirming both Christ and the church and renouncing Satan's power in their lives, each one entered the water. "Jessie, upon your profession of faith, I baptize you in the name of the Father, of the Son, and of the Holy Spirit," the elder said, and he immersed her.

After each was baptized, other elders gathered and placed their hands on the heads and shoulders of each of the new faithful. In this they were both ordained into service in the church and also accepted with the right hand of fellowship into the church. They changed clothes then shared bread and fruit of the vine and sang hymns of joy.

Jessie smiled as her older sister said, "Arise, shine, for the light of the Lord is upon you." Her sister kissed her on the cheek, as did each member, to show their fellowship. Finally, an elder said,

> We now receive you into the fellowship of the church. We make a covenant with you as we renew our own covenant with our Lord: to bear one another's burdens, to share in the experience of forgiveness, to share in the abundance of this world's goods, to assist each other in times of need, to share our joys and our sorrows, and in all things to work for the common good, thus manifesting God's presence among us to His glory. As we unite with each other now, may we all be joined with Christ our Lord.[3]

1998 in Uganda

Deron Smith, a missionary in Uganda, preached in an African village where there was no water suitable for baptism—only a shallow spring for drinking water.

"What if we dig a pit and fill it with water for the baptism?" Deron said. They laughed. He said the pit would remind them that baptism is like a burial that symbolizes the story of Jesus' death and resurrection and signals a new life within us.

They dug a pit and filled the provisional baptistry with water from the spring. A crowd gathered to watch the spectacle of a grave baptism. With the baptismal plunge and lift of every person, the crowd surrounding the grave erupted in wild laughter, slapping their knees and smiling. They delighted in watching each person exit the water, spitting and spewing. They had never seen anyone baptized like this before.

The event and this story have been very meaningful to the people in those villages. Baptizing in a grave, they told the story of Christ's death, burial, and resurrection. Those being baptized grasped the reality that they were truly being buried in union with Christ. If they were buried in union with Christ's death, they would surely also be united with him in his resurrection. With this hope, they turned to a new life and a new ethic for living.

July 5, 1978
I (Greg) joined the body of Christ on a sweltering summer night in 1978. I remember talking to my mother about "getting baptized." The lines of the conversation are fuzzy but my mother lovingly listened and guided me in "counting the cost" of following Jesus. Did I understand what I was doing? My father also stood by me in the baptismal experience. He held my hand as I gripped the back of the pew and my knuckles turned white. When I took a step, he practically sprung to the aisle and led me with conviction to the front of that small Northeastern Oklahoma congregation.

I stood in front of the congregation and "made the good confession" that Jesus is Lord. Then all eyes turned toward a door—a veil of sorts—that led to a sacred room where I was fitted with a white baptismal smock while the church sang, "I have decided to follow Jesus." A deacon, meanwhile, removed large sheets of Styrofoam that covered the baptistry. The congregation knew this meant business. When a female was baptized, the Lydias and Eunices and Dorcases of the church made sure the girls had enough covering and towels, and in the sacred room they'd say the angels were singing over this new child.

Standing in the baptistery with me, Dad confirmed my confession and with quick instructions on plugging my nose—though he himself had taught me how to hold my breath years before in a pool—dad quoted the baptismal injunction of Christ in the Great Commission (Matt. 28:19): "Greg, based on your confession, I now baptize you in the name of the Father, the Son, and the Holy Spirit."

Dad plunged me under the water momentarily and raised me back to the surface and hugged me. His shirt was wet with water and tears. Water dripped inside his duck waders. My cousin, the same age, was also baptized that night by my uncle. The congregation formed a circle, held hands, and my father explained that this circle of faith goes around the world and anywhere the new Christian went, brothers and sisters in Christ are part of this circle.

On that humid summer night in 1978, the congregational embrace and exhortations finished, my family went home by way of the ice cream parlor. The angels were singing, and we mortals ate ice cream. We didn't know what else to do. I remember sitting at that school desk in the ice cream shop, hair wet from the baptism, wondering what I had gotten myself into, feeling awkward about the attention put on me, eating my banana split. I was ten! My interest in using that plastic banana split boat as a pirate ship in the creek behind my house nearly eclipsed my reflection on the baptism. But the water—whether in a baptistry or stream or river—has never left my consciousness since that night.

Each of the above four baptism stories illustrate practically how rituals surrounding baptism connect us to God in Christ through the Spirit and to the body of believers in Christ. When we think of our stories, we think of the persons who baptized us, the witnesses, the words that were said, the expressions of faith. Our story becomes one with God's story of redemption. When we share our stories, we not only participate in Christ but God also adds our story to the redemptive-historical narrative he has been telling since before the world began and the waters proceeded out of the throne of God.

Practical Steps to Navigate the River

Practically, how can we make the symbolic event of baptism come alive for each believer? How can churches take symbols related to baptism and use them ceremonially to powerfully impact the body of Christ? While we believe baptism is much more than symbolic, it can still be highly symbolic and therefore vivid, meaningful, and memorable. We now turn to practical steps for churches to develop their own baptismal ceremonies.

Develop Locally Meaningful Symbols and Rituals of Baptism

Ceremony and ritual shape the atmosphere and thus the symbolism and theological depth of the event. But the symbols and rituals must be intentionally and locally meaningful. Does importing the idea from Africa of digging a hole for baptism make sense for most American churches? No. Someone might say, "We can't dig a ditch in our churchyard. We'd have to call the utilities and the city planner to dig a hole! True, the call here is not to follow the above examples exactly but to contextualize the symbolic meaning of baptism. In other words, make baptismal ceremonies locally meaningful.

For example, rather than digging a grave, a church could develop the idea of being clothed with Christ (Gal. 3:26-27) with a set of new clothes for the newly baptized believer. A ceremonial robe, reminiscent of the prodigal son and Joseph's colorful coat, could be draped on the new believer.

For rituals to be locally meaningful, leaders must direct the congregation toward these powerful ceremonies and rituals. For example, we might reflexively applaud a baptism, but how do the leaders call us to respond? Are we simply doing what our culture calls for? Are we truly deepening the meaning of baptism by applauding? It is a kind gesture but nothing different from our culture. What or who are we applauding? God? The decision? The person getting baptized? Rather than reflex actions, we ought to carefully and intentionally discern how we might make baptism locally meaningful, then lead congregations intentionally toward deeper ceremonies that express the rich symbolism and theological impact of baptism in the life of the believer and the congregation.

Put High Value on Ritually Celebrating Baptism

Many churches value baptism doctrinally but not ceremonially. Most people we interviewed for this book hunger for holy moments or events that give them identity and assurance of relationship with God. We all want those moments in our churches. Baptism in many churches, however, comes at the end of a worship time as an unplanned event. Pressure to conclude the service on time leaves little room for ceremony. Perhaps the service must end in consideration of the children's nursery or worship. Baptism is also practiced privately in small groups then simply announced in the bulletin.

Yet we clearly value ritual and ceremony in other pursuits. Each year we attend dozens of birthday parties, banquets, school and church activities. Even faith communities that highly value baptism rarely celebrate baptism with as much enthusiasm and investment of time and energy as a youth group or school awards banquet. When we want to convey that an event—such as a birthday, anniversary, Christmas, or accomplishment—is important, we build traditions and ceremony. Baptism, too, ought to be celebrated for the identity-shaping event that we claim it is. Dodd, Lewis, and Tippens say, "We must rediscover the emotional and spiritual power of conversion. Baptism, and the events leading up to and following it, must be seen as profoundly significant."[4]

Why not throw a party for the newly baptized member? In our churches, we gather and celebrate everything from birthdays to the Super Bowl to secular holidays. Why not celebrate the initiation of one just born into the kingdom of God? One church we know of has a time of fellowship after a baptism to exhort the newly baptized member with prepared or spontaneous blessings. Perhaps this could be called a "shower of blessing" for the newly baptized believer. When a member of a church is sick, we send flowers. Why not apply some of these kindnesses and markers of importance for those who are baptized? Cards, flowers as symbols of new life, or anything that celebrates new life would be appropriate for reinforcing the moment of baptism.

Why not make a person's first communion as a baptized disciple a community occasion for celebration? A church potluck could celebrate few more worthy occasions than the baptism of a new child into the family of God. Early Christians, and even the Greek Orthodox Church today, include the first communion as a ritual part of baptism. With each candidate, a church leader baptizes, anoints with oil, lays on hands, and gives the first Eucharist (communion). Early Baptists also laid hands and anointed. The welcome circle referred to earlier was a kind of "Great Commission" to go out into the world, to launch out in faith and to join a community of believers wherever we go, to share what we know about the Lord. By intentionally sharing the Lord's Supper together after a baptism, believers would be brought into the communion of the body of Christ with additional vivid ceremony and symbolism. Additional words about the new Christian and the connection to Christ could be spoken over the bread and wine.

Stand for baptisms. The South MacArthur Church of Christ in Irving, Texas, stands during baptisms. Before the baptism they sing "Holy Ground," and after the baptism they sing "Arise, my Love!" John Ogren, one of the ministers, says "there is a palpable sense of solidarity and joy in these moments," but he adds that "we could do more to make baptism an occasion for unbelievers present to hear the gospel and witness it enacted."[5] Church leaders ought to encourage more public baptisms and give less way to the will of those in the church who want to make the occasion as private as possible. We need to go back down to the river in public view.

Welcome circle. In some churches, the one baptized is welcomed after baptism with a circle of fellowship. Members hold hands and surround the auditorium. They sing joyful songs, with lines such as, "I have decided to follow Jesus…no turning back," and "Happy day! When Jesus washed my sins away." This brief post-baptismal ceremony usually includes singing, prayer, and greeting the one(s) baptized. At least this much celebration is fitting for the event of baptism, and churches ought to develop their own practices that bring honor to God, encourage the new Christian, and build up the body of Christ.

Speak and Write Meaningful Words of Blessing

What we say shapes how believers view their new life in Christ and the significance of what they are doing. How much more, then, would a new believer be encouraged if the church planned a time after baptism to publicly bless the new Christian, pray for him or her, and speak blessings from Scripture? The priestly blessing from Numbers 6:22-27 is one example of a blessing for new Christians. Another example is Paul's prayer for the Ephesian church (Eph. 3:14-21).

Spoken words. What words should we speak at baptisms? The church has taken Christ's words in Matthew 28:19 and developed the formula, "I baptize you in the name of the Father, the Son, and the Holy Spirit for the remission of your sins." While this formula is not specifically stated as what we should say before baptism, the importance of the Lord's commission and the names into which we are baptized make this a powerful declaration of what God is doing in baptism. Typically in Churches of Christ, a minister or elder will ask the baptismal candidate, "Do you believe with all your heart that Jesus is the Son of God?" The person receiving baptism replies, "Yes," or "I believe." Acts 8:37 is one of the models for this practice, which is printed in the NRSV and NIV as a footnote. The earliest manuscripts do not include the verse but KJV and ASV were early English versions that did include it. The verse describes an exchange between Philip and the eunuch about baptism: "Philip said, "If you believe with all your heart, you may." The eunuch answered, "I believe that Jesus Christ is the Son of God." Romans 10:9 is another source that leads us to ask for the "good confession": "because if you confess with your lips that Jesus is Lord and believe in your heart that God raised him from the dead, you will be saved."

Written words. Dodd, Lewis, and Tippens suggest having family and friends write or speak exhortations to the baptized person as one way to ritualize baptism and make it more meaningful. Many churches provide cards for members to encourage one another or to share their faith with unbelievers in Christ. These words can also be read in a special ceremony after the baptism.

Make the Event Communal

While many baptisms in Churches of Christ are performed by the preacher or in small groups, baptism ought to be a communal event for the whole body of Christ as much as possible. We do not come to Christ as isolated members for a private faith but as members of one body with a common faith in Christ. The community of faith has a vital role to play in shaping and nurturing through a return to the rich language of conversion in scripture and rituals surrounding the baptismal event.

Intentionally communal. Baptism was never intended to be a private ceremony but rather a public declaration of God's grace. In many churches baptism is subjugated to an "after services" private occasion. On the one hand, some practice a strict urgency for baptism and only wait to ascertain how much the disciple knows before going into the water. On the other hand, some ministers agree to set appointments for baptism at times when only a few members will be present. Practicing baptism either urgently when no one is around or setting an appointment when few are present, may further reduce the faith to a private affair. Baptism should be a public witness to faith and God's work in the one going down in the river. While the propensity of new members may be to make as little fuss as possible and lower the attention focused on them in this vulnerable moment, this occasion should be an important communal event through which the community commissions the person to a life of faith.

Coming closer. Larger churches will have to work to make the experience intentionally communal. Many of the congregation may not know the one being baptized; the person may not want to be baptized in front of many people. In many large churches there is applause for a baptism but the majority of members walk out without as much as shaking the hand, embracing, or saying a word to the new member. We have ministered in churches where the baptistry was fifty feet away from the front pews. The baptistry was simply too far away to experience and support the new disciple in this important moment. One youth group in a Houston, Texas, church began a tradition of gathering around the baptistry. Now the church calls the entire congregation to the front for baptisms.

Teaching moment. Watching a baptism is also a powerful teaching moment for our children. Yet many churches hurry through the moment at the end of a service or plan it for another time. Some churches, in fact, do plan baptisms for a special service, where they emphasize the meaning of baptism in the preaching, singing, and communion.

Connect the Event with the Life of the Disciple

How can we express the importance and urgency of following Jesus Christ and submitting to baptism within cultural and religious narratives that view such rituals as old fashioned or merely symbolic? Baptism in scripture and today is both an urgent call and a divine comfort to those who would put their faith in Christ. Baptism as pictured in Acts was done urgently when a person expressed faith in Christ. The disciples apparently did not hesitate to baptize 3,000 on the day of Pentecost. These baptisms as well as Lydia's, the Jailor's and the Ethiopian's appear to be immediate (Acts 2:41; 8:36-38; 16:14-15, 33).[6] In the Gospel of Mark the two-fold question is continually asked, "Who is Jesus? And what does it mean to follow him?" When a person answers these questions with genuine faith in Christ, baptism ought to be an expression of that faith that is not deferred for months or even years. Faith in Christ is an urgent call down in the river to pray.

Fear, however, may supplant urgency when baptism is foisted on young seekers as the line in the sand or the ultimate end of one's spiritual journey, rather than a transformational moment that is part of the faith journey. For instance, many of us shared a common fear as children growing up in strict Evangelical and Fundamental churches: hell. The urgent message we received as pre-teens was that our souls hung in the balance between heaven and hell. We had to act urgently, and the church would sing extra verses of "Just As I Am" as long as it took to get us to "come forward," repent of our sins, confess that Jesus is Lord, and submit to immersion. The teaching we received focused on following biblical commands that could save our souls. The waters of baptism could extinguish those flames. So we were baptized as pre-teens. Baptism scared the (fear of) hell out of us. Though our faith was small and our fears childlike, they were still real. We turned away from sin and acknowledged our need for a redeemer whom we met in the waters of baptism. We feared God's judgment and sought his redemption. Yet God did much more for us in baptism than we originally thought.

Repudiating sin. The early church included a denunciation of Satan and the powers of evil in the life of a candidate for baptism. Making a covenant is no trifle. The two parties walking through two halves of a slaughtered animal often sealed ancient Hebraic covenants with a saying such as this: "May this happen to me if I do not keep this covenant!" Paul, in his letters, often points back to baptism as he exhorts Christians in the early churches. The implication is that their baptism ought to be memorable, and in case it wasn't, Paul exhorts them to remember and attach great significance to their baptism as a break from their past lives, a shaping influence on their lives now, and a vivid symbol of their coming resurrection with Christ.

Follow Through Toward Discipleship

The disconnect in our practice of baptism in the church is that we often speak of baptism as a beginning for a believer, but we leave her with little else than a towel and a blow dryer to get her through the new life. How is the church to be held accountable not only to make disciples but also to keep them as disciples?

How can we practically make baptism a moment of discipleship?

Bible study. If baptism is to connect more fully with discipleship, churches should establish a flexible agenda of Bible study and shepherding before and after baptism. In some cases more study and shepherding can be done before baptism. In others, more can be done after. Baptism, says Timothy George, "should be related directly to the discipline and covenantal commitments of the congregation.

The role of catechesis in the process of baptismal preparation is also crucial if we are to avoid trivializing the meaning of baptism."[7]

Mentors. Another way to connect baptism to discipleship is to coordinate a group within the church to mentor a new believer in faith. Ananias and Barnabas led Saul through the early days of his calling and transformation (Acts 9:17, 27), and Paul mentored others, including Timothy. Christians need one another to navigate the waters ahead of them. Paul would have never preached a day had the Lord not confronted him, had Ananias not laid hands on him to give him the Holy Spirit (Acts 9:17), had Barnabas not defended him to fellow Christians. Even Paul had mentors, and new Christians in particular need them as well.

Persevere. We have a tendency to feel relief that a disciple has gone into the waters. This relief, however, causes us to drop our guard. Some of us were handed a book, such as *Now That I'm a Christian*, to study on our own. In most cases, the Bible study before baptism is done with great fervor and personal attention. Often, after baptism, churches hand new disciples a booklet and send them on a solo journey.

Baptism is a moment of discipleship decision, and we ought to focus on this moment intensely. Baptism marks a radical shift from anything that would separate us from the love of Christ. Discipleship, on the other hand, is a process.

Remember who you are. When a young woman we know became involved with a boyfriend, became pregnant, and suffered the shame of her sin slowly becoming visible to the congregation, she was reminded of her baptism. The church had supported her and loved her. Her lasting and true union is with Christ and nothing can separate her from him—neither life, nor death, nor pregnancy out of wedlock, nor anything else. This does not excuse her action or the action of the boyfriend but is intended as a reminder of who she is called to be. Christ still holds the power over shame and sin and continually washes her by his blood, just as baptism cleansed her of sin when she was immersed. We want to re-connect those in such crises with the effective sign of baptism as a continual renewal and re-clothing. We want to remember that we were clothed with Christ and the old life can again be laid in the grave of baptism. We must remember who we are.

Much of who we are may only be known in hindsight, but ritual helps establish and lock in this meaning for believers in Christ. For example, at a church camp in the hills of Northeast Oklahoma we would sing Galatians 2:20 over and over, faster and faster. The words are burned into our minds now. As children, we enjoyed the ritual of singing together. Yet in later years, in reflecting on our stories and reading the text again, the song now means everything to us:

> I am crucified with Christ: nevertheless I live; yet not I, but Christ liveth in me: and the life which I now live in the flesh I live by the faith of the Son of God, who loved me, and gave himself for me. (Gal. 2:20, KJV)

Conclusion

We can make the event of baptism more meaningful by carefully discerning how to practice it in the local church. We all practice rituals. Our rituals, however, must be formed intentionally from theological, symbolic, and practical concerns. Any practice that is developed must honor God and serve God's purposes of transformation and relationship. We have laid out several ways churches are doing this and failing to do this. Finally, we have suggested ways for churches to begin practically making baptism a genuinely transformational moment for disciples to plunge into the divine community.

****

Principle

When giving God honor guides development of our rituals, we can move toward more intentionally and fully connecting baptism with a rich mixture of theological meaning and practical concerns. We may be guided in our developing baptismal ceremonies by asking the question, Does the specific ritual embody the theological values of baptism?

Prayer

Lord, connect us to our baptism. Help our church to more fully connect baptism to theology, community, symbol, and discipleship. Clothe us, renew us, wash us, plunge us in the flood of eternal life, and raise us out of the river to stand on the distant shore before your throne! Amen.

Questions

1. What are the defining moments of your life? A death or marriage or a religious experience? Was it your baptism? A prayer? The Spirit moving in your life or through the word of God?

2. Why were you baptized? What effect do you believe your baptism had on your life? What, in baptism, did God do for you?

3. How does your church promote baptism as a meaningful event?

4. What symbolism came along with the event of your baptism?

5. What are some ways baptism can be practiced as the important event that it ought to be in the church?

6. How can we make baptism meaningful, symbolic, communal, and tied once again to discipleship?

13 / Revisioning the River

"It is a strange gap in the baptismal teaching," says Karl Barth, "of all Confessions—the Reformed included—that the meaning and work of baptism have never been understood in principle as a glorifying of God, that is as a moment in His self-revelation." [1]

While baptism does affect us, a far greater thing occurs, says Barth: at the moment of baptism, God gets his just due for what he has done for us in Christ.

Certainly initiating souls into the kingdom of God brings God glory, but in the process of doing this, do we give God his due? Renewing the full biblical, symbolic, theological practice of baptism in the church, we believe, will ultimately bring God glory.

****

How can we revision baptism in a way that ultimately will bring glory to God, reflect the normative teaching and practice in Scripture, and flow out of theological conviction rather than simple concerns for expediency in churches?

Revisioning a High View of Baptism

We have gone down in the river to pray. At the river we have caught a glimpse of how to revision a high view of baptism. A high view approaches baptism as the normative means through which God mediates his grace to those who have faith. Further, a high view approaches baptism as not merely symbolic but effective, by the power of the Spirit, to produce what it symbolizes. For example, baptism not only symbolizes washing but is an actual cleansing of sins. As James McClendon says, baptism is an effective sign, "for it is the nature of signs not only to betoken but to do something, to convey something."[2]

We are calling for a higher view of baptism in the church. We believe baptism needs to be revisioned in at least four ways.

Revision Baptism as Transformation

The early church practiced baptism in a mission context. New believers were converted and initiated into Christ and the faith community. Through the centuries, however, baptism has been used less as a means of conversion and more as a means of initiation or an act of obedience to a church ordinance. Many find the language of conversion incongruent with what is really happening in children growing up in faith. While we do not want to lose the language of conversion, we do want to view baptism as an objective sign of God's transformation. This is not meant to overstate the role of baptism so that it replaces or diminishes the fruit of the Holy Spirit as an objective sign of assurance and a seal of our inheritance.

The language affects how we view baptism. And the way baptism has been spoken of and viewed over the centuries has become devalued in most churches. For many Catholics, baptism has become a way to celebrate the birth of a baby, get a Christian name, and invite friends and family to the occasion. Baptism has lost its original meaning for many Catholics first as a means of mediating God's grace for those who believe the effects of original sin to be so pervasive that we are lost without this divine pouring of sacramental water. Baptizing infants, for many Presbyterians and Methodists, has become more of a social event than a divine mediation. For many Baptists, baptism has become a sectarian entry rite into the local church or a nice occasion to re-affirm belief or publicly confess a salvation already accepted upon saying the sinner's prayer.

In many Churches of Christ, baptism has become a technical hoop through which to jump toward salvation. Lack of ceremony surrounding baptism has also devalued baptism as an important moment in the church. Many of us learned about baptism in camps that argued with other churches about the correct mode (immersion) and its essentiality. Yet, paedobaptists (baptize infants) and credobaptists (baptize adults) have strayed from a transformative understanding of baptism. Paedobaptists tend to view baptism as initiation. Credobaptists tend to view baptism symbolically, as enrichment or full obedience in Christian life. Because of this situation, we believe baptism should be revisioned as the powerful conversion-initiation rite for which we have precedent in the New Testament. R.E.O. White summarized the biblical teaching or practice of conversion-baptism or conversion-initiation like this:

> The full rite of Christian initiation emerges from Luke's account as comprising the hearing of the gospel, repentant acceptance of God's word, baptism, reception of the Spirit, entrance to the church and to the New Age of eschatological fulfillment.[3]

White describes a fuller conversion-baptism narrative, which we believe is for the purpose of transformation—God's ultimate goal. We believe the church must revision baptism as transformation.

Revision Baptism as an Effective Sign

The central question here is, "What does baptism really do?" We have emphasized throughout this book that in order to understand what baptism does, we must first step back and ask, "What has God done?" The way we view the effectiveness of baptism grows out of our belief that God is truly doing something through baptism, not merely giving us an eloquent symbolic practice nor a random command. On the contrary, we believe God has given baptism as an effective sign of our transformation as we are planted with Christ in union with him, reclothed, renewed, forgiven, and blessed with the Holy Spirit. The Spirit assures us of salvation and sanctifies us for God's ongoing presence in our lives.

By revisioning baptism as an effective sign of God's transformation, we believe we are returning to a more biblical picture of baptism's role in conversion and its close relationship to faith and the Holy Spirit—the gracious meeting of God's Spirit and our faith is closely tied to baptism. "God's gracious giving to faith," says Beasley-Murray,

> belongs to the context of baptism, even as God's gracious giving in baptism is to faith. Faith has no merit to claim such gifts and baptism no power to produce them. It is all God, who brings a man to faith and to baptism and in his sovereignty has been pleased so to order his giving. Faith therefore ought not to be represented as self-sufficient; Christ comes to it in the Gospel, in the sacraments, in the Church, and it needs them all. Nor should baptism be regarded as self-operative.[4]

We believe too much turf in Evangelical churches has been yielded to the capitulating language of baptism as a symbol or an added event following salvation rather than the language of baptism as a means through which God imparts an objective sign of his grace to us. In Stone-Campbell churches, on the other hand, fulfilling the command of baptism has been isolated as the deciding factor in one's assurance and standing before the Lord and church. It has become the final and most important step in a five-step plan.

Baptism is both a symbolic act of the church and an effective action of God through his redeeming work in Christ. Baptism is a normative means through which God mediates his grace to us, but God is not limited by this means. Baptism is bound up with faith and a proper treatment of one must include the other. Baptism must be re-cast as initiation-conversion rather than simply a church ordinance or command to be technically accomplished. Baptism is an effectual sign, not merely the thing signified but a means through which God gives us his grace.

Revision a Non-Sectarian Application of Baptism

The central question here is, "Can we practice adult immersion as normative without being sectarian?" For instance, a perception of many Christians in Churches of Christ is that since we practice adult immersion, also called believer's baptism, it follows that we necessarily believe all other interpretations or practices lead to hell. Some friends come by this notion honestly because they have crossed paths with a member of the Churches of Christ who has no room for differing interpretations of scripture, ignorance, or errors of others. We believe we are fallible and therefore want to be gracious in how we discuss baptism with those who differ from our belief in believer's immersion. We believe the immersion of those who believe in Christ as an effective sign of God's transformation is the normative teaching and practice in the New Testament and ought to be today. At the same time, we believe baptism may be taught and practiced in a non-sectarian way. But often baptism is practiced in sectarian ways. For example, some Baptist churches and Churches of Christ do not accept a person's baptism unless performed in that particular tradition.

Tied to the central question is the related one, "Is baptism essential for salvation?" To ask the question is not wrong but to persist in rejecting the overriding weight of New Testament and church normative teaching and practice on baptism as part of the whole narrative of conversion is to deny the very faith one claims to profess. When we marry, do we ask, "Do I have to have sex with you for our marriage to work?" We do not want to take the analogy too far—it breaks down, but the point is that baptism is a gift of grace that is no mere item on a checklist but an transformative moment for every disciple of Christ to participate with their Lord in dying to sin, being re-clothed, forgiven, and empowered by the Holy Spirit.

We believe we are not able nor should we attempt to nail down the winds of God's Spirit. He saves who he wants to save. Paul alluded to this unfathomable mercy of God, "So then he has mercy on whomever he chooses, and he hardens the heart of whomever he chooses" (Rom. 9:11-18).

Our appeal is to the mercy of God not only for the "unimmersed" but for all of us. Our salvation rests in God's mercy poured out on us in Christ. To say one has faith in Jesus Christ is to actively respond to the full narrative of conversion. Baptism is an essential event within the whole normative conversion narrative in Scripture. Conversion, transformation, and sanctification are all parts of discipleship that draw us near to God for relationship with him. These prepare us for God's holy presence. Baptism is the normative means through which God mediates his grace through our faith in Christ. God is not, however, limited by that. We say that not because we are embarrassed to say something more hard and fast but for theological reasons. God's grace and mercy, we believe, will not be fenced in by our attempts to discern his mysteries and hold them in our hands and in our baptisteries. In the case of someone not baptized because of ignorance, error, or for any other reason God deems acceptable, we leave these in the hands of God, where we believe these matters belong. "So it depends not on human will or exertion, but on God who shows mercy" (Rom. 9:16). We, too, will fall at God's feet and appeal to his mercy and the blood of our savior. Until then, we will live expectantly, faithfully, and we will respond to the full narrative of conversion and sanctification as disciples who want to be in God's presence forever. Yet we will practice baptism as a grace for humanity, not a line in the sand.

This does not mean that we will agree with everything taught in every Christian tradition. In fact, even within the Stone-Campbell Movement, there is wide diversity in baptismal views. Certainly on baptism, we differ with other Evangelical churches and Catholic churches in significant and important ways. Yet we do share a common faith in Christ, and on that basis we walk the same journey toward transformation in Christ. With Christ as our foundation, we respectfully join the conversation with others both within our own movement and in all churches.

Revision "One Baptism" of Ephesians 4

The central question here is, "If there truly is 'one baptism' and Christ prayed for unity in John 17, on what basis can we have unity in the doctrine and practice of baptism in Christian churches?" Baptismal teachings and practices in churches worldwide are diverse and complex. We cannot accomplish a full vision of unity on earth. Christ's prayer will be fully accomplished in the end times. Yet we faithfully pray, attend to, and seek this unity.

Is there a basis for unity? Yes. We believe that just because there is disunity in the church does not mean we back down from proclaiming that baptism now saves us by the power of the resurrection of Christ (I Pet. 3:21-22). In the same breath, however, we proclaim that God is merciful and understands what we do not. We believe the words God spoke to Moses also speak to this context: "I will have mercy on whom I have mercy, and I will have compassion on whom I have compassion." So it depends not on human will or exertion, but on God who shows mercy (Rom. 9:15-16). We will proclaim the mystery that while God has chosen to mediate his grace through faith and the sign of baptism, he is still sovereign over the means of imparting or mediating his grace and salvation.

So, to the question of, "Can one be saved without being baptized?" we answer with a question, "Is God not still Lord of salvation?" He works according to his own good pleasure. Our role is to proclaim this sovereignty and grace. The normative New Testament way this grace is expressed in the life of a converting individual is through faith, repudiation or repentance of sins, and immersion.

We could be more unified and more faithful to the prayer of Jesus in John 17 if we accept that faith, repentance, renewal by the Holy Spirit, and baptism are all part of the entire narrative of conversion and that the order is less important than the understanding that God is sovereign and will accomplish what he promised in his time. There is no unified scriptural sequence of salvation in the New Testament. There is a normative order of penitent response to the gospel proclamation that includes submitting to baptism and Holy Spirit pouring. The sequence is ultimately mysterious. This is not to say that there are no steps of conversion but that the process is more mysterious and unbound by time than we may have originally expressed in previous attempts to lead our children or Christ-seekers down in the river to pray.

How does the list of "ones" in Ephesians 4 relate to this discussion? Anthony R. Cross calls both infant and adult baptizing churches back to the New Testament pattern of conversion-initiation by viewing the "one baptism" of Ephesians 4 as more than symbol, more than initiation, but as a conversion-initiation that is not bound by time or order but by a return to teaching and practicing baptism as a part of the journey of faith as described in the New Testament. Cross, in developing a proposal for returning to "one baptism" of Ephesians 4, says few churches—infant or adult baptizing—actually practice the "one baptism" about which Paul speaks. On the one hand, churches that practice infant baptism have minimized the role of faith, and the strong connection in the New Testament between faith and baptism continues to point toward believer's baptism. Infant baptism has no biblical precedent but is only argued on the basis of practical or theological concerns. We believe, with Cross, Beasley-Murray, and R.E.O. White, among others, that New Testament references to baptism refer to adult baptism. On the other hand, churches that practice adult baptism have also devalued baptism by reducing it to a mere symbol, outward expression of faith, or optional practice if it works for them in their particular faith walk.

Ultimately, we see unity in Christ as relational rather than technical. Baptism serves that unity. It points toward it and embodies it. Thus, we speak of baptism as God's transforming work not only in terms of individuals but also of the church. The church is unified through the sign of our common faith in Christ and one Spirit. This unity, however, is not only for the present times but also for the future. This unity is eschatological in character—we are in process of unity, just as we are in process of sanctification. In other words, just as individuals are justified, are being sanctified and wait expectantly for the end times when Jesus will return, so also the church has been set right and through the power of the Spirit is moving toward unity. We wait in hope for full unity in the eschaton. We work with God's Spirit towards this unity, but we recognize it is always ongoing yet imperfect in this present world but will be complete and continuous in the end times.

Common Questions

Questions such as the following have been asked for centuries. While we attempt to be biblical, theological and practical, these responses are not the final word on the matter. We believe local churches are autonomous in the sense that each body ought to gather and discern their own beliefs and practices from Scripture. Yet, in reality, we are interdependent and help one another discern the meaning of God's word. We are ever subject to reform (*semper reformandum*).

1. How do you decide when a child is mature enough to be baptized?

Approaches to sharing faith with children are diverse. Some Methodists baptize infants as an initiatory rite of including the child in the community of faith, not out of fear for their eternal destiny. William Willimon and his wife handed down their faith by baptizing their children as infants in the Methodist tradition. He said they had thought to wait until the child could make a faith decision but later decided that this would be less than straightforward about their desire to pass on their faith in Christ to their children. The child would be later led to own this faith when capable of disciple-ability. Many Independent Baptists defer initiation of infants but immerse their children as soon as they are able to reason independently, understand right and wrong, and accept Jesus Christ as their personal savior. By some reports, these children are as young as five years old. A Church of the Nazarene member we interviewed said she was baptized several years after she was saved. She was a teenager and made the decision on her own to be baptized on a night at her church when several others were being immersed.

In the Stone-Campbell Movement, the focus has been on the "age of accountability" as a stage of maturity in which a child "knows the difference between right and wrong." In many Churches of Christ, children in particular are asked questions to ensure that they have "counted the cost of discipleship" as they "make this important decision." At times a preacher, parent, or teacher asks the child questions before baptism, such as, "Do you know this is a lifetime commitment?" and "Do you understand what Jesus has done for you?" Urgency is often placed on the decision of children at the age of accountability. Few want to stand in the way of God's work of moving the child to himself, but some actually try to "talk them out of it," and if they cannot, they reason that they must be truly committed. Many pre-teens and teenagers are baptized at Bible camps and retreats. There seems to be no consensus in Churches of Christ about whether children should submit to parental approval, decide completely on their own, or to seek parental or adult advisement.

To illustrate this dilemma, a 35-year-old who had grown up as a son of a Church of Christ preacher, told us this story. We will call him Mike. When he was ten years old, Mike wanted to be baptized.

His father, the church preacher, talked him out of it. Consequently, Mike resisted being baptized. He held off through his teenage years, to his father's consternation. Mike was embarrassed that he had gone forward and was refused baptism. He resented his father's holding him back, and he decided that he would not later be forced into baptism. Once past the "age of accountability," the preacher very much wanted Mike to be baptized. Mike did not want to be pushed into it. Finally, when Mike was in college and up against life forces he felt he could no longer handle, he decided—again—to be baptized. He went to his father and said, "Let's go. I want to get baptized." They went together and Mike was baptized that day.

In a near opposite experience, another parent in a Church of Christ told us his son wanted to be baptized when he was nine. With Christmas approaching, the nine-year-old said he wanted to be baptized on Christmas Eve, to symbolize the birth of Christ and his own re-birth. While the parents wanted him to count the cost of his commitment, they felt he was determined to be baptized, even had his own agenda to be baptized in a doubly symbolic way on Christmas Eve.

My (Greg) children are nine, six, and four. None have been baptized. John Mark's children are teenagers and have been baptized. We pray for our children every day to be transformed in a new relationship with God as they grow older. We do want our children to be baptized but also transformed, sanctified and continually moving toward the Father, Son, and Holy Spirit. We want them to be baptized in the context of appealing to God's grace through their faith, not baptized as a way to be relieved of the twelve-year-old and attendant parental angst about passing the "age of accountability" without being baptized.

We do not want our children to be baptized for remission of the "sin of not being baptized." We pray that they will develop faith as they grow. Their faith decision may not be a sudden decision or conversion that reflects the darkness to light, idolatry to worshiping God, death to life contrasts of Scriptural conversion. Their faith may come more as maturing participants. Parents must discern what teaching a child needs and at what point to convey that message. But they must also respond to faith expressed by their children and adjust teaching and Spiritual formation to their maturity level.

So, what is the right age of maturity for a child to be baptized? We have seen a variety of approaches in age level, from infancy to adulthood. We have seen different ways of viewing a person, ranging from a baptized-into-the-community infant, a non-member, a prospect, a potential disciple, a maturing participant. In answering this question, we have tried to provide parents and church leaders with information upon which to base their own decision. We would not want to limit this answer to a range of ages that Scripture does not specify. Little if any evidence in Acts would suggest that children were baptized. We believe faith is a strong connection to baptism, that one who is going down in the river must be one who is going down in faith, seeking to plunge into the divine community and into the body of Christ. If a child, teenager, or adult thinks independently, repents of sins, and by faith comes believing Jesus is the Son of God, we could not hold that person back from the waters of baptism. Our responsibility is to focus our children on faith in Christ. That faith will bring our children to baptism at the right time. We believe God's grace is not riding on the edge of our human discernment. God sees in places where we cannot. We believe God will receive with grace a child who dies, even though not baptized. Furthermore, both adults and children are in the hands of God who judges with justice and grace (Exodus 34:6-7; Revelation 22:12-15).

2. Should we baptize infants?

Baptizing infants arises from a high view of baptism. We do not advocate baptizing infants. Rather, we believe adults who are expressing their faith in Christ should be baptized. Those who baptize infants, however, help teach us this high view of baptism, because they view baptism solely as a gift from God that is bestowed on the infant through the agency of the church and believing parents. It is impossible for infant baptism to be viewed as a work of the infant. The problem with this view, however, is that it excludes the faith of the one being baptized. True, one who is baptized as an infant may later live out faith, and we appreciate the perspective of those who baptize their infants out of an appeal to God for his gracious work in the lives of their children. This is indeed a theocentric understanding of baptism. We too affirm the theology that God is at work through baptism and that baptism is a sign, seal and means of grace. We, however, also affirm that this divine work is through faith. Just as we are saved by grace through faith, so baptism is effectual by grace through faith. To emphasize the necessity of personal faith for baptism no more de-emphasizes the divine work through baptism than does the necessity of faith de-emphasize the reality of God's gift of salvation through faith.

We believe our children, as maturing participants in the faith, are part of the kingdom of God. When their faith matures to the point that they seek baptism, we believe God works through their faith to transform and renew their lives. Their baptism affirms their discipleship and it becomes their personal decision to follow Jesus into water in order to follow him to the cross.

Many baptistic churches find ways to affirm the participatory role of their children in the life of the church. Many pray over their children at birth or have an annual day of prayer for newborns within that year. Churches should invite children to participate in the life of the church and affirm their presence. And they should encourage their children to affirm their faith through baptism when they are able and willing to count the cost of discipleship.

3. So, what is the plan of salvation?

There is an undeniably normative, or ideal, process in Scripture through which God joins his people again in a new covenant relationship. We should not, however, overstate this or attempt to own the process as if we could manipulate God's own choosing, mercy, or judgment or as if we could take Paul's various writings in different contexts and place them together to form a plan of salvation that is foolproof in all cases. God is not limited by this process and can choose and save whom he wants to choose and save.[5] God did not explicitly outline a precise five-step "plan" in Scripture. Instead, we have constructed a "plan" out of biblical materials.

The conversion narratives in Acts do not all conform to one consistent order. The normative order of conversion narratives is gospel proclamation, repentance, faith, immersion, and pouring out of the Spirit on new believers. The texts do not, however, explicitly call for this specific order in absolute terms (Acts 2:38; 8:15-16; 10:44-48; 22:16). While narratives in Acts do not agree in the order of conversion, they consistently portray adults responding penitently in awe and faith to proclamation of the gospel, receiving baptism in water and being renewed by the Holy Spirit. Paul says, "So faith comes from what is heard, and what is heard comes through the word of Christ" (Rom. 10:17). The word of Christ is proclaimed and demands a decisive "Yes!" in the life of a disciple. What is heard comes from Christ—we are saying "Yes" to him. For Paul, "...baptism was the moment and context in which it all came together," says D.G. Dunn, "so that the image of 'baptized into' Christ was given its deeper resonance."[6]

The Stone-Campbell Movement has generally worked with a step mentality. Originally, these steps were six in number and equally balanced between the human response and the divine gift. For example, Alexander Campbell enumerated them as: faith, repentance, immersion, remission of sins, the gift of the Holy Spirit and eternal life.[7] However, for pedagogical purposes, Walter Scott enumerated five in his five-finger exercise: faith, repentance, baptism, remission of sins and the gift of the Holy Spirit.[8] However, by the late nineteenth century, epitomized by T. W. Brent's *Gospel Plan of Salvation*,[9] the five steps had been recalibrated as hear, believe, repent, confess and be baptized.[10] Unfortunately, the five steps were now taught as five human acts rather than as human response and divine gift. The divine part was left out of the equation and a subtle shift took place so that now the "plan" of salvation was focused on human response rather than divine initiative (grace) and gift (salvation).

K.C. Moser noticed this shift toward human response. He wrote, *The Way of Salvation* (1932) and *Christ Versus a Plan* (1952), in which he pointed to Jesus Christ as our only way of salvation, not a plan. He said a blueprint does not save us. Jesus saves us. C. Leonard Allen outlined four reasons K.C. Moser rejected the "plan theory."[11]

- [The plan theory] removes Christ and the cross from first place and puts central emphasis on the "plan."
- The "plan theory" views the conditions of salvation as arbitrarily given by God.
- The "plan theory" makes the "plan" the means of salvation, not Christ crucified.

- The "plan theory" misconceives the meaning of saving faith and obedience to Christ.

Jack Cottrell suggests a revised "plan of salvation" and he also puts the phrase in quotes: "Baptism," he says, "is not the means of receiving salvation, but simply (by God's decree) the time or occasion for receiving it. A suggested (revised) 'plan of salvation' is that a sinner is saved by grace (as the basis), through faith (as the means), in baptism (as the occasion), for good works (as the result)."[12]

The problem with any formula, though Cottrell's language does not itself do this, is that it easily reduces faith, repentance, and baptism to stepping-stones to heaven rather than gifts to us through which God transforms us and invites us into a covenantal relationship. Any "plan" that is portrayed as the way to heaven that does not take great pains to tie faith and baptism to the work of God, Christ, and Holy Spirit concerns us. For instance, Peter says, "Baptism now saves us." Then he quickly says, "It saves us by the power of the resurrection" (1 Pet. 3:21-22).

God does have a plan, and it is for us to return to his redemptive story again and again. God's redemptive ways resist human attempts to contain his grace in an exactly ordered plan. As long as we are the ones developing the order of salvation, it is destined to be flawed. God's mercy meets humanity's faith in the person of Christ and the Holy Spirit.[13] God expects us to image his mercy in our lives—the criteria of human action in the few examples we have in the Bible of God's judgment are merciful, faithful, sanctified lives (Matt. 25:31-46; Rev. 22:14-15). God gets the last word on this. He will save those he wants to save (Rom. 9:14-18).[14]

4. At what point in time are we saved?

We need to take off our watches for this discussion. God is not bound by our mechanical clock. We were given a booklet on baptism that listed eight of nine questions that began with, "At what point..." For instance, "At what point is a person saved? At what point is a person's sins forgiven? At what point does a person receive the Holy Spirit?" This struck us as odd that nearly every question about baptism began with a focus on an exact point in time.

The redemptive work of God is a historical reality but not bound by time. God has been planning our redemption since before creation. We are not saying that we ought to ignore questions about when we are saved or at what point we receive the Holy Spirit. The question of "When, Lord?" has always been on the lips of God's people, either in terms of when God will bring the end of time or when he will redeem his people. We ought, however, to re-phrase our questions, because the way we phrase them often affects the answers. What if we re-phrased each of the questions that begin, "At what point..." with "What has God done?" So that the questions become "What has God done to save me? What has God done to wash away my sins?" This would re-focus our reflection on God's actions to save us and our receiving of his grace.

At what second are we saved? We do know the promise God has given by grace through faith expressed in baptism. We experience the journey of redemption through important events of repentance, renewal by the Holy Spirit, and baptism. God's redemption includes but is not limited to those events. The moments we repent of sins, trust in Jesus Christ to forgive us, and receive the Holy Spirit, and receive baptism are all part of the conversion narrative. Only God knows exactly when someone on this conversion journey is saved, though we know that those who are obedient in baptism through faith are forgiven and receive the gift of the Holy Spirit according to God's promise (Acts 2:38). We want to follow the whole conversion narrative. Our submission to this narrative is part of the journey of faith.

5. Is baptism a symbol, sacrament, sign, or all of the above?

The answer to this question lies in the definition of symbol, sacrament, and sign. On the one hand, if baptism is viewed purely as a symbol, it may be God-given but it is enacted by humanity. On the other hand, if baptism is viewed solely as a sacrament, or means of grace, it may be performed by a person but grace is mediated wholly by God.

Symbol and theology come together at the river. In baptism, the ground and means of grace unite mysteriously through faith in Christ. In other words, baptism is both an act of God and human beings. James McClendon, Jr. says, "human action and divine action converge in baptism." We agree. Therefore, we do not view baptism as purely symbolic or purely sacramental. We still view baptism through the lenses of symbol and sacrament. Yet in baptism symbol and sacrament unite. In baptism the divine action of God meets the humble "yes" of humanity. We agree with McClendon, who says that "baptism is not just the act of a candidate and a human administrator, but is an act of God: 'Baptized into union with him, you have all put on Christ like a garment' (Gal. 3:27)."[15]

We prefer to call baptism an "effectual sign."[16] Baptism is not merely the thing signified. In other words, God actually effects what baptism symbolizes. We believe baptism is an effectual sign of God's grace—a sign that actually effects what it symbolizes. When we go down in the river, we not only symbolize death with Christ—we do actually die to sin with him, are buried with him, and are raised to new life with him. The saving act is not the actual water—it is not magical—but we believe baptism in water is a performative sign through which God has chosen to mediate his grace through faith in Jesus Christ.

In the Stone-Campbell churches, where the attempt to emulate the early church has been important, the focus has moved away from the debate over symbol and sacrament and centered on the essentiality of baptism for salvation because it is a command or ordinance to be obeyed unswervingly. Teaching related to baptism has de-emphasized both the symbolic and sacramental sides in favor of viewing baptism as a command of Jesus the church is to carry out in much the same way that the church would carry out a hypothetical command of Jesus to jump through a hoop three times. Yet, reducing baptism down to a command does not solve the dilemmas of what baptism accomplishes, what it symbolizes, and whether it is God's work or our work. Even if considered as a command, is it a symbolic command or sacramental command?[17]

Chapter seven described how Alexander Campbell shifted from his Zwinglian view of baptism as a symbol of God's work in us to a view that sees our baptism as an actual means through which we receive forgiveness of sins. Baptism is a truly effective symbol through which God empowers his people by bestowing a visible sign of his assurance that is mediated through the grace of baptism of water and the Spirit.

In viewing baptism as a sign, we view God graciously giving us the very things that baptism symbolizes. In baptism, God shares with us the gracious gifts of union with Christ in his death washing of forgiveness, burial and resurrection with Christ, being reclothed, initiated into the body, forgiveness of sins and receiving the fire of the Holy Spirit, making a covenant appeal to Christ and the resurrection of Christ that saves us (Rom. 6:3-5, Titus 3:5-7; Col. 2:12; Gal. 3:27; 1 Cor. 12:13; Acts 2:38-39; 1 Pet. 3:21). God through baptism both symbolizes and gives these gifts.

6. When is "rebaptizing" a person legitimate or necessary?

This question has at least two dimensions. Some seek rebaptism because they feel that their first immersion as a child or in a different church tradition was defective. Others feel their infant baptism was genuine baptism and see no need to express their faith through "another" baptism.

Some adults are reimmersed because they believe their baptism as a pre-teen was for less than laudable motives. Some associate their baptism with a kind of "following the crowd" syndrome, or some believe their baptism was purely an emotive response to the passionate appeal of a persuasive evangelist. Other adults are reimmersed because they believe they lacked a sufficient understanding of the meaning of baptism. For example, they may, in agreement with John Thomas (see chapter 7), believe that one must understand that baptism is the moment of salvation in order for God to work effectively through it. Consequently, they are reimmersed.

Both of the above situations, we think, miss the point. The efficacy of baptism does not depend upon what we believe about baptism but whether we believe in Christ. The object of faith is Christ, not baptism. The efficacy of baptism is the efficacy of faith, and faith is effective when it is directed at Christ's work for us. The important question, then, is whether we trusted in Christ for our salvation when we were immersed. We should not focus on the perfection of faith since that is unattainable. Rather, we focus on the object of faith—in whom does faith trust? When we remember our faith in Christ at our baptism, then our baptism is a divine promise to us.

We all were baptized with mixed motives and misunderstandings of baptism. While we may have been persuaded by an evangelist or peers, or moved by the emotional drama of the occasion (including the fear of going to hell if we were not baptized that very night!), the significant point is that when we were immersed we trusted in Christ. If that trust was present at our baptism, whether other motives were there or not, then God was graciously present through that faith. God's promise in baptism is attached to faith and where faith is present at baptism God is present. Generally speaking, if one has enough faith in Christ to be baptized in submission to God's command, then God will graciously receive that faith no matter what other misunderstandings or inferior motives are present. Enough faith to act is sufficient faith.

If faith, however, is so central as a means for baptismal efficacy, what does this say about infant baptism? Should those baptized as infants be immersed as believers and thus be "rebaptized?"

We appreciate how significant infant baptism is for believers who were initiated into the Christian faith by their parents. We value parents and grandparents who seek to introduce and nurture their children in the faith. We would not want to devalue the nurture and training that those so raised have received. Further, we would not want anyone to repudiate the values that their baptism represented and which their parents sought to inculcate in them. Infant baptism is not totally devoid of significance. At the very least it functions as an infant dedication, though advocates believe it is much more.

We do believe, however, that infant baptism is defective and does not reflect a biblical baptismal theology. We call those baptized as infants to express their own personal faith and discipleship through immersion. By so doing, we do not believe that anyone renounces all that was part of their past. Indeed, they affirm their past by a continued, though fuller, commitment to Christ.

McClendon refers to the immersion of a believer who was first baptized as an infant as baptismal "repair." Rebaptism is not a denial of one's life of faith up to that moment, but a reaffirmation of faith. The "appropriate remedy for an impaired baptism," McClendon writes, is repetition whereby "this repetitive act regularize[s] the original one rather than" denying "its [impaired] existence" so that "baptismal repair" acknowledges "the earlier rite and the genuine faith that has appeared."[18]

We affirm the rebaptism of those baptized as infants for the same reason we reject the rebaptism of those who were baptized as believers. Baptism is effective through faith, just as grace is received through faith. Every immersion that expresses faith in Christ is effective by the grace of God, but no baptism without faith is effective. We call the church to "one baptism."[19]

7. Who may administer baptism?

Since the early second century baptism has been administrated by clerics. Ignatius, for example, ruled that no baptism should take place without the approval of the Bishop (Letter to Smyrna 8:2). From that time on the provenance of baptism has belonged to the clergy—only they may administer the grace of baptism. Due to the historic church's understanding of baptismal necessity, emergency baptisms by lay people (even midwives) have been authorized. Some, however, like Calvin, objected to the practice because they did not believe salvation hung absolutely on baptism.

One of the greatest strengths of the Stone-Campbell Movement is its emphasis on the priesthood of all believers. One of the fundamental expressions of this perspective is how the liturgy or worship of the church is conducted—it is stripped of any overt clericalism. The administration of the Lord's Supper, for example, is not limited to ministers, elders or evangelists. Rather, believers serve the Supper. Likewise, baptism is not limited to ministers, elders or evangelists. Rather, believers baptize believers. Indeed, fathers often baptize their sons, or the one who brought them to Christ is the one who baptizes. This has been a cherished value among Churches of Christ and has been part of their history from the beginning.[20]

This priestly privilege, however, has been generally limited to men. Women have been excluded from the administration of baptism to their daughters or to those whom they disciple. The main rationale for this exclusion is that women should not have "authority" over men, which is based upon a particular reading of 1 Timothy 2:12. But baptism does not involve authority—either clerical or gender. John the Baptist did not have "authority" over Jesus when he baptized him. The baptizer is a servant, a tool in God's handiwork—not the agent of God's grace. Faith is the means of grace in baptism, not the baptizer. Baptism is God's work, and it is neither the authority nor the work of the baptizer or the baptizee. The issue is not one of gender, but the nature of baptism. To center the meaning and legitimacy of baptism on the administrator is to subvert the place of God in the baptismal rite. We see no reason why women should not baptize their daughters whom they nurtured in the faith, and we see no reason why women should not baptize those they lead to faith in Christ.

8. Is salvation an event or a process?

Salvation is both an event and a process. Paul describes salvation in the past, present and future tenses in his letters (Eph. 2:8; 2 Cor. 2:15; Rom. 5:10). Salvation is something we have experienced, continue to experience and will yet more fully experience in the future. This is a process, but it is punctuated with events. Both the process and the events are important.

It is a process of transformation. We are continually transformed into the image of Christ by the power of the Spirit as we live in faith. This process will be complete when we are made like Christ in every way. God will finish his work in us through the full sanctification of body, soul and spirit when Christ returns to raise his people from the dead. However, this process includes significant events. It includes frequent encounters with God in prayer and worship, whether personal or communal.

But God has also ordained some concrete, visible events through which he encounters his people. Some call them "sacraments" and others "ordinances." God encounters us at his table where God communes with us through bread and wine.[21] The table is the gospel in bread and wine; it is communion with God in concrete, visible form. But the first concrete encounter with God is through baptism, which is the gospel in water. Through baptism we are united with Christ and experience the grace of the gospel. Consequently, in Romans 6 Paul points back to this event in order to encourage Christians to continue the process of salvation (transformation). Baptism is a life-changing event, but it is part of the process of transformation.

Is there process before baptism? Yes, because faith leads us to baptism and God is active in bringing people to faith by his Spirit and leading people to baptism. The Spirit of God is active before baptism. For example, we all pray for God's Spirit to surround our children and mature them in faith, even before their baptism. We pray for God to lead people to faith and then once in the process of faith we pray for God to mature their faith by his Spirit. Ultimately, however, faith acts in the baptismal event, and the Spirit also acts in the baptismal moment. Salvation is not an either/or, but a both/and. It is process and event—neither should be devalued.

The Future of Baptism

The river that begins and ends at the throne of God has cut a broad path through the canyons of church history. The river beckons us to be unified in its flow, to dive in and drown our old life. We believe it's time for revival in the camps and another preaching down in the river. Baptism is a hopeful and effective sign of God's work in us through faith in Christ. We must begin anew to acknow-ledge that baptism is a vital part of conversion but that God is not bound by our attempts to pinpoint the exact minute at which one is saved. We can affirm with confidence that believer's baptism is a conversion-initiation. Baptism is for transformation and is the normative teaching and practice of Scripture. And we believe this should be the normative practice in the church today. The particular time-sequence, exceptions, and mysterious ways through which God chooses to mediate his grace and redeem people must be left to his good pleasure and divine will.

Baptism, however, is not simply about what God did in the past. Baptism is a glorious sign of future hope through the rising of Christ. Robert Lowry wrote about the vivid end-times image that prompted him to write the hymn, "Shall We Gather at the River." A pastor at Hanson Place Baptist Church in Brooklyn, New York, Lowry said he was resting when a powerful image engulfed his imagination. He wrote:

> One afternoon in July 1864, the weather was oppressively hot, and I was lying on a lounge in a state of physical exhaustion…My imagination began to take itself wings.

> Visions of the future passed before me with startling vividness. The imagery of the apocalypse took the form of a tableau. Brightest of all were the throne, the heavenly river, and the gathering of the saints…I began to wonder why the hymn writers had said so much about the "river of death" and so little about the "pure water of life, clear as crystal, proceeding out of the throne of God and the Lamb." As I mused, the words began to construct themselves. They came first as a question of Christian inquiry, "Shall we gather?" Then they broke in chorus, "Yes, we'll gather." On this question and answer the hymn developed itself. The music came with the hymn.[22]

Here are the words that flowed from his pen, words that have beckoned many down to the river side:

> Shall we gather at the river,
> Where bright angel feet have trod,
> With its crystal tide forever
> Flowing by the throne of God?

Our faith seeking understanding asks the question: "Is there any unity to be had at the river, where Catholics, Baptists, Methodists and 'Campbellites' have trod? Is there yet one baptism along with one faith, one Lord, one Spirit, one body, one hope? If we are to live the prayer of Jesus in John 17 for unity, we must ask this question and answer resoundingly, in the words of Lowry's refrain:

> Yes, we'll gather at the river,
> The beautiful, the beautiful river;
> Gather with the saints at the river
> That flows by the throne of God.

There is another shore that we hope and long for: the other side, where we—who have been saved by God's grace—will stand. Lowry's song continues to float over the river.

> At the smiling of the river,
> Mirror of the Savior's face,

Saints, whom death will never sever,
Lift their songs of saving grace.

REFRAIN
Soon we'll reach the shining river,
Soon our pilgrimage will cease;
Soon our happy hearts will quiver
With the melody of peace.

Shall we gather at the river speaks to the unity that we hope for in the end times. Christ's prayer for believers in John 17 may not have been entirely a vision of earthly unity. On this shore we have a few unity picnics in the midst of all the lines in the sand. We rejoice in those opportunities to share the vision of Christ for the unity of his body. Yet like each individual who is being transformed from one degree of glory to the next, so the whole body of Christ is being transformed, sanctified, and will be glorified. This full unity, however, will be known only on the other shore. Lowry's song is a vivid vision of the end times, when we will meet our Lord. And finally the community of Father, Son, and Holy Spirit will be fully joined with the community of faith. We will also join with the faithful who have gone before us and those who may come after us. Only then will we have complete unity.

We have called the church back to the riverbanks, but we also point to that distant shore that John saw in a vision and recorded in Revelation 22:1-5:

> Then the angel showed me the river of the water of life, bright as crystal, flowing from the throne of God and of the Lamb through the middle of the street of the city. On either side of the river is the tree of life with its twelve kinds of fruit, producing its fruit each month; and the leaves of the tree are for the healing of the nations. Nothing accursed will be found there any more. But the throne of God and of the Lamb will be in it, and his servants will worship him; they will see his face, and his name will be on their foreheads. And there will be no more night; they need no light of lamp or sun, for the Lord God will be their light, and they will reign forever and ever.

The river flowing by the throne of God is a victorious vision for Christians. God's river does not flow into a salty sea, though we could sing songs of the depth of his grace like the ocean. Instead, the image is of an ever fresh river, flowing. God's grace flows from the throne through time and through the city he is preparing for his chosen and faithful ones. Both shores of the river are now blessed with the trees of life and their fruit. The trees produce the leaves of healing for the nations. No longer will disunity abide by the river. Nothing accursed will be on these riverbanks.

The throne of God is down in the river. The angel showed John a city, a street, and a river that flowed down the middle of the street. In a wide place in the river was the throne. Later in verse 3, John simply says the throne is in it. The Lamb is on the throne. The one with whom we have been buried, planted, is the one who has been first raised up by God and seated on the throne. He will bring us to the other shore, lift us as he had been lifted from the depths. And on his shores of grace and life we shall rest and be healed by the trees of life. Unity and healing will not be complete until we reach the other shore. We have both been emotionally, spiritually, and physically moved by God's grace, and only because of this grace can we rise up to stand before the throne.

When we dove into the river to find Christ, we found that life itself has dashed us on the rocks, drowned us, and its roaring white waters have swept us downstream. The destructive drowning pull of sin is no match for the redeeming power of God's grace through faith in Christ Jesus. A song by Debbie Dorman, "Had it not been the Lord,"[23] has helped both of us express this grace:

> Had it not been the Lord who was on our side
> Had it not been the Lord who was on our side
> The water would have engulfed us
> We would have surely died
> Had it not been the Lord who was on our side
>
> Blessed be the Lord who would not give us up
> Blessed be the Lord for his unfailing love
> The snare is broken and we have escaped
> Our help is in the name of the Lord
> Blessed be the Lord

We have been down in the river to seek the kingdom of Christ. We dove into the divine community and have not been abandoned in the depths. "The water would have engulfed us," says the song. "We would have surely died, had it not been the Lord who was on our side." We would have drowned. We were swept away, consumed by the power of hell and sin and darkness, but by the "long gentle hand" of Jesus, we are saved. Young Bevel dove into the river to find that kingdom of peace with God. Perhaps Christ did meet Bevel in the depths. He said the kingdom belongs to such as these who by simple trust in God, live. Perhaps we too are not far from the kingdom. Christ has by his death and resurrection moved us toward the kingdom. By God's grace we can see the other shore that is without lines in the sand. Christ who met us in the depths will also meet us on that shore. If we have met him in the depths, surely we will stand with him on that shore.

****

Principle

When we revision "one baptism" as transformation but allow God to inhabit the mystery of the time-sequence of conversion, we will move toward greater unity that Christ prayed for in John 17.

Prayer

Lord, our world is ripped to shreds and divided along battle lines of war, ethnic hatred, political opinions, and religious dogma. Shall we gather at the river? Are you calling us to both a firm belief in baptism's role in conversion and a strong pull toward unity? How can two seemingly opposed ideas co-exist among Christians? Yet you prayed, Jesus, for unity and called us to make disciples on the basis of faith in you, teaching of all that you've commanded, baptism, and renewal by the Holy Spirit. We know you did not call us to make disciples who are not unified, yet we are perplexed by the lack of unity we see among Christians. How much longer, Lord, will this be? Show us the path of greater unity while helping us keep biblical integrity. Lord, we long to be with you on that distant shore! Amen.

Questions

1. How can you revision baptism in your church?

2. What is the primary Scriptural symbol through which you view baptism? Your baptism specifically?

3. Is baptism a work of humans or a work of God? Why?

4. How can we believe and practice immersion as vital without applying it in sectarian ways that deny God's sovereignty over his judgment of humanity?

5. Can we have unity on earth? How can we see or promote glimpses of the end-times unity in our beliefs and practices today?

Suggested Reading

Biblical

Beasley-Murray, G. R. *Baptism in the New Testament.* Grand Rapids: Eerdmans, 1962.

Cullmann, Oscar. *Baptism in the New Testament.* London: SCM, 1950.

Hartman, Lars. *'Into the Name of the Lord Jesus': Baptism in the Early Church.* Edinburgh: T. & T. Clark, 1997.

Wedderburn, A. J. M. *Baptism and Resurrection: Studies in Pauline Theology Against Its Graeco-Roman Background.* Tübingen: J. C. B. Mohr, 1987.

White, R. E. O. *The Biblical Doctrine of Initiation.* London: Hodder & Stoughton, 1960.

Historical

Aland, Kurt. *Did the Early Church Baptize Infants?* London: SCM, 1963.

Baker, William R., ed. *Evangelicalism & the Stone-Campbell Movement.* Downers Grove, IL: InterVarsity, 2002.

Cross, Anthony R. *Baptism and the Baptists: Theology and Practice in the Twentieth Century.* Carlisle: Paternoster, 2000.

Jeremias, Joachim. *Infant Baptism in the First Four Centuries.* London: SCM, 1960.

McDonnell, Kilian and George T. Montague. *Christian Initiation and Baptism in the Holy Spirit in the First Eight Centuries.* 2nd ed. Collegeville, MN: Liturgical Press, 1994.

Porter, Stanley E. and Anthony R. Cross. *Baptism, the New Testament and the Church: Historical and Contemporary Studies in Honour of R. E. O. White.* Sheffield: Sheffield Academic Press, 1999.

White, James F. *The Sacraments in Protestant Faith and Practice.* Nashville, TN: Abingdon, 1999.

Theological/Practical

Barth, Karl. *The Teaching of the Church Regarding Baptism.* London: SCM, 1948.

Beasley-Murray, G. R. *Baptism Today and Tomorrow.* London: Macmillan, 1966.

Bridge, Donald and David Phypers. *The Water That Divides: The Baptism Debate.* Downers Grove, IL: InterVarsity, 1977.

Jewett, Paul K. *Infant Baptism and the Covenant of Grace.* Grand Rapids, MI: Eerdmans, 1978.

Schlink, Edmund. *The Doctrine of Baptism.* St. Louis, MO: Concordia, 1972.

Stookey, Laurence Hull. *Baptism: Christ's Act in the Church.* Nashville, TN: Abingdon, 1982.

Root, M. and Saarinen, R., eds. *Baptism and the Unity of the Church.* Grand Rapids, MI: Eerdmans, 1998.

Willimon, William. *Remember Who You Are: Baptism, A Model for Christian Life.* Nashville, TN: Upper Room, 1980.

Recent Stone-Campbell Works

Bryant, Rees. *Baptism, Why Wait? Faith's Response in Conversion.* Joplin, MO: College Press, 1999.

Cottrell, Jack. *Baptism: A Biblical Study*. Joplin, MO: College Press, 1989.

Fletcher, David, ed. *Baptism and the Remission of Sins: An Historical Perspective.* Joplin, MO: College Press, 1990.

McNicol, Allan J. *Preparing for Baptism: Becoming Part of the Story of the People of God.* Austin, TX: Christian Studies Press, 2001.

Olbricht, Owen D. *Baptism: New Birth or Empty Ritual?* Delight, AR: Gospel Light, 1994.

Riley, Tom. *Dying to Live Again: The Grace of Baptism.* Webb City, MO: Covenant Publishing, 2000.

Smith, F. LaGard. *Baptism, the Believer's Wedding Ceremony.* Nashville, TN: Gospel Advocate, 1993.

Watkins, Keith and La Taunya Marie Bynum. *Baptism and Belonging: A Resource for Christian Worship.* St. Louis, MO: Chalice Press, 1991.

Williamson, Clark. *Baptism: Embodiment of the Gospel.* St. Louis, MO: Christian Board of Publication, 1987.

Notes

Chapter One

1. Flannery O'Connor, "The River," *The Complete Stories* (New York: Farrar, Straus and Giroux, 1971). Originally published in 1953 in a volume of short stories entitled, *A Good Man Is Hard To Find, And Other Stories* (New York: Image Books, 1970).

2. O'Connor, "The River."

3. When we speak of God's intentions and goals, we must stay as close as possible to God's own words, revelation in Christ, and redemptive history, and far from attaching our own human characteristics, desires, and feelings onto the Father, Son, and Holy Spirit. When we try to peg God's goals and intentions, we must move with caution.

4. A helpful book for me (Greg) was Jack Cottrell's *Baptism: A Biblical Study* (Joplin, M0: College Press, 1989), 1-21. I'm also grateful for Rees Bryant's *Baptism, Why Wait? Faith's Response in Conversion* (Joplin, M0: College Press, 1999) for a comprehensive view specifically of conversion in the Old Testament and New Testament from a missions perspective. The book is good reading for churches thinking about both local and worldwide evangelism.

5. Beasley-Murray has been the "go to" source on baptism since the 1960s. Few Church of Christ preachers are without a copy of this Baptist writer's *Baptism in the New Testament* (Grand Rapids: Eerdmans, 1962).

6. For a look at one unifying effort on baptism, see *Baptism and the Unity of the Church*, eds. Michael Root and Risto Saarinen (Grand Rapids: Eerdmans, 1998). Also see http://www.wcc-coe.org/wcc/what/faith/bem3.html.

7. David Fletcher and John Mark Hicks, "Introduction," in *Baptism and the Remission of Sins: An Historical Perspective*, ed. David W. Fletcher (Joplin, M0: College Press, 1990), 9f. Their introduction was helpful in my (Greg) understanding of how Churches of Christ have taken neither the Orthodox sacramental view nor the strictly Evangelical (symbolic) view. Churches of Christ are a strange mix and rejection of these two, because we have largely rejected the "magical" view of the sacraments but have tied legal exactitude of baptism to salvation. We have rejected the strict "ordinance view" of Evangelicals, yet maintain strong ties to faith and believer's baptism. We have rejected infant baptism. Anglican N.P. Williams said Restorationists (he was speaking specifically of the Disciples) rejected infant baptism as the fundamental

error of Christendom because it sets within the Christian system a standing contradiction to the gospel: no strong tie to faith (other than parents) and God's personal relationship with his people.

8. As quoted by Karl Barth, *The Epistle to the Romans*, trans. by Edwyn C. Hoskyns (6th ed., London: Oxford, 1933), 96.

Chapter Two

1. "A Day in the Life of Hananiah Nothus," a fictional member of the Qumran community in the region of the Dead Sea whose life is reconstructed based upon known archaeological and historical sources, available at http://www.mfa.gov.il/mfa/go.asp?MFAH0dqe0.

2. Jon A. Weatherly, "The Role of Baptism in Conversion: Israel's Promises Fulfilled for the Believer in Jesus," in *Evangelicalism & the Stone-Campbell Movement*, ed. William R. Baker (Downers Grove, IL: InterVarsity Press 2002), 162. Weatherly refers to A. J. M. Wedderburn, *Baptism and Resurrection: Studies in Pauline Theology Against Its Graeco-Roman Background*, Wissenschaftliche Untersuchungen zum Neuen Testament 2 (Tubingen: Mohr-Siebeck, 1987) as the "definitive treatment." According to Wayne Meeks' review in the *Journal of Biblical Literature* 108 (December 1989), 744, Wedderburn established "his principal points beyond dispute."

3. See Wayne Grudem, *The First Epistle of Peter*, TNTC (Downers Grove, IL: InterVarsity, 1988), 163-64.

4. John E. Colwell, "Baptism, Conscience and the Resurrection: A Reappraisal of 1 Peter 3:21," in *Baptism, the New Testament and the Church: Historical and Contemporary Studies in Honour of R. E. O. White*, JSNTSup 171, ed. Stanley Porter and Anthony R. Cross (Sheffield: Sheffield Academic Press, 1999), 227.

5. E. P. Sanders, *Judaism: Practice & Belief, 63 BCE–66 CE* (Philadelphia: Trinity Press International, 1992), 225.

6. Robert L. Webb, *John the Baptizer and Prophet: A Socio-Historical Study*, JSNTSup 62 (Sheffield: JSOT Press, 1991), 106.

7. Webb, 107.

8. On the Second Temple period, see Webb, 108-162.

9. See some of the standard, but recent, encyclopedias for discussion, e.g., *Anchor Bible Dictionary*. Also, Sanders, 222-229, provides a good summary.

10. See the example at http://members.aol.com/uticacw/baptist/baptism3.html.

11. William S. LaSor, "Discovering What Jewish Miqva'ot Can Tell Us About Christian Baptism," *Biblical Archaeology Review* 13 (January/February 1987), 52-9.

12. Ronny Reich, "The Great Mikveh Debate," *Biblical Archaeology Review* 19 (March/April 1993), 52.

13. Bargil Pixner, "Jerusalem's Essene Gateway: Where the Community Lived in Jesus' Time," *Biblical Archaeological Review* 23 (May/June 1997), 22-31, 64, 66, available at http://www.centuryone.org/essene.html, including a picture of a *mikveh* with

descending and ascending steps.

14. Herbert Danby, *The Mishnah, Translated from the Hebrew with Introduction and Brief Explanatory Notes* (London: Oxford University, 1933), 742.

15. Sanders, 228.

16. Sanders, 228-29.

17. Ehud Netzer, "A Synagogue from the Hasmonean Period Exposed at Jericho," available at http://www.bibleinterp.com/articles/Synagogue.htm.

18. Bill Grasham, "Archaeology and Christian Baptism," *Restoration Quarterly* 43.2 (2001), 115, citing *B. Yoma* 30a.

19. However, the Sibylline Oracles, lines 151-72, may establish the practice as early as 80 A.D.

20. See Joan E. Taylor, *The Immerser: John the Baptist within Second Temple Judaism* (Grand Rapids: Eerdmans, 1997), 64-69.

21. For example, David Dockery, "Baptism," *Dictionary of Jesus and the Gospels*, eds. Joel Green and Scot McKnight (Downers Grove, IL: InterVarsity, 1992), 55-58. But for a contrary opinion, see Taylor, 76-88.

22. http://www.cresourcei.org/phototour/pfintro.html provides a clear picture of steps into a Qumran *mikveh*. So far ten have been discovered.

23. See G. Vermes, *The Dead Sea Scrolls in English* (New York: Penguin, 1962), 77-78.

Chapter Three

1. This is a summary of Acts 2:1-47.

2. N. T. Wright, *The New Testament and the People of God* (Minneapolis: Fortress, 1992).

3. Jon A. Weatherly, "The Role of Baptism in Conversion: Israel's Promises Fulfilled for the Believer in Jesus," in *Evangelicalism and the Stone-Campbell Movement*, ed. William R. Baker (Downers Grove, IL: InterVarsity, 2002), 173. I am indebted to Weatherly's thematic perspective.

4. See the discussion of Max Turner, *Power from on High: The Spirit in Israel's Restoration and Witness in Luke-Acts*, Journal of Pentecostal Theology Supplement 9 (Sheffield: Academic Press, 1996).

5. Adela Yarbro Collins, "The Origin of Christian Baptism," *Studia Liturgica* 19.1 (1989), 35.

6. Cf. Robert Webb, *John the Baptizer and Prophet: A Socio-Historical Study*, Journal for the Study of the New Testament Supplement 62 (Sheffield: JSOT Press, 1991), 193.

7. Kilian McDonnell, "Jesus' Baptism in the Jordan," *Theological Studies* 56.2 (1995), 210.

8. G. R. Beasley-Murray, *Baptism in the New Testament* (Grand Rapids: Eerdmans, 1962); R. E. O. White, *The Biblical Doctrine of Initiation* (London: Hodder & Stoughton), 1960. Note the judgment of M. J. Walker, "Baptist Worship in the Twentieth

Century," in *Baptists in the Twentieth Century*, ed. K. W. Clements (London: Baptist Historical Society, 1983), 24-25: "[they] brought the sacrament of baptism out of the Zwinglian shadows and made us see that here was indeed a place of rendezvous between God and man, an integral part of that process of conversion by which a man or woman is raised from death to life in Christ, is cleansed of sin, made a member of the body of Christ and endowed with the gift of the Spirit."

9. For example, Robert H. Stein, "Baptism and Becoming a Christian in the New Testament," *Southern Baptist Journal of Theology* 2.1 (1998), 6-17. The Baptist evangelical H. Wayne House, "An Evangelical Response to Baird & Weatherly," in *Evangelicalism and the Stone-Campbell Movement*, 188: "I enthusiastically acknowledge, contrary to the common practice in Baptist churches, that the early church would not have understood a person claiming to be a Christian who was not baptized."

10. These are the traditional "conversion narratives" in Acts, though others might be included. For example, the lame man in Acts 3:16 who is healed (saved) by faith, Sergius Paulus who hears and believes the teaching about the Lord in Acts 13:6-12, and Dionysius and Damarius who believe the preaching of Paul regarding the resurrection of Jesus in Acts 17:34. For a full discussion of conversion narratives in Acts, see Allen Black, "The Conversion Stories in the Acts of the Apostles: A Study of their Form and Function" (Ph.D., Emory University, 1985).

11. Joel B. Green, "From 'John's Baptism' to 'Baptism in the Name of the Lord Jesus': The Significance of Baptism in Luke-Acts," in *Baptism, the New Testament and the Church: Historical and Contemporary Studies in Honour of R. E. O. White*, JSNTSup 171, ed. Stanley E. Porter and Anthony R. Cross (Sheffield: Sheffield Academic Press, 1999), 161. This perspective is increasingly more common. For example, Kilian McDonnell and George T. Montague, "A Response to Paul Turner on Christian Initiation and Baptism in the Holy Spirit," *Worship* 71 (January 1997), 53, maintain that Acts 2:38 is "paradigmatic" and "normative." For a fuller explanation of their views, see their *Christian Initiation and Baptism in the Holy Spirit: Evidence from the First Eight Centuries*, 2nd ed. (Collegeville, MN: Liturgical Press, 1994).

12. Green, 161 (italics his).

13. See J. W. Roberts, "Baptism for the Remission of Sins—A Critique," *Restoration Quarterly* 1.4 (1957), 226-234 and J. C. Davis, "Another Look at the Relationship Between Baptism and Forgiveness of Sins in Acts 2:38," *Restoration Quarterly* 24.2 (1981), 80-88.

14 See Carroll D. Osburn, "The Third Person Imperative in Acts 2:38," *Restoration Quarterly* 26.2 (1983), 81-84 and Ashby L. Camp, "Reexamining the Rule of Concord in Acts 2:38," *Restoration Quarterly* 39.1 (1997), 37-42.

15. Timothy George, "The Reformed Doctrine of Believer's Baptism," *Interpretation* 47 (July 1993), 248.

16. Frederick W. Norris, "'Christians Only, but Not the Only Christians' (Acts 19:1-7)," *Restoration Quarterly* 28.2 (1985-86), 97-105.

17. Weatherly, 169.

18. Alexander Campbell, "Remarks on the Above," *Millennial Harbinger* 11 (March 1840), 127-8, preferred the term "disciple" for the unimmersed and tended to reserve the name "Christian" for those who fully practiced the New Testament order. Cf. "A Voice From the North," *Millennial Harbinger* 11 (June 1840), 276-7: "No one, then can be called a Christian, in the Antiochian sense, who does not resemble them in knowledge and faith, and manners, though he may be scripturally called a disciple of Christ."

Chapter Four

1. As quoted by Karl Barth, *The Epistle to the Romans*, trans. by Edwyn C. Hoskyns (London: Oxford, 1933), 96.

2. Beasley-Murray examines at least sixteen references that move from the strongest and most likely references to the weakest and least likely references to baptism. The order is from most prominent and strong to less prominent and weaker statements. Romans 6:1f; Gal. 3:26-27; Colossians 2:11f, 1:13f; 1 Cor. 6:11, 12:13; 2 Cor. 1:22; Eph. 1:13, 4:30; 1 Cor. 1:11-17; 1 Cor. 10:1f; 1 Cor. 15:29; 2 Cor. 7:14; Eph. 4:5, 5:25-27; 1 Timothy 6:12-13; 2 Timothy 2:11-12; Titus 3:5-7. See his classic study of baptism, *Baptism in the New Testament* (Grand Rapids: Eerdman, 1962).

3. For more on the social setting of Romans, see James C. Walters, *Ethnic Issues in Paul's Letter to the Romans: Changing Self-Definitions in Earliest Roman Christianity* (Harrisburg, PA: Trinity Press International, 1993).

4. See Richard P. Carlson, "The Role of Baptism in Paul's Thought," *Interpretation*, 47 (July 1993), 257.

5. I first encountered this idea in Phillip Yancey's *What's So Amazing About Grace?* (Grand Rapids: Zondervan, 2000).

6. Beasley-Murray, *Baptism in the New Testament*, 154.

7. Paul uses similar language in Romans 13:14 in the imperative tense in a section on the new ethic in Christ with no apparent allusion to baptism. The sense is that one can "put on" (*enedysasthe*) Christ in baptism and "put on" the new identity and ethical life.

8. Indicative and imperative is not a new idea. The structure of biblical ethics could be put in this paradigm, and specific actions or imperatives of God in the Old Testament can also be seen this way. The Ten Commandments, for instance, were predicated by a prologue, a historical demonstration of God's deliverance of Israelites from Egypt. The indicative shows what God has done. The imperatives are the commands or God's requirements on the basis of the indicatives. See Brevard Childs, *The Book of Exodus*, Old Testament Library (Philadelphia: Westminster, 1974), 401. Michael Parsons, "Being Precedes Act: Indicative and Imperative in Paul's Writing," *Evangelical Quarterly* 88 (April 1988), 99-127.

9. Watchman Nee, *Sit, Walk, Stand* (Wheaton, IL: Tyndale House, 1977).

10. Bornkamm, *Paul*, 203.

11. See Morton Scott Enslin, *The Ethics of Paul* (New York: Abingdon, 1957), 67; M. Cary and T. J. Haarhoff, *Life and Thought in the Greek and Roman World* (London: Methuen & Co., 1940; reprint, 1957), 330-31.

12. J. L. Houlden, *Ethics and the New Testament* (Harmondsworth, Middlesex, England: Penguin Books, 1973), 34.

13. Carlson, 257.

14. Cf. J. Paul Sampley's *Walking between the Times: Paul's Moral Reasoning* (Minneapolis: Fortress Press, 1991) for a discussion of how Paul's moral reasoning occurs in the context of "no longer," "already," and "not yet."

Chapter Five

1. As quoted by Everett Ferguson, *Early Christians Speak* (Austin: Sweet Publishing, 1971), 57.

2. See David F. Wright, "How Controversial Was the Development of Infant Baptism in the Early Church?" in *Church, Word, and Spirit: Historical and Theological Essays in Honor of Geoffrey W. Bromiley*, ed. James E. Bradley and Richard A. Muller (Grand Rapids: Eerdmans, 1987), 45-63.

3. See Jack P. Lewis, "Baptismal Practices of the Second and Third Century," *Restoration Quarterly* 26 (1983), 1-18.

4. Everett Ferguson, "Baptismal Motifs in the Ancient Church," *Restoration Quarterly* 7 (1963), 202-16.

5. J. Jeremias, *The Origins of Infant Baptism* (London: SCM Press, 1960), 70, 74.

6. Everett Ferguson, "Inscriptions and the Origin of Infant Baptism," *Journal of Theological Studies* ns30 (1979), 37-46.

7. Ferguson, "Inscriptions," 44.

8. Ferguson, "Inscriptions," 44.

9. Ferguson, "Inscriptions," 45.

10. The fourth-century historian Eusebius describes the circumstances of his baptism in his *Ecclesiastical History* (6.43).

11. David F. Wright, "The Origins of Infant Baptism—Child Believer's Baptism?" *Scottish Journal of Theology* 40 (1990), 1-23 and "Infant Dedication in the Early Church," in *Baptism, the New Testament and the Church: Historical and Contemporary Studies in Honour of R. E. O. White*, ed. Stanley E. Porter and Anthony R. Cross (Sheffield: Sheffield Academic Press, 1999), 352-78.

12. Session 6, Chapter 4, available at http://history.hanover.edu/texts/trent/ct06.html.

13. James F. White, *The Sacraments in Protestant Practice and Faith* (Nashville: Abingdon, 1999), 32.

14. Bonaventure, *Commentary on the Book of Sentences*, 3, a.2, q.2, writes: "The method of dipping into the water is the more common, and therefore the fitter and

safer," and Aquinas, *Summa Theologica*, 3, q.66, a.7, writes: "Christ's burial is more clearly represented by immersion: wherefore this manner of baptizing is more frequently in use and more commendable."

15. See, for example, the "agreed statement" of the North American Orthodox-Catholic Theological Consultation, June 3, 1999 available at http://www.geocities.com/Atrium/8410/baptism.html.

Chapter Six

1. As quoted by Hans J. Hillerbrand, ed., *The Reformation: A Narrative History Related by Contemporary Observers and Participants* (Grand Rapids: Baker, 1978), 233.

2. See Gerald S. Krispin, "Baptism and *Heilsgewissheit* in Luther's Theology," *Concordia Journal* 13 (April 1987), 106-118.

3. *The Babylonian Captivity of the Church*, 9.3, available at http://www.ctsfw.edu/ etext/luther/babylonian/babylonian.htm.

4. Luther, *Small Catechism*, available at http://www.lcms.org/bookofconcord/smallcatechism.asp#baptism.

5. *Augsburg Confession*, art. 13, available at http://www.lcms.org/bookofconcord/augsburgconfession.asp#article13.

6. Luther, *Sermon on the Holy and Blessed Sacrament of Baptism*, in *Luther's Works* 35 (Philadelphia: Muhlenberg, 1959), p. 36.

7. Luther, *Large Catechism*, available at http://www.lcms.org/bookofconcord/largecatechism/6_baptism.asp.

8. *Babylonian Captivity*, 3.33.

9. "Reformed theology" is a broad tradition that includes Presbyterians, Baptists and even Anglicans to some degree. It is not a synonym for "Calvinism," though all Calvinists are Reformed.

10. http://members.tripod.com/~lexpbc/baptism.htm.

11. *Baltic Confession*, art. 33, available at http://www.reformed.org/documents/BelgicConfession.html#Article%2033

12. See Jack Cottrell, "Baptism According to the Reformed Tradition," in *Baptism and the Remission of Sins*, ed. David W. Fletcher (Joplin, MO: College Press, 1990), 39-81, for a thorough discussion of Zwingli. My summary is heavily dependent upon Cottrell's work.

13. Zwingli, "Of Baptism," in *Zwingli and Bullinger*, ed. G. W. Bromiley, Library of Christian Classics (Philadelphia: Westminster, 1953), 130.

14. Zwingli, "An Account of Faith," in *The Latin Works of Huldreich Zwingli*, ed. William John Hinkle (Philadelphia: Heidelberg, 1922), 2:46.

15. Zwingli, "Commentary on True and False Religion," in *The Latin Works of Huldreich Zwingli*, ed. C. N. Heller, 3:184. Cottrell, 55, translates a passage from Zwingli's letter to Thomas Wyttenbach, June 15, 1523 in *Werke* (CR), 8:86, which significantly illustrates this point: "Therefore it is faith which is required there, which if

it is so great, that it has need of no certain point of time or (no certain) place or person or any other thing, by which, through the circumstance itself, it would desire to be made assured and secure, it has no need of baptism. But if he is still a little too simple-minded and unsophisticated, and needs a demonstration, let the believer be washed, so that now he knows that he is cleansed by faith within just as he is by water without."

16. Calvin, *Institutes of the Christian Religion,* Library of Christian Classics 20; ed. John T. McNeill and trans. Ford Lewis Battles (Philadelphia: Westminster, 1960), 2:1289. An older translation of the *Institutes* is available at http://www.reformed.org/books/institutes/.

17. Calvin, *Commentaries on the First Twenty Chapters of the Prophet Ezekiel,* accessed at http://www.ccel.org/c/calvin/comment3/comm_vol23/htm/ix.xiv.htm.

18. Calvin, "The Best Method of Obtaining Concord, Provided the Truth Be Sought Without Contention," in *Selected Works of John Calvin: Tracts and Letters* (Grand Rapids: Baker, reprinted 1983), 2:573, available at http://www.blessed-hopeministries.net/bestmeth.htm.

19. Available at http://www.creeds.net/reformed/frconf.htm.

20. Available at http://anglicansonline.org/basics/thirty-nine_articles.html.

21. Cottrell, 70-73, argues that Calvin's position ultimately reduces to Zwingli's.

22. Calvin, *Commentary upon the Acts of the Apostles* (Grand Rapids: Eerdmans, reprint 1949), 1:118. Available at http://www.ccel.org/c/calvin/comment3/comm_vol36/htm/ix.vii.htm.

23. Calvin, "The True Method of Giving Peace to Christendom and Reforming the Church," in *Selected Works,* 3:275.

24. Zwingli admitted that "for some time I myself was deceived by the error and thought it better not to baptize children until they came to the age of discretion" (quoted by Bromiley, p. 139).

25. Wayne Pipkin and John Howard Yoder, eds., *Balthasar Hubmaier: Theologian of Anabaptism,* Classics of the Radical Reformation, 5 (Scottdale, PA: Herald, 1989), 280.

26. The Mennonite *Dordrecht Confession of Faith* of 1632 states: "Concerning baptism we confess that penitent believers, who, through faith, regeneration, and the renewing of the Holy Ghost, are made one with God, and are written in heaven, must, upon such Scriptural confession of faith, and renewing of life, be baptized with water, in the most worthy name of the Father, and of the Son, and of the Holy Ghost, according to the command of Christ, and the teaching, example, and practice of the apostles, to the burying of their sins, and thus be incorporated into the communion of the saints; henceforth to learn to observe all things which the Son of God has taught, left, and commanded His disciples." Available at http://www.bibleviews.com/Dordrecht.html

27. The *New Hampshire Baptist Confession of Faith* (1833): "We believe that Christian Baptism is the immersion in water of a believer, into the name of the Father, and Son, and Holy Ghost; to show forth, in a solemn and beautiful emblem, our faith in the crucified, buried, and risen Saviour, with its effect in our death to sin

and resurrection to a new life; that it is prerequisite to the privileges of a Church relation." Available at http://www.carmichaelbaptist.org/Articles%20of%20Faith/nhcof.htm.

28. Available at http://www.anabaptists.org/history/schleith.html

29. This is evidenced by various quotes from the three in this chapter.

30. Wes Harrison, "The Renewal of the Practice of Adult Baptism by Immersion during the Reformation Era, 1525-1700," *Restoration Quarterly* 43 (2001), 95-112, surveys the story of immersion during the Reformation.

31. Available at http://justus.anglican.org/resources/bcp/Baptism_1549.htm.

32. Available at http://justus.anglican.org/resources/bcp/Baptism_1552.htm.

33. Available at http://www.gty.org/~phil/creeds/bc1644.htm.

34. See the interesting data available at http://www.blessedhopeministries.net/bhisv118.htm.

35. Available at http://www.opc.org/documents/WCF_text.html.

36. Available at http://www.covenanter.org/Westminster/directoryforpublicworship.htm#baptism.

Chapter Seven

1. As quoted by William Baxter, *Life of Walter Scott* (Nashville: Gospel Advocate, reprint n.d.), 113. See John Mark Hicks, "The Recovery of the Ancient Gospel: Alexander Campbell and the Design of Baptism," in *Baptism and the Remission of Sins*, ed. David W. Fletcher (Joplin, MO: College Press, 1990), 145-7, available at http://johnmarkhicks.faithsite.com/content.asp?CID=10075.

2. Samuel E. Hester, "Advancing Christianity to Its Primitive Excellency: The Quest of Thomas Grantham, Early English General Baptist (1634-1692)" (Th.D., New Orleans Baptist Theological Seminary, 1977), 60, as cited by Lynn A. McMillon, "The Restoration of Baptism by Eighteenth and Nineteenth Restorers in Britain," in *Baptism and the Remission of Sins*, ed. David W. Fletcher (Joplin, MO: College Press, 1990), 89.

3. McMillon, 101.

4. T. F. Torrance, *Scottish Theology* (Edinburgh: T. & T. Clark, 1996), 37.

5. See Derek B. Murray, "An Eighteenth Century Baptismal Controversy in Scotland," 419-429 and Kenneth Roxburgh, "Open and Closed Membership Among Scottish Baptists," 447-466, in *Baptism, the New Testament and the Church: Historical and Contemporary Studies in Honour of R. E. O. White*, JSNT, 171, ed. Stanley E. Porter and Anthony R. Cross (Sheffield: Sheffield Academic, 1999).

6. The Christian Church (Disciples of Christ), the Churches of Christ, and the Churches of Christ and Christian Churches (Independent) are the contemporary descendents of the Stone-Campbell Movement.

7. Alexander Campbell, "Calvin on Baptism," *Millennial Harbinger* 4 (November 1833), 543-47, quotes Calvin's *Institutes*, 4.15.1-5 and comments: "We leave it to the

good sense of the reader, whether John Calvin ought not to be called a Campbellite as well as the Apostle Peter." See also Richard L. Harrison, Jr., "Early Disciples Sacramental Theology: Catholic, Reformed and Free," *Mid-Stream* 24 (July 1985), 255-92.

8. Alexander Campbell, *Debate on Christian Baptism* (Pittsburg: Eichbaum & Johnston, 1822; reprint ed., Hollywood: Old Paths Book Club, n.d.), 136-7.

9. Campbell, *Debate*, 170-1.

10. Campbell, *Debate*, 241, 244.

11. See Hicks, "The Recovery of the Ancient Gospel," 117-37.

12. Thomas Campbell, "Essay on the Proper and Primary Intention of the Gospel, and its Proper and Immediate Effects," *Christian Baptist* 1 (1 September 1823), 35.

13. Alexander Campbell, *A Public Debate on Christian Baptism* (London: Simpkin & Marshall, 1842; reprint ed., Kansas City: Old Paths Book Club, n.d.), 116-7.

14. Campbell, *Public Debate*, 125.

15. Campbell, *Public Debate*, 118.

16. Alexander Campbell, "A Catalogue of Queries—Answered," *Christian Baptist* 6 (2 February 1829), 164.

17. Alexander Campbell, "Reply to the Above," *Christian Baptist* 4 (4 June 1827), 229. On the significance of this shift, see John Mark Hicks, "The Role of Faith in Conversion: Balancing Faith, Christian Experience and Baptism," in *Evangelicalism & the Stone-Campbell Movement*, ed. William R. Baker (Downers Grove, IL: InterVarsity, 2002), 91-124 and "'God's Sensible Pledge': The Witness of the Spirit in the Early Baptismal Theology of Alexander Campbell," *Stone-Campbell Journal* 1 (1998), 5-26, available at http://www.spaceports.com/~scj/pledge.html

18. "Conscience," *Christian Baptist* 3 (6 February 1826), 150.

19. Campbell, "Ancient Gospel—No. I," *Christian Baptist* 5 (7 January 1828), 128-130; "Ancient Gospel—No. II," 5 (5 February 1828), 164-168; "Ancient Gospel—No. III," 5 (3 March 1828), 179-182; "Ancient Gospel—No. IV," 5 (7 April), 221-223; "Ancient Gospel—No. V," 5 (5 May 1828), 229-232; "Ancient Gospel—No. VI," 5 (2 June 1828), 254-257; "Ancient Gospel—No. VII," 5 (7 July 1828), 276-279; "Ancient Gospel—No. VIII," 6 (4 August 1828), 14-17; "Ancient Gospel—No. IX," 6 (6 October 1828), 72-74; and "Ancient Gospel—No. X," 6 (3 November 1828), 97-100.

20. Campbell, "No. II," 166.

21. Campbell, "No. V," 232.

22. Campbell, "No. VI," 254, or a "medium of remission…the means through which, by faith, we are forgiven" (Campbell, "Reply to C.F.," *Christian Baptist* 7 [1 February 1830], 181).

23. Campbell, "No. VII," 277.

24. Andrew Broaddus, *A Reply to Mr. A. Campbell's M. Harbinger, Extra on Remission of Sins, Etc.* (Richmond, VA: Religious Herald, 1831), 5, 8, 19-24.

25. Campbell, "The Extra Defended," *Millennial Harbinger* 2 (October 10, 1831), 14.

26. Campbell, "Extra Defended," 16-17, 37.

27. See James Baird, "The Role of Baptism in Conversion: Baptism & Its Substitutes as Rituals of Initiation in American Protestantism," in *Evangelicalism & the Stone-Campbell Movement*, 176-86.

28. Campbell, "No. V," 231.

29. See John Mark Hicks, "Alexander Campbell on Christians Among the Sects," 171-202 (available at http://johnmarkhicks.faithsite.com/content.asp?CID=10070), Roderick Chestnut, "John Thomas and the Rebaptism Controversy (1835-1838)," 203-40, and Jerry Gross, "The Rebaptism Controversy Among Churches of Christ," 297-332, in *Baptism and the Remission of Sins*. My summary is indebted to their research.

30. Campbell, however, addressed it early as a potential misapplication of his views; cf. "Rebaptism," *Millennial Harbinger* 2 (1831), 482 and "Dialogue on Re-Immersion," *Millennial Harbinger* 3 (1832), 223.

31. Thomas, "The Cry of 'Anabaptism,'" *Apostolic Advocate* 1 (October 1834), 122.

32. Thomas, "Re-immersion and Remarks," *Apostolic Advocate* 2 (1 September 1835), 102.

33. Campbell, "Susan," *Millennial Harbinger* 6 (September 1835), 418.

34. See Lipscomb, "What Constitutes Acceptable Obedience?" in *Salvation From Sin*, ed. J. W. Shepherd (Nashville, TN: Gospel Advocate, 1913), 208-234, available at http://www.mun.ca/rels/restmov/texts/dlipscomb/dlsin.html.

35. Jimmy Allen, *Rebaptism? What Must One Know to Be Born Again* (West Monroe, LA: Howard, 1990), 10.

36. Shelemiah, in "Any Christians Among the Protestant Parties?" *Millennial Harbinger* 8 (September 1837), 411. Chestnut, p. 238, n.85, has identified "Shelemiah" as Louisa A. Anderson who was a member of Thomas' circle. The Lunnenberg correspondence materials are available at http://www.bible.acu.edu/stone-campbell/ Etexts/lun16.html.

37. Campbell, "Any Christians Among the Protestant Parties," *Millennial Harbinger* 8 (September 1837), 411.

38. Campbell, "Protestant Parties," 412.

39. Campbell, "Any Christians Among the Sects?" *Millennial Harbinger* 8 (December 1837), 563-4.

40. Campbell, "Re-Immersion and Brother Thomas," *Millennial Harbinger* 7 (February 1836), 62.

41. Campbell, "Reply to James Fishback—No. 1," *Millennial Harbinger* 3 (July 1832), 304.

42. Campbell, *The Campbell-Rice Debate* (Lexington, KY: A. T. Skillman & Son, 1844), 519-20

43. Campbell, "Re-Immersion and Brother Thomas," 62.

44. Campbell, "The Three Kingdoms," *Christian Baptist* 6 (1 June 1829), 268.

45. Campbell, "Christians Among the Sects," *Millennial Harbinger* 8 (November 1837), 506-508.

46. Campbell, "Any Christians Among the Sects?" 565.

47. Campbell, "Protestant Parties," 412. Also Campbell, "Mr. Meredith on Remission," *Millennial Harbinger* 11 (December 1840), 544: "I have taught from the first day in which I preached baptism for remission of sins, taught that, without previous faith and repentance, baptism availed nothing—that a man was virtually, or in heart, in the new covenant, and entitled to its blessings, when he believed and repented; but not formally nor in fact justified or forgiven till he put on Christ in baptism; that if by any insuperable or involuntary difficulty he could not be baptized, and were in the mean time to die, he would be in heart right with God, and would be accepted through the Beloved."

48. See Gary Holloway, "Not the Only Christians: Campbell on Exclusivism and Legalism," *Christian Studies* 15 (1995-1996), 46-54.

49. Moses Lard, "Do the Unimmersed Commune?" *Lard's Quarterly* 1 (September 1863), 41.

50. Letter from J. W. McGarvey to Hugh B. Todd, January 19, 1895, as quoted by W. L. Butler, "No Correction Needed," *Gospel Advocate* 37 (12 December 1895), 790.

51. See James B. North, "The Open Membership Controversy and the Christian Churches," in *Baptism and the Remission of Sins*, 333-366.

52. Disciples Commission on Theology, "A Word to the Church on Baptism," available in Clark Williamson, *Baptism: Embodiment of the Gospel* (St. Louis, MO: Christian Board of Publication, 1987), pp. 46-60.

53. For example, among Churches of Christ, see Mike Cope, "Christians-Only—Not the Only Christians," *Wineskins* 3.3 (1997), 7 and F. LaGard Smith, *Who Is My Brother?* (Nashville: 21st Century Christian, 1997), 17-50.

54. Henry Webb, "Baptism, an Issue Among Disciples" (paper presented at meeting of the Stone-Campbell Dialogue, Cincinnati Bible College, November 27-28, 2000), available at http://www.disciples.org/ccu/documents/dialpapwebb.htm.

55. J. W. McGarvey, "Is Baptism a Positive Institution?" *Apostolic Times* 5 (26 June 1873), 4, claims that there was a time "when every preacher in the Reformation had one or more discourses on Positive institutions, and with many it was a favorite subject."

56. See John Mark Hicks, "The Gracious Separatist: Moral and Positive Law in the Theology of James A. Harding," *Restoration Quarterly* 42.3 (2000): 129-47, available at http://johnmarkhicks.faithsite.com/content.asp?CID=17867.

57. Benjamin Franklin, "Positive Divine Law," in *Gospel Preacher: A Book of Twenty-One Sermons*, vol. 2 (Cincinnati: G. W. Rice, Publisher, 1877), 193, available at http://www.mun.ca/rels/restmov/texts/bfranklin/tgp2/TGP209.HTM.

58. Franklin, "Positive," 194-217.

59. Franklin, "Positive," 215-6.

60. Harding, "Should Unbaptized Sectarians be Called Upon to Lead the Prayers of the Lord's House?" *Gospel Advocate* 25 (22 February 1883), 118.

61. Harding, *The Harding-Nichols Debate* (1888; reprint ed., Nashville, TN: Gospel Advocate, 1947), p. 77.

62. Harding, "Should the Unbaptized," 118.

63. Harding, "Does Ignorance Excuse Them?" *Gospel Advocate* 24 (30 November 1882), 758.

64. Harding, "Union Meetings," *Gospel Advocate* 25 (27 June 1883), 410.

65. Harding, "Questions from Brother T. M. Sweeney, and Answers," *The Christian Leader and the Way* 29 (25 September 1905), 8.

66. Harding, *Debate on Baptism and the Work of the Holy Spirit* (1889; reprint ed., Nashville: Gospel Advocate, 1955), 256-7.

67. Harding, *Debate on Baptism*, 267.

68. Campbell, "Calvin," 547.

69. See Douglas A. Foster, "Churches of Christ and Baptism: An Historical and Theological Overview," *Restoration Quarterly* 43.2 (2001), 79-94.

70. Campbell, "Mr. Meredith on Remission," 545.

71. See, for example, the teaching document of the Oak Hills Church of Christ in San Antonio, Texas, which is available at http://www.oakhillschurchofchrist.org. See Hicks's critique in "The Role of Faith in Conversion," 114-5.

Chapter Eight

1. Some versions read "save from wrath and make me pure" rather than "cleanse me from its guilt and power."

2. Jack Cottrell, "The Role of Faith in Conversion," in *Evangelicalism & the Stone-Campbell Movement*, ed. William R. Baker (Downer's Grove, IL: InterVarsity, 2002), 89.

3. Paul Althaus, *The Theology of Martin Luther* (Philadelphia: Fortress, 1966), 356. We also noted in chapter seven how Scottish baptismal theology was described by T. F. Torrance as the sacrament of justification.

4. Luther, *Large Catechism*, available at http://www.lcms.org/bookofconcord/largecatechism/6_baptism.asp.

5. I have adapted this chart from Jack Cottrell.

Chapter Nine

1. Frederick Buechner, *Wishful Thinking: A Seeker's ABC*, revised and expanded (New York: Harper San Francisco, 1993), 6.

2. See Stanley J. Grenz, *Theology for the Community of God* (Nashville, TN: Broadman & Holman, 1994), 574f.

3. James D. G. Dunn, like Barth, is concerned that the church has given undue

credit to water baptism where credit for the Yes and the "seal" of God on his people is due to the Holy Spirit.

4. William Willimon, *Remember Who You Are: Baptism, a Model for Christian Life* (Nashville: Upper Room, 1980), 87.

Chapter Ten

1. Campbell, *Christian Baptism* (1851; reprint ed., Nashville: Gospel Advocate, 1951), 202.

2. Campbell, "Any Christians Among the Protestant Parties," *Millennial Harbinger* 8 (September 1837), 412.

3. See James Baird, "The Role of Baptism in Conversion: Baptism & Its Substitutes as Rituals of Initiation in American Protestantism," in *Evangelicalism & the Stone-Campbell Movement,* ed. William R. Baker (Downers Grove, IL: InterVarsity, 2002), 176-86.

4. There are some exceptions to this unanimity. For example, Quakers, the Salvation Army, and some extreme dispensational theologians do not practice water baptism in any significant form. These groups are outside the framework of our discussion in this chapter.

5. See the discussion by John Mark Hicks, *Yet Will I Trust Him: Understanding God In a Suffering World* (Joplin, MO: College Press, 1999), 51-81.

6. Available at http://www.religiousdebates.com/graceframe.htm.

7. John Mark Hicks, *1 & 2 Chronicles* (Joplin, MO: College Press, 2001), 464-478.

8. John Mark Hicks, "The Sabbath Controversy in Matthew: An Exegesis of Matthew 12:1-14," *Restoration Quarterly* 27 (1984), 65-74.

9. Some believe that Matthew's main point is that David is a messianic figure and this is why the actions of Jesus' disciples are analogous. However, Matthew does not appeal to this aspect, though it may be true. Rather, Matthew pinpoints the rationale in Hosea 6:6 and thus sees the disciples' action as a function of mercy. In this context, Jesus offers a "mercy" principle for applying Sabbath regulations: "It is lawful to do good on the Sabbath" (Matt. 12:12). Anyone may do what is lawful on the Sabbath and it is always lawful to "do good" or show mercy on the Sabbath. The principle of mercy is built into God's law because it serves his goals even when the law does not explicitly mention the principle or potential exceptions.

10. See Hicks, *1 & 2 Chronicles,* 145-49.

Chapter Eleven

1. Carl Spain, "Modern Challenges to Christian Morals" in *Christian Faith in the Modern World: The Abilene Christian College Annual Bible Lectures 1960* (Abilene Christian College Students Exchange, 1960), 198-231. Available at http://www.mun.ca/rels/ restmov/texts/race/haymes15.html.

2. Don Haymes, Introduction to the Text of Carl Spain's "Modern Challenges

to Christian Morals" in *Christian Faith in the Modern World: The Abilene Christian College Annual Bible Lectures 1960* (Abilene Christian College Students Exchange, 1960), 198-231. Available at http://www.mun.ca/rels/restmov/texts/race/ haymes15.html.

3. God promised Abraham then later circumcised him and even later the law entered the scene. Paul says the entrance of the covenant doesn't nullify the basis of what pleased God: Abraham's faith. Abraham was not perfect or sinless. He, rather, believed God would do what he said he would do. He believed God kept his promises—however imperfect that looked over his years of nomadic wandering. He still left Ur, the most telling event of his faith journey.

4. "The inability of the churches mutually to recognize their various practices of baptism as sharing in the one baptism, and their actual dividedness in spite of mutual baptismal recognition, have given dramatic visibility to the broken witness of the Church. The readiness of the churches in some places and times to allow differences of sex, race, or social status to divide the body of Christ has further called into question genuine baptismal unity of the Christian community (Galatians 3.27-28) and has seriously compromised its witness. The need to recover baptismal unity is at the heart of the ecumenical task as it is central for the realization of genuine partnership within the Christian communities." Quoted from World Council of Churches Faith and Order, "Baptism, Eucharist and Ministry," Faith and Order Paper No. 111. Available at http://www.wcc-coe.org/wcc/what/faith/bem3.html.

5. Our point is that baptism should not divide us, but it often does. For a good picture of how baptism has divided the Christian world, see Donald Bridge and David Phypers, *The Water that Divides: The Baptism Debate* (Downers Grove, IL: InterVarsity, 1977). They discuss how baptism has divided churches along the lines of symbol vs. sacrament as well as infant vs. believer's baptism. Usually extreme sacramentalists baptize infants. They say, "Baptism does not bring salvation automatically, by the work being worked, but neither is it merely symbolic. It is a sacrament that brings grace through faith. It is part of the obedience of faith. The act of baptism demonstrates that faith is active for salvation" (181).

6. Leonard Allen's opening remarks in the Preacher's Forum of the 2002 Abilene Christian University Lectures. Available at http://www.missiology.org/MMR/mmr27.htm.

7. Rodney Clapp, *A Peculiar People: The Church as Culture in a Post-Christian Society* (Downers Grove, IL: InterVarsity, 1996), 99-102.

8. Churches are called Evangelical for three primary reasons: they take Scripture as true and normative for faith and practice, they believe Jesus is exactly who he says he is, and they believe they ought to share the message of Scripture and of the gospel of Christ with the world. For a helpful discussion on Evangelicalism, particularly as it relates to groups such as the Stone-Campbell Movement, see *Evangelicalism and the Stone-Campbell Movement*, ed. William R. Baker (Downers Grove, IL: Intervarsity, 2002).

9. James D. G. Dunn, *The Theology of Paul the Apostle* (Grand Rapids: Eerdmans,

1998), 449.

10. Infant baptism is difficult to consider here, because it involves more the faith step of parents and the fulfilled mission of the church than it does the faith response of a believer.

11. Thomas Halbrooks, "Children and the Church: A Baptist Historical Perspective," *Review and Expositor* 80.2 (Spring 1983), 179-188.

12. Halbrooks, 180.

13. Halbrooks, 183.

14. Lewis Craig Ratliff, "Discipleship, Church Membership, and the Place of Children Among Southern Baptists" (Th.D., Southern Baptist Theological Seminary, 1963), 130, 137, 140, 143, 181. I am grateful to Thomas Halbrooks' research in this area, and I relied on his reading of Ratliff for the point about the age of "disciple-ability."

15. David K. Lewis, Carley H. Dodd, and Darryl L. Tippens, *The Gospel According to Generation X: The Culture of Adolescent Belief* (Abilene, Texas: ACU Press, 1995), 138-162.

16. Lewis, Dodd, and Tippens, *Gospel,* 148.

17. Lewis, Dodd, and Tippens., *Gospel,* 142.

18. Ralph C. Wood, "Baptism in a Coffin," *Christian Century* 109 (21 October 1992): 925-26.

19. William Willimon, *Remember Who You Are: Baptism, a Model for Christian Life* (Nashville: Upper Room, 1980), 23.

Chapter Twelve

1. Timothy George, "Reformed Doctrine of Believers' Baptism," *Interpretation* 47 (July 1993), 242f.

2. Statements taken from a litany developed by Harold Bauman for use in the Assembly congregation, Goshen, Indiana and quoted in James H. Waltner, *Baptism and Church Membership*, Worship Series No. 3 (Newton, Kansas: Faith & Life Press, 1979), 34-36.

3. Waltner, 34, quoting *The Mennonite Hymnal,* no. 725. See also Marlin Jeschke's *Believer's Baptism for Children of the Church* (Scottdale, Pennsylvania: Herald Press, 1983) for more on the concept of "crossing over" from childhood innocence to owned faith.

4. This section is informed by David K. Lewis, Carley H. Dodd, and Darryl L. Tippens, *The Gospel According to Generation X: The Culture of Adolescent Belief* (Abilene, Texas: ACU Press, 1995), 138-162.

5. John Ogren, "Missional Worship," *new WINESKINS* 6.4 (Sep/Oct 2002), 16.

6. James D.G. Dunn, *The Theology of Paul the Apostle* (Grand Rapids: Eerdmans, 1998), 449.

7. George, "Reformed Doctrine," 242f.

Chapter 13

1. Karl Barth, *The Teaching of the Church Regarding Baptism*, trans. Ernest A. Payne (London: SCM, 1948), 31.

2. James Wm. McClendon, Jr. *Doctrine: Systematic Theology* (Nashville: Abingdon, 1994), 388-389.

3. Anthony R. Cross, "'One Baptism' (Ephesians 4:5): A Challenge to the Church," in *Baptism, the New Testament and the Church: Historical and Contemporary Studies in Honour of R.E.O. White*, ed. By Stanley E. Porter and Anthony R. Cross (Sheffield: Sheffield Academic Press, 1999), 173.

4. Beasley-Murray, *Baptism in the New Testament* (London: MacMillan, 1963), 273.

5. Jon A. Weatherly, "The Role of Baptism in Conversion: Israel's Promises Fulfilled for the Believer in Jesus," in *Evangelicalism & the Stone-Campbell Movement*, ed. William R. Baker (Downers Grove, IL: InterVarsity, 2002), 174.

6. James D. G. Dunn, *The Theology of Paul the Apostle* (Grand Rapids: Eerdmans, 1998), 457, cautions us in deriving theology from Paul with two points: 1) Include all parts of the conversion narrative. "Otherwise, the wholeness and the richness of Paul's conceptuality and theology can be gravely diminished." 2) Realize that Paul emphasized different elements of the conversion narrative in different contexts. He goes on to say that this ought not to keep us from having a rich sacramental theology of baptism, particularly drawn from Colossians 2:11-12 and Romans 6:3-4, but we must be careful not to attribute theological schemas to Paul where he simply did not elaborate.

7. Alexander Campbell, "Ancient Gospel—No. IX," *Christian Baptist* 6 (6 October 1828), 128.

8. Alexander Campbell, "To Epaphras—No. I," *Millennial Harbinger* 3 (July 1832), 298.

9. T. W. Brents, *The Gospel Plan of Salvation* (16th ed.; Nashville: Gospel Advocate, 1973; reprint of 1874 edition). His chapters focus primarily on human responsibility in the "plan": faith, repentance, confession and baptism. Even his chapter on the "Holy Spirit" is more about "hearing" than it is the convicting work of the Spirit and his indwelling, transforming life in the believer. Thus, his exposition of the "plan" is anthropocentric rather than theocentric.

10. See the discussion of M. Eugene Boring, *Disciples and the Bible: A History of Disciples Biblical Interpretation in North America* (St. Louis: Chalice Press, 1997), 395-400.

11. C. Leonard Allen, *Distant Voices: Discovering a Forgotten Past for a Changing Church* (ACU Press, 1993). For a discussion of K. C. Moser's life and work, see John Mark Hicks, "The Man or the Plan? K. C. Moser and the Theology of Grace Among Mid-Twentieth Century Churches of Christ," available at http://www.mun.ca/rels/restmov/texts/moser/jmhindex.html.

12. Jack Cottrell, "The Role of Faith in Conversion," in *Evangelicalism and the Stone-Campbell Movement*, ed. William Baker (Downers Grove, IL: InterVarsity Press, 2002), 89.

13. McClendon, 388-89, uses an illustration of front door conversion and back door conversion.

14. Cambpell, "Three Kingdoms," *Christian Baptist* 6 (1 June 1829), 286, argues that the "kingdom of glory" is inherited by those who through "good works," "piety," and "humanity" feed the hungry and clothed the naked. In other words, according to Campbell, transformed living is more important than immersion.

15. McClendon, 388-89.

16. McClendon, 388-89.

17. Rees Bryant's discussion on sacrament, symbol, and ordinance is helpful in understanding and distinguishing how God works through baptism. See *Baptism, Why Wait? Faith's Response in Conversion* (Joplin, MO: College Press, 1999), 87-103.

18. McClendon, 396.

19. See Anthony R. Cross, "'One Baptism' (Ephesians 4:5): A Challenge to the Church," 173-209, for a defense of this perspective while looking at other possible solutions.

20. Alexander Campbell, *A Debate Between Rev. A. Campbell and Rev. N. L. Rice on the Action, Subject, Design and Administrator of Christian Baptism* (Louisville, KY: A. T. Skillman & Son, 1844), 567-610, denied the following proposition in his debate with the Presbyterian Rice: "Baptism is to be administered only by a Bishop or Ordained Presbyter."

21. See John Mark Hicks, *Come to the Table: Revisioning the Lord's Supper* (Orange, CA: New Leaf Books, 2002).

22. http://www.cyberhymnal.org/htm/s/w/swgatriv.htm.

23. Used by permission. Copyright 1998 Debbie Dorman. See http://www.debdorman.com.